Patriarchy and Incest from Shakespeare to Joyce

Patriarchy and Incest

University Press of Florida
Gainesville
Tallahassee
Tampa
Boca Raton
Pensacola
Orlando
Miami
Jacksonville

Jane M. Ford

from Shakespeare to Joyce

03 02 01 00 99 98   6 5 4 3 2 1

LIBRARY OF CONGRESS CATALOGING-IN-PUBLICATION DATA

Ford, Jane M.
Patriarchy and incest from Shakespeare to Joyce / Jane M. Ford.
p. cm.
Includes bibliographical references (p.   ) and index.
ISBN 0-8130-1595-2 (alk. paper)
1. English literature—History and criticism. 2. Shakespeare, William, 1564–1616—
Knowledge—Psychology. 3. Joyce, James, 1882–1941—Knowledge—Psychology.
4. Fathers and daughters in literature. 5. Literature—Psychological aspects.
6. Patriarchy in literature. 7. Incest in literature. I. Title.
PR408.F36F67   1998
820.9'3520431—dc21   98-13226

Jane M. Ford is visiting scholar in the Literature Department at the
University of California, San Diego.

The University Press of Florida is the scholarly publishing agency for the State University
System of Florida, comprised of Florida A & M University, Florida Atlantic University,
Florida International University, Florida State University, University of Central Florida,
University of Florida, University of North Florida, University of South Florida, and University of West Florida.

University Press of Florida
15 Northwest 15th Street
Gainesville, FL 32611
http://nersp.nerdc.ufl.edu/~upf

For Barbara, Bill, Brian, and Ann

Contents

Preface

When questioned about the origins of my interest in the topic of fathers and daughters, I am confronted with those fragments from the past which, as they accumulate, often lead into unexplored avenues and unexpected areas of interest. In this case, the fragments extend consciously back to my adolescence, and certainly unconsciously beyond that. Early on, I was struck by the fact that my grandmother, the youngest of five girls in a family early bereft of their mother, married a friend and contemporary of her father's—a father to whom she was deeply attached. There was never any indication from her that it was a love-match. I was also impressed by an old photo of her with the handwritten inscription on the back: "Your father carried this in his pocket always." But the portrait was of a mature woman, not of a small child.

I also often pondered the deep distress of an acquaintance's father when she first began to date, and his later genuine anguish when she married, sensing that it was disproportionate and verged on hysteria. I had been impressed by reading of the suicide of Henry Adams's wife following her own father's death; had been appalled by Charles Laughton's vitriolic portrayal of Elizabeth Barrett Browning's father, and relieved at her rescue by a suitor. I was not unaware of the attraction that men who resembled my own father held for me.

Years later, my husband, one of the early devotees of Joyce who first read *Ulysses* in a copy smuggled from Europe in a brown paper wrapper, wrote an essay on incest as the answer to the riddle of the Prankquean in *Finnegans Wake*, a novel now commonly acknowledged as "riddled" with incest. Later, while rereading *Ulysses*, I began to ponder possible reasons for Bloom's having sent his daughter Milly to live and work fifty miles from Dublin in the small town of Mullingar at the age of fourteen. A trip to Mullingar helped me to gauge the distance from Dublin and judge the significance of the exile Bloom had imposed on his daughter.

Freud once said of his case histories, "I read them over and over until they begin to speak to me." This, in effect, was what I had done with *Ulysses*, believing that highly receptive, repeated readings of literary works of substance yield results similar to those Freud experienced with his case histories. Contrary to certain modern theories which dismiss the importance of the author, I believe that the psyche of the writer reaches out to the psyche of the reader across the bridge of the written page and something happens which accounts not only for the wide diversity of responses and interpretations of all literary works so fascinating to reader-response theorists, but also for the similarities. Rereading led to my realization that the theme of incest occurred not only in *Finnegans Wake*, but in *Ulysses* also.

I began my research for "Why Is Milly in Mullingar?" with some compunction; I felt as though I were accusing an old friend. Subsequently, I made it the central focus of my reading to seek out and analyze the opposition between the father and the suitor for possession of the daughter in Shakespeare's plays and in each novel I read, usually finding some variation of the pattern. Sometimes, as in certain novels by Henry James, it seemed to be all the narrative was about. In other novels, such as Joseph Conrad's *Lord Jim*, the theme was an obscure and scarcely noted aspect of the plot. My interest grew with each new work I read, and with many old ones to which I returned. My investigations gradually assumed the nature of what Northrop Frye had dubbed "literary anthropology."[1]

I had also long been responsive to many of Sigmund Freud's observations, particularly those pertaining to the oedipal triangle, and I found that his theory and the literature complemented each other in a reciprocal fashion—a circular argument some might say. Since Freud had been led into the development of his theories through literature, this seemed a natural progression. Although both Freud and Otto Rank had long ago pointed out the prevalence of the theme of incest in poetry and drama, less work had been done on the novel in which the theme is frequently more muted, apparent only as a subtext.

I have sometimes met with resistance on the part of male readers, especially regarding controversial interpretations of novels such as *Bleak House*, *The Golden Bowl* and *Ulysses*, but women readers have been very receptive. Older women particularly, who lived their young lives in the early twentieth century, have been intrigued and asked to read what I had written even when unfamiliar with the literature being cited.

The problem of incest has surfaced at many levels in recent years, sometimes eliciting substantial anxiety and distress. Newspaper and popular magazine articles have gradually come to terms with its previously unacknowledged prevalence in our society, as indicated by a selection of recent headlines: "Dad Wonders Why He Hurt His Little Girl," "Breaking the Incest Taboo: Those Who Crusade for Family 'Love' Forget the Balance of Family Power," "British Panel Asks Changes in Laws on Sex in Family," "Seeing Father Again Frightens Daughter," "Court Is Told Incest Triggered Slaying of Five," and "Incest: A Chilling Report." These are not headlines from the *National Enquirer*, but from major city newspapers and such magazines as *The Progressive*, *Ms*, and *Lear's*.

More open discussion has had varied results. Films such as *Chinatown*, the French *Murmur of the Heart* and more recently *L'Ombre du Doute* (Shades of Doubt) have dealt with incest openly, and in the case of *Murmur* even lightheartedly. In recent years, the law-making bodies of both England and Sweden have heard strong arguments in favor of legalizing incest between consenting adults. Recent additions to the popular literature have been biographies of various prominent people who now wish to divulge all. A California defense attorney endeavored to save his client from a jail sentence for fraud by pleading her early molestation by her father, and this type of legal defense for everything up to and including murder has multiplied substantially. The recent proliferation of arguments between those defending methods used in repressed-memory cases and those condemning them has raised questions that plagued Freud many years ago.

One issue which this study recalls is that of the function of language and narration in the management of anxieties and defenses. Many artists have used narration as a method of repeatedly dealing with subject matter that is rarely discussed openly. Freud and Breuer, in their early case studies of hysteria in young women, recognized the strong father attachments involved, but they also recognized the temporary, therapeutic effects of the patient's opportunity to *narrate* the material. It has been a common-place observance among writers that once they have completed a novel, they seldom think about it again, in fact, sometimes forget it entirely; the writing has served its purpose.

Hysteria has largely disappeared as a clinical phenomenon and focus has shifted to other problems such as schizophrenia. Comparisons have been made between the language of *Finnegans Wake* and that of schizo-phrenics, with the artistic control by the author of the novel being the main distinction between the two. The language in other novels such as *The Golden Bowl* and the second half of *Ulysses*, while not achieving the obscurity and density found in *Finnegans Wake*, has many similar char-acteristics. One novel which deals with father/daughter incest simply and straightforwardly presents the daughter participant as intermittently schizophrenic—F. Scott Fitzgerald's *Tender Is the Night*.

Focus on the incest theme in literature is in no sense meant to exclude the importance of various other factors in the creation of a work of art. In Freud's terms, each work is "overdetermined," its creation serving mul-tiple purposes for the artist. But I am inclined to agree with the premise that "clarification is attained by intense concentration on one or another aspect of an author's work."[2]

Acknowledgments

I wish to thank Shari Benstock and Grace Eckley with whom I first studied James Joyce at Drake University. I also wish to thank the faculty of the Department of English at State University of New York at Buffalo for their guidance and advice when I was first engaged in research for this project: Leslie Fiedler, William Fischer, Joseph Fradin, Norman Holland, George Levine, Murray Schwartz, Mark Shechner, and David Willbern. I espe-cially wish to acknowledge the characteristically encouraging role played by the late Berni Benstock in his early support of my work on *Ulysses*. Zack Bowen and Peter Rudnytsky were especially helpful in suggestions for improving the manuscript. My faithful Mullingar correspondent, Leo Daly, contributed many valuable insights and perspectives over the years.

The cooperation of many libraries was invaluable, especially access to the Joyce manuscripts held by the Poetry Collection of the Lockwood Library of State University of New York at Buffalo. I am also indebted to the National Library of Ireland, the Huntington Library in California, the Rosenbach Museum and Library in Philadelphia, the Harry Ransom Humanities Research Library at the University of Texas in Austin, the

Berg Collection of the New York Public Library, the library at San Diego State University, and the Geisel Library at the University of California, San Diego.

Prior to the publication of the English translation of Rank's work by Johns Hopkins University Press, I was fortunate in having a series of colleagues who provided translations of segments of the German for me: Eleanor Garner, Jean Kimball, and Albert Richards. Barbara Ford aided me with the French, Mary and Avrum Stroll with the Italian, Betty Fraser with manuscript preparation, and Ariss Treat with proofreading.

The names of myriad colleagues from the International James Joyce Society and the University of California, San Diego—especially Alice Marquis and Chris Norris—who contributed their valuable insights and support are too numerous to mention. I was also helped along the way by grants from both the Kolar Foundation and the Helen Hawkins Grant Fund, administered under the aegis of San Diego Independent Scholars.

I express my gratitude for permission to quote from *Ulysses* (copyright 1934 by James Joyce, reprinted with the permission of the Wylie Agency, Inc., acting on behalf of the Estate of James Joyce). I acknowledge permission to quote from *Finnegans Wake* (copyright 1939 by James Joyce, reprinted with the permission of the Wylie Agency). I also acknowledge permission to reprint from *Finnegans Wake*, by James Joyce (copyright 1939 by James Joyce, copyright renewed 1967 by Giorgio Joyce and Lucia Joyce, used by permission of Viking Penguin, a division of Penguin Books USA Inc.). I am grateful to the *James Joyce Quarterly* for permission to reprint that portion of the present text that appeared as "Why Is Milly in Mullingar?" (14.4 [Summer 1977]: 436–49).

I gratefully acknowledge permission to reprint segments of Otto Rank's *The Incest Theme in Literature and Legend: Fundamentals of a Psychology of Literary Creation*, translated by Gregory C. Richter with an introduction by Peter L. Rudnytsky (copyright 1992, Johns Hopkins University Press, Baltimore, Maryland).

We have reproduced the portrait long believed to be of Beatrice Cenci by Guido Reni which hangs in the Galleria Nazionale d'Arte Antica in the Palazzo Barberini in Rome by permission of the Ministry for Cultural and Environmental Affairs, Florence, Italy. (Reproduction by any means is prohibited.)

A more freudful mistake
James Joyce, *Finnegans Wake*

Introduction
Father/Daughter Incest:
Theory, History, and Sociology

Father/daughter incest, a topic rarely discussed only a few years ago, has become the focus of an increasingly substantial body of sociological, psychoanalytic, and clinical discourse; the subject of modern novels, TV docudramas, and films. More recently it has been a favored subject for literary criticism with a variety of theoretical bases, particularly those of the feminists and/or psychoanalysts. The old argument that the study of any literary work is sufficient unto itself is maintained by only a few diehards. Literature is not created in a vacuum and the New Historicists in particular have restored to criticism the importance and value of placing literature in its appropriate historical/sociological context, which by definition opens to a broad range of theoretical approaches, including psychoanalytic theory. Since the application of such theory to an individual or a situation is by its very nature historical, a combination of the sociohistory of the incest theme in literature and the relevant psychoanalytic theory that applies to it seems an appropriate development. The logical extension of this premise would include pertinent psychobiographical data concerning both those who first recognized and recorded the theme in literature, and the artists who utilized it in their work.

Focus on the persistent recurrence of the incest theme in literature is not new, since it was elaborated upon by both Otto Rank and Sigmund Freud. Sophocles contributed much more than just the name "Oedipus" to psychoanalytic theory. Literature was not only the precursor of such theory, in a sense it spawned it. Otto Rank's seminal work, *Das Inzest-Motiv in Dichtung und Sage* (1912), was acknowledged by Freud soon after its publication: "Among the strictly scientific applications of analysis to literature, Rank's exhaustive work on the theme of incest easily takes the first place."[1] Peter Rudnytsky concurs: "This judgment remains true today. In its encyclopedic erudition, interpretive brilliance, and theoretical cogency *The Incest Theme in Literature and Legend* is the greatest and most important single work of psychoanalytic literary criticism."[2]

In contrast to Freud's clear writing, Rank's unusually convoluted style discouraged a complete translation for many years, keeping the work from becoming available in English until 1992. Rudnytsky points out that although psychoanalysis and literary criticism have undergone radical changes since 1912, Rank's work expresses "a theoretical position that will always have to be taken into account when literary issues are debated" (xxi). The definitive value of Rank's work on legend and myth, combined with his forays into modern literature and case histories, along with his predictions for the future, guarantees the work's continued importance. When I came upon Rank's volume during my own recognition and development of the theme, I realized that his observations provided a rich historic background for my own.

Rank's survey of the theme in more modern literature involved primarily German novels and dramas through 1911. He had also used German translations of Shakespeare, Byron, Shelley, and Ibsen, and although he made cursory references to certain English literature (Wilde's *Salome*, Shaw's *Misalliance*), there is no mention of three major writers: Charles Dickens, Henry James, and Joseph Conrad. As Shakespeare had done before them, these three novelists focused on father/suitor rivalry for possession of the daughter, with the theme sometimes treated in terms of surrogates for father and daughter, particularly in the works of Henry James. The use of surrogates distances potentially threatening material for both the artist and the reader; Rank would have viewed it as another example of repression.

Literature involving incest usually treats one or more of three heterosexual possibilities: mother/son, brother/sister, or father/daughter. Sociological studies indicate a correlation between the numeric frequency of actual cases and the literary depictions. Mother/son incest occurs the least frequently in both. Otto Rank defines the essential difference between father/daughter and mother/son incest which contributes to the discrepancy in occurrence:

> The incest between son and mother, as well as the fantasies that replace it, are considered by consciousness probably owing first to physiological sensations—as a more serious infraction than a union between father and daughter. The internal, physical blood relationship that unites the son with the mother is of course not present to the same degree in the kinship between father and daughter.[3]

Himself the product of a patriarchal society, Rank points out that the father's authoritarian position carries a weight with the daughter which would not obtain when the male participant is younger and in the role of son. He also observes that "in legends and folktales the father's attraction to the daughter plays a much greater role than in myths, where the son's relationship to father and mother is dominant," giving as an example the legend of King Apollonius of Tyre, which underlies Shakespeare's *Pericles* (304). Early literature focusing on fathers and daughters often dealt impersonally with a series of suitors who are successively defeated by obstacles set up by the possessive father, with a final, victorious suitor sometimes emerging as the young hero. Modern developments of the theme usually involve a single suitor viewed by the father as an adversary.

The fact that brother/sister incest has traditionally been regarded as the least reprehensible of the three variations probably accounts for its more overt and frequent treatment in literature; Rank devotes 170 pages to "The Relationship between Siblings," but a scant thirty-seven pages to fathers and daughters. Probably fewer actual sibling cases come to the attention of authorities because incest between brothers and sisters does not carry the same onus as incest between fathers and daughters, which more frequently than not constitutes abuse of power and authority and is a more traumatic experience for the female participant. Actual cases that command legal attention today consist almost exclusively of those involving fathers/stepfathers and daughters.

In addition to Rank's chapter on fathers and daughters, other such literary examples are located in his final chapter, "The Incest Theme in Contemporary Literature." The modern works in the earlier chapter do not always feature conscious incest as a fait accompli; sometimes it is much desired but never achieved. Rank concluded the earlier chapter with Ibsen's *Rosmersholm* which he viewed as representative of a gradual repression of the incest theme in literature and his chapter on modern literature begins with other Ibsen plays.[4] He follows this with a survey of twenty-nine literary examples, fourteen of which involve siblings, nine of which involve mother/son incest, but only four of which involve a father and daughter. This series includes one narrative reminiscent of a personally observed situation that I mentioned in the preface. In "The Wedding Night," the mother fails in her attempt to seduce her husband following their daughter's wedding earlier in the day because the situation reminds him too vividly of the fact that "his daughter was in the desiring, ardent arms of a man" (561).

Although variations on the father/daughter theme are central to at least twenty-one of Shakespeare's plays,[5] Rank's discussions of Shakespeare concern themselves mainly with the rivalry between father and son for the mother. His pages devoted to fathers and daughters only include *The Merchant of Venice* as exemplifying the ordeal of the suitor, and *Pericles* briefly, as an example of use of the Apollonius legend. He refers to *The Tempest* only in a footnote, although the play provides an important variation on the theme.[6]

My work focuses only on literature written in English by male artists and primarily involving fathers and daughters. This seemed an important prerequisite to me for any future consideration of the theme in women writers. Although many earlier writers such as Boccaccio and Chaucer treated the theme, Shakespeare serves as a particularly valuable touchstone for two reasons: (1) the prolific nature of his work with its wealth of plots and (2) his acknowledged importance for all subsequent artists who wrote in English. Many other novelists might have been chosen, but since selection is imperative, the five artists here under consideration provide a nice diversity of family dynamics across a broad time span. Shakespeare, Dickens, and Joyce all had daughters; Conrad had only sons, and James never married.

Having benefited so extensively from representations of incest in mythology and literature, Freud, citing Rank's work, commented on "the extent to which the interest of creative writers centers around the theme of incest and how the same theme, in countless variations and distortions, provides the subject-matter of poetry."[7] He was also interested in how this had come about and this led to speculation by both Rank and Freud regarding creativity:

Up till now we have left it to the creative writer to depict for us the "necessary conditions for loving" which govern people's choice of an object, and the way in which they bring the demands of their imagination into harmony with reality. The writer can indeed draw on certain qualities which fit him to carry out such a task: above all, on a sensitivity that enables him to perceive the hidden impulses in the minds of other people, and the courage to let his own unconscious speak.[8]

The origins of the incest taboo have long been the focus of a broad spectrum of disciplines ranging from anthropology to philosophy, and a variety of scholars, in addition to Freud, have turned their attention to it: Socrates, Plato, Aquinas, Frazer, Levi-Strauss, and Lacan. The confusion it has engendered as an interdisciplinary puzzle was indicated by L. Levy-Bruhl: "The famous question of the ban on incest, this much discussed problem, the solution to which ethnologists and sociologists have so long sought after, has no answer."[9] A major source of the confusion has been the wide variations in the taboo itself, with ranges from "totemic exogamy, the prohibition of sexual intercourse between members of the same clan" (SE, 13:7) to religious restrictions on marriage between godparents.

Freud cites some of the variations in taboo emphasis: the separation of boys from mothers and sisters from puberty on, restrictions on certain cousins, tribes in which "a father may never be alone in the house with his daughter, nor a mother with her son," and others in which the onus falls on a man's relations with either his sister-in-law or his mother-in-law (SE, 13:10–14). Researchers have ultimately found the multiple discrepancies in the taboo both tantalizing and frustrating; how can one draw conclusions when the findings are so inconsistent? Even the assumption that there is always some taboo is not accurate; for example, nineteenth-century Aleuts of Kodiak practiced all forms of incest with no restrictions, and the Dyaks of Borneo have no concept of incest. Maisch concludes that "the concept is a relative one."[10] Pun intended?

Since lack of consistency in the incest taboo constitutes the only consistency, a common suggestion is that it derives not from some inherent moral code, but from man's need for self-imposed limitations and boundaries, separating him from the animal world wherein most sexual activity is indiscriminate. The derivation of the word "incest" supports this, coming as it does from the Latin *incestum* or "unchaste." This was the name of the girdle of Venus "which in lawful marriage was worn by the woman and loosened by the husband as an omen of conjugal and parental happiness; its disuse in an unlawful marriage rendered it 'incestuous or ungirdled'."[11]

The cultural history of incest involves both the taboo against it and the incestuous relationship as a special privilege. From very early times, the prerogative of defloration of the virgin was the privilege of an authority figure: an elder, a priest, or a holy man, followed later by the *jus prime noctis* of medieval feudal lords. In ancient Ireland, the prince married the princess and the king sometimes married his daughter.[12] A similar pattern was maintained in parts of Africa, and brother/sister marriages were accepted in Egypt.[13] In some cultures, incest is permitted only on special occasions: "to achieve prosperity," "to promote successful hunting," or "to make the tribesmen bulletproof" (Masters, 41, 42).

Incest behavior was common in Renaissance Italy, the most famous example being the Borgia Pope Alexander VI (1492) who is believed by most historians to have fathered a child by his daughter. Lucretia Borgia (who died in 1519) "was the daughter of her father, Alexander VI, as well as his lover, and as her brother's lover, she was her father's daughter-in-law. Reference to these relationships was made in her epitaph:

"Hic jacet in tumulo Lucretia nomine, sed re
Thais, Alexandri filia, sponsa, nursus.

"[Here lies entombed one named Lucretia—in truth
Thais, Alexander's daughter, wife, and daughter-in-law.]"
(Rank, 312–13)

This summary is at the heart of the riddle posed by the incestuous daughter for her suitors that occurs in many versions of the Apollonius legend, extending at least back to the Middle Ages and appearing finally in Shakespeare's *Pericles*. A friend of Joyce's reported the writer's comments on the Borgia case: "Nevertheless, I don't like Rome. . . . The Rome of the popes appeals to me more because it reminds me of that pig of a pope, Alexander VI, lying in the arms of his daughter and mistress, Lucretia Borgia."[14]

Incest was also accepted by the Persians, Incans, ancient Arabians, Indo-Europeans, pre-Mosaic Hebrews (Maisch, 23), and until 1892 by the Mormons.[15] The Greeks accepted only brother/sister incest, and that reluctantly (Maisch, 23). Cardinal Richelieu had incestuous relations with his daughter, as did Duke Philippe d'Orleans, of Voltaire's time, with two daughters (Maisch, 32). The importance of the concept of incest as privilege will be apparent in my analysis of the literature, particularly in Henry

James's *The Golden Bowl*. Incest eliminates the admission of a stranger into an established bloodline—a crucial point when that bloodline is already deemed optimal.

Rank explains the occurrence of incest in a wide range of classical myths: "[T]he development of myths and religions, as well as artistic activity, is intended to . . . justify male sexual fantasies" (300). Acceptance of the Adam/Eve story in Genesis automatically posits incest as the very foundation of the races of men. Although the Bible is obscure as to Cain's reasons for murdering Abel,[16] the Mohammedan version attributes the murder to an incestuous conflict over their own twin sisters (Masters, 14). Since Eve produced only male children at the outset, it is not difficult to read this first murder in terms of rivalry over the mother. Cain is suddenly furnished with a wife, but the next time we learn of Eve's bearing a child, it is Seth, another male; there is no reference to Eve's having given birth to a female child. The blatantly incestuous father in the Marquis de Sade's *Eugénie de Franval* (1788) relies on this to rationalize his behavior: "Was it not necessary to resort to such methods to populate the world? And what was then not a sin, can it now have become one? What nonsense!"[17] Was "Original Sin" in fact incest?

The wide variations in the taboo are equaled only by the range of explanations proffered for such taboos, reasons which might appear humorous to the modern reader. However, violations punishable by suicide-on-demand, castration, beheading, or other means of execution are by and large not humorous. The undesirable contraction of the family circle was spelled out in Plutarch's objection that "a girl who married her father would have no family to run home to in case of a domestic squabble" (Masters, 57). A similar concern was expressed to Margaret Mead by the Arapesh of New Guinea: "What, you would like to marry your sister! . . . Don't you want a brother-in-law? Don't you realize that if you marry another man's sister and another man marries your sister, you will have at least two brothers-in-law, while if you marry your own sister you will have none? With whom will you hunt, with whom will you garden, whom will you go to visit?"[18] Although amusing to us now, these were not negligible reasons in tightly enclosed societies. James Joyce posits another rationale, quoting Thomas Aquinas on incest: "[He] likens it in his wise and curious way to an avarice of the emotions. He means that the love so given to one near in blood is covetously withheld from some stranger who, it may be, hungers for it."[19]

There has been much controversy over whether the incest taboo is the result of an innate revulsion, but this has been effectively refuted for most authorities by the long history of stringent laws and punishments invoked to control the compelling attraction that sometimes exists between family members. Related to this controversy has been the disagreement among investigators over the probability of a progressive dulling of sexual desires among family members who have grown up together. Jeremy Bentham was one of the first to promulgate this theory,[20] which appears to have an element of truth, related to the observed occurrences of incest following the separation of related parties and their subsequent reunion—a predisposing factor in much of the literature:

> All types of incest are likely to occur when near-relatives are reunited after a lengthy separation, especially if the separation occurred in the childhood of one or both of the participants. It is quite easy to understand. . . . For psychological reasons, knowledge of the intimate blood-bond is conducive to affection. But this affection is not diluted in its sexual aspects, or diverted into non-sexual channels, as happens over a period of years in the day-to-day life of the family. . . . Unless the incest prohibition has great force within such persons, sexual intercourse is likely to take place. (Masters, 82)

Weinberg's findings corroborate this: "German soldiers separated from their families during the First World War often had relations with their maturing daughters when they returned home" (117). Boose, citing more recent studies carried out at Massachusetts General Hospital, revealed a new category, "divorce incest," in which incest did not occur until after the divorce or separation took place.[21] Although the report attributes this to possible paternal revenge, the element of reunion following separation is possibly also a factor.

Masters mentions the function of narcissism in incest, since relatives separated for a period of time see reflections of each other: "Plato also remarked that, lacking an incest prohibition, each individual would marry that person who most closely resembled himself—probably his sibling, his parent, or his child" (55). As in Oedipus Rex, incest participants in literature often discover the incriminating relationship only after incest has already occurred. The attraction toward someone who resembles oneself is simply another manifestation of the Oedipus complex.

We can only conclude that the incest taboo, in spite of its many variations in form (or perhaps because of them), represents a basic human need to impose order. Since the family unit represents man's most fundamental attempt at social order, incest represents a major violation of that order. As Maisch stresses, incest is not a *cause* of family disintegration, but a *symptom* of a "disturbed family order" that already exists (145). It would seem to be another chicken/egg conundrum. Although from the nineteenth century on, there were thought to be genetic grounds against incest—the threat of defective offspring—more recent research has questioned this (Maisch, 43). Repetition of genetic codes can work either way, and we are thrown back on the pragmatic basis, the preservation of the integrity of the family unit.

Masters summarizes: "The family would be disrupted, and in some cases destroyed, were its members permitted sexual access to one another. . . . The always precarious harmony of the family unit could not survive the tensions" (60). Weinberg maintains that incest confuses the child (and all familial roles), minimizes deference to parents, isolates the family, limits contacts with the outside world, intensifies rivalry, and reduces family cooperation and harmony (258). The experiments with more open sexual access within the hippy communes seems to have borne this out.

Recent case studies (many done by women) emphasize the permanent psychological damage done to the child—usually the daughter—in spite of the fact that a few writers on the subject still maintain that the abolishment of all sexual taboos would make for a happier society. These theorists (predominantly male) ignore the basic fact that forced participation of a child in adult sexual activity results in actions that are both premature and inappropriate for that stage of development. The daughter is deprived of her prerogative of a natural, progressive maturation, of the opportunity for sexual participation when she is ready for it, and of freedom of choice. Herman stresses the resulting permanent damage: "Thus did the victims of incest grow up to become archetypally feminine women: sexy without enjoying sex, repeatedly victimized yet repeatedly seeking to lose themselves in the love of an overpowering man, contemptuous of themselves and of other women, hard-working, giving, and self-sacrificing."[22]

The fact that this sexual exploitation of young female members of the society is a major component of patriarchal structures has been pointed out by a number of authorities:

The adult male's diminished capacity for affectionate relating prevents him from empathizing or identifying with his victim; without empathy, he lacks a major internal barrier to abusive action. At the same time, because other types of relationships are restricted, the need for a sexual relationship with a compliant and submissive female is exacerbated. Hence it is that adult men so frequently seek out sexual relationships not only with adult women who are younger and weaker than themselves, but also with girl children. (Herman, 56)

I would add here the importance of a submissive object as a possible requirement for the maintenance of male potency for certain individuals. Although a marriage may begin with a compliant, submissive female partner, a long-term relationship usually dulls this aspect of the relationship and the male need for someone to look up to him and to some extent remain subservient is no longer satisfied.

The wide variations in the taboo and in the rationale for it are paralleled by the history of its legal restrictions and punishments. Even the Oedipus myth is not exempt, for although Freud selected the Sophoclean version in which Oedipus blinds himself, the Homeric version entailed no such punishment and Oedipus becomes king and reigns in honor for many years.[23] An earlier version entailed the immediate rape of the mother following the father's murder (Rank, 218).

Taylor points to a shift in Greek thought between Homer (1200 B.C.) and Sophocles (500 B.C.). In Hebrew law, the strictures against incest came about gradually and there is no indication of legal or moral infraction in the story of the seduction of Lot by his daughters as they dwelt together in a cave following the destruction of Sodom and Gomorrah (Genesis 19.31–36). The mother is indeed absent, having been turned into a pillar of salt, and the daughters were the instigators, thinking that their father offered their only hope of propagating the human race.

Although many references have been made to this biblical occurrence of father/daughter incest (c. 1898 B.C.), an important element of the story is frequently overlooked: Prior to the daughters' seduction of their father, Lot had offered his hospitality to "two angels." The men of Sodom surround Lot's house and demand that he send the men outside so that they might "know them" (Genesis 19.5). But Lot refuses to do so and replies: "Behold now, I have two daughters which have not known men; let me, I pray you, bring them out unto you, and *do ye with them as is good in your eyes*: only unto these men do nothing" (Genesis 19.9, emphasis mine). His daughters are spared this fate by the intervention of the "angels," who orchestrate their escape with their father.

By about 1490 B.C., the restrictions against incest, homosexuality, and bestiality were established, a shift that appears to have occurred in the Hebrew culture much earlier than in the Greek. As the world population gradually increased, the need for simply increasing and multiplying diminished—a factor ignored by de Sade—encouraging the introduction of restrictions on sexual mating. In spite of the long history of these changes in attitudes and in the laws put into effect to reflect them, contemporary sociological investigators have observed that, even today, participants in certain incest cases were unaware of any wrongdoing until they were arrested.

Writers as far back as Plato saw the artist's role as didactic in his depiction of incest in literature: "In *Laws*, he indicated that Athenian playwrights had an obligation to portray incest perpetrators as committing suicide" (Masters, 23). In world literature, incest participants are usually punished. Primitive societies held a wide variety of superstitions concerning the disasters that would befall the group if incest were allowed to occur. These included the sun falling from the sky, earth tremors and volcanic explosions, flooding, and failures of harvest. Some thought the incestuous union could produce only monsters (Maisch, 39–40).

The connection between incest and limitations and boundaries is illustrated by the custom that "in the northern Gilbert Islands, the incest participants were . . . set adrift in the ocean. . . . Death was inevitable."[24] Decapitation, a classic castration substitute, served as punishment for incest in such disparate cultures as the Chinese and the Scottish (Masters, 205). All authorities cite the frequent occurrence of compulsory suicide as a major form of punishment (Weinberg, 9–11), although the Romans sometimes accepted "an expiatory sacrifice. . . . to the goddess Diana" (Masters, 41). The death penalty for incest was enforced in Switzerland as late as the seventeenth century, and in Germany until the end of the nineteenth century. Only in 1887 did Scotland switch from the death penalty to life imprisonment, and some term of imprisonment is the most common form of punishment today (Maisch, 31, 32).

In the United States, definitions of incest vary. Some states stipulate a blood relationship, some vaginal penetration, and most require that the victim be a minor. Prison terms run the gamut from a limit of eighteen months in Indiana to ten years in Kansas, with many states settling at five years.[25]

The gradual evolution of legal modifications in both Greek and Hebrew cultures has been paralleled in most other civilizations, with the Catholic Church exhibiting perhaps the widest swings. Although by 800 A.D., the Pope forbade marriage to the seventh degree of kindred (a restriction later extended to godparents and witnesses), dispensations were sold (Weinberg, 18–20). Incest in the early Middle Ages was fairly common and both the Inquisition and witch-hunts frequently involved either incest or homosexuality (Maisch, 26–28). Bloch emphasizes a shocking increase in incestuous unions during the eighteenth century in France.[26] In spite of the church's restrictions, at least two popes were involved in incest; one of them, Pope John XXII (1316–34), was relieved of the pontificate for that reason (Maisch, 30).

Significant legal measures coincide historically with two major literary periods: the Elizabethan and the Victorian. In 1583, approximately eleven years prior to Shakespeare's first play, Elizabeth created a Court of High Commission to penalize incest, and during the Interregnum (1642–60), the death penalty was in effect (Weinberg, 23). Between Elizabeth's Act of 1558 and 1908, jurisdiction oscillated between the ecclesiastical and the civil courts. The Punishment of Incest Act was passed in 1908 and was in turn repealed by the Sexual Offenses Act of 1956, which established a maximum penalty of seven years or possible life imprisonment if the girl was under 13 (Maisch, 223, 224). For a period of time, there had been great resistance to establishing legal strictures on the grounds that calling attention to the offense would only lead to more frequent occurrences.

The enforcement of legal restrictions gradually resulted in more cases being brought before the courts. The resulting sociological data on the incidence of father/daughter incest provides a valuable context for the recurrence of the theme in literature. The lack of correspondence between literature and general life experience would notably diminish literature's impact. Joyce reflects this connection when he says of Shakespeare: "He found in the world without as actual what was in his world within as possible" (U, 9.1041–42).

The sociological and clinical data concerning fathers and daughters is usually concerned solely with those two principals, since the incestuous relationship is initiated prior to the daughter's encounters with potential suitors. In fact, one of the primary functions of an established incestuous relationship is the isolation of the daughter from potential suitors. Ward comments: "Many of the Father-rapists give 'keeping her away from those other men out there' as the reason why they raped her in the first place."[27] The sad fact is that the early age at which the father often begins to approach his daughter sexually would preclude her having encountered suitors.

Rank concluded his chapter on "The Relationship Between Father and Daughter" with a series of thirteen case histories culled from newspaper accounts from various European cities between 1907 and 1910. Illustrating the common relationship between violent death and incest, five cases ended in murder, one in suicide, and three in infanticide, including one case in which five successive infants were destroyed (333–36). Tolstoy had earlier depicted this grim reality in *The Power of Darkness* (1888) which encompassed murder of the elderly husband, incest, and infanticide. Eugene O'Neill's *Desire under the Elms* (1924) offered a later variation on the lurid plot.

Recent research "surmised that somewhere in the neighborhood of one million American women have been involved in incestuous relations with their fathers, and that some 16,000 new cases occur each year." Herman goes on to add that the estimates are conservative and that the real incidence may actually be considerably higher (14). Even reports sent from Ireland, that bastion of restrictive sexual practices, have indicated an alarming increase in the incidence of incest.[28]

Although the authority factor cannot be discounted in any father/daughter relationship, it is more oppressive in some than in others, with three general types emerging: (1) the tyrannical father, (2) the loving-protective father, and (3) the truly mutual love affair. Any consideration of the father/daughter relationship must take into consideration the factor of autonomy in two aspects: its function in inducing the daughter's cooperation, and its function as a prerequisite for the father's own sexual potency. Although many fathers regard sexual relations with the daughter as a natural prerogative (Weinberg, 160), there sometimes exists a more nearly mutual relationship, which probably passes undetected by the community. Weinberg describes this relationship: "When the daughter reciprocates the father's sexual attentions, she experiences few conflicts. Relatively isolated from boys, she regards sexual compliance as one more filial function. She acquires a wifely role, or may conceive of herself as her father's 'lover'" (163).

But such instances constitute the minority. In most cases, as Maisch points out, the girl is trapped in the situation against her will and the father rarely gives the girl up voluntarily (193, 195). This is corroborated by Herman: "In no case was the incestuous relationship ended by the father. The daughters put a stop to the sexual contact as soon as they could, by whatever means they could. . . . Though all the daughters eventually succeeded in escaping from their families, they felt, even at the time of the interview, that they would never be safe with their fathers, and that they would have to defend themselves as long as their fathers lived" (95).

The precipitating factors in actual cases of father/daughter incest are the same factors that are found in literature: an "absent" mother, a nubile daughter, and some radical polarization in familial attachments. In the literature, the mother is frequently physically absent, often, in fact dead.

Less frequently, she is absent only as an effective agent of action. Rank suggests the underlying reason: "The mother's death when her daughter reaches marriageable age not only is an expression of the father's wish to exchange his spouse for his daughter but . . . also corresponds to the jealous wish of the daughter, who wishes to take her mother's place with the father (identification)" (309). Henry VIII acted out this fantasy rather than simply transmuting the impulse into literature.

The involved daughter is usually very passive (for a variety of reasons) and either dependent on or intimidated by the father. This passivity is explained by Meiselman: "To truly understand the passivity of the daughter, one needs to imagine the situation as it is perceived through the eyes of a child. Especially in a paternalistic family, the daughter has been taught to obey her father in all situations, to anticipate punishment for any show of defiance, and to believe that what her father does is unquestionably in her best interests."[29]

Ward expands on this explanation, tying it directly to the girl's development in a paternalistic culture: "The internalization of passivity by women differs in degree along a spectrum; it is a direct result of a male supremacist cultural system that indoctrinates women to exist only as the playthings or nurturers of men" (171). Rank mentions yet another dimension: "Even in the few mythological passages in which the loving passion seems to be presented from the viewpoint of the daughter, one has the impression that this is only a justification of the father's shocking desires; an attempt is made to shift the blame for the seduction onto her" (300).

An additional factor is the importance of the feminine desire for masculine approval, especially as fostered in a paternalistic atmosphere. Also, even when the mother is not physically absent, she is often as passive and as psychologically incapable of standing up to the father as the daughter is, thus depriving the daughter of protection. The economic dependence of both women must also be factored in. The "absence" of the mother is thus not necessarily physical, although in literature, it usually is. There is always some disruption in the husband/wife relationship before the incest occurs; absence often entails estrangement only. On occasion the substitution of the daughter is either actively or passively promoted by the mother. No matter what the duration of the parental estrangement has been, it is sufficient to alter the father's attitudes toward his daughter's newly developed sexual potential. Statistics on the daughters' ages at the outset vary. Maisch cites the average as 12¼ (102), while Herman maintains that 80% were under thirteen years when first approached by their fathers, with the average age being nine years (83).

Citing the average age of the father as 43.5, and of the daughter as 15.3, Weinberg summarizes the conditions that obtain in actual cases, conditions that can be transposed onto certain literary examples: "The father initiated incest at a period of life when his usefulness to industry had declined, when his wife's attraction had diminished, when extrafamilial women were less accessible, and when his daughters had become biologically mature" (44). In most instances, there is also an economic factor at work, since "extrafamilial women" usually cost money in one way or another and require more elaborate planning. In some societies, father/daughter incest served as a form of birth control, with the father moving from daughter to daughter as each began to menstruate.

The recurrent preoccupation on the part of various writers throughout an extensive body of literature with the triangular father/daughter/suitor configuration suggests the importance of the Oedipus complex in the individual's selection of subsequent love-objects. This corroborates Freud's delineation of its function in "Contributions to the Psychology of Love" and elsewhere. In spite of continued controversy over the validity of the Oedipus complex and its variety of interpretations, I assume Freud's concept of it as a "given." Although Freud explored more extensive ramifications of the historical and anthropological aspects in "Totem and Taboo," its most basic concepts are adequate. René Girard, in his brilliant discussion of desire in the novel, sums this up: "From a Freudian viewpoint, the original triangle of desire is, of course, the Oedipal triangle. The story of 'mediated' desire is the story of this Oedipal desire, of its essential permanence beyond its ever changing objects."[30] Freud discusses the function of the complex in the choice of love-objects:

Analytic researches have discovered how universal and how powerful the first attachments of the libido are. It is a question of sexual wishes active in childhood and never relinquished—in women generally a fixation of the libido upon the father . . . *wishes that often enough were directed to things other than coitus, or that included it among others only as a vaguely conceived aim.* A husband is, so to speak, never anything but a proxy, never the right man.[31] (emphasis mine)

Consideration of the mutual relationship between father and daughter leads to the concept of the "inverted triangle." The daughter's original attachment for her father has never been deflected toward another person. But it is maintained by many psychoanalytic authorities that in some cases, the father's prolonged attachment for the daughter is a *reversal* of an unresolved mother/son attachment. There are two ways of coming to this position: the wife (the mother of the daughter) was herself a "proxy" for the man's own mother. Consequently, the daughter is one of a series, and thus replaces both the original and the proxy. Ernest Jones offers a more complex explanation, later elaborated by devotees of transactional analysis:

> I have, for instance, invariably found that a man who displays an abnormally strong affection for his daughter also gives evidence of a strong infantile fixation in regard to his mother (often with an insufficient affection for his wife due to the same cause). In his phantasy he begets his mother (e.g., in the form of a rescue), becomes thus her father, and so arrives at a later identification of his real daughter with his mother. *Such people fit into the situation either of parent or of child, but only imperfectly into that of a marital partner.*[32] (emphasis mine)

Jones's explanation provides an interesting basis for potential deficiencies in primary marital relationships.

By extending this theory, if the daughter has replaced the mother in the earlier oedipal triangle, the suitor as a proxy for the man's own father explains the hostility on the part of the father toward the suitor. "The suitor's struggle with the father of the beloved corresponds to the son's struggle with his father" (Rank, 313). As in other displacements, the original feelings are intensified and can be openly expressed to an extent that was not possible in the initial triangular conflict. The inverted triangle repeats an earlier conflict when as son the man was helpless, but now as father he is in the position of power within the triangle. Also, when the daughter has reached puberty, the wife has reached an age at which she begins to suggest the man's own mother, a fact which may inhibit his relationship with her and cause him to seek satisfaction in his daughter or in a daughter-substitute. This is augmented by an increased awareness of his own mortality. That the artist projects these same anxieties and conflicts into his creative work will become evident in reviewing the literature in the ensuing chapters.

Yung and easily freudened
James Joyce, *Finnegans Wake*

1

Some Literary Variations on the Incest Theme

"Novelists, playwrights, poets and literary critic/essayists have made a greater contribution to the understanding of incest than have scientists and scholars" (4). Masters's conclusion, echoing Freud's, no longer has the validity it once had, but creative artists will always be recognized as the precursors of subsequent explorers of the subject. However, many of these novelists, playwrights, and poets veiled and obscured the theme. Freud, writing about father/daughter incest in Ibsen's *Rosmersholm*, corroborated Rank's earlier observation when he stated that "everything that refers to it in the play is, so to speak, subterranean and has to be pieced together from hints."[1]

Freud contended that readers failed to acknowledge the pervasiveness of the incest theme in literature because of "the distaste which human beings feel for their early incestuous wishes, now overtaken by repression" (SE, 13:17). As will be seen in the case of Joseph Conrad, sometimes the artists themselves ignored or denied the presence of the theme in a given work, and they are often joined by literary critics. It is important here to define what constitutes the presence of the incest theme in a given literary work. Joseph Conrad was technically correct when he denied the incestuous nature of his novel since actual incest did not occur in *Almayer's Folly*, and this is true in much of the literature to be considered here. Literature to which the incest theme might be attributed would include not only overt incest, but any abnormal attachments on the part of fathers and/or daughters which permanently inhibit their ability to relate to each other appropriately and to establish viable relationships with others.

Although Rank surveyed literature other than myth and legend, his life span restricted him to a limited period of modern literature. Frequently, even in the presence of the father/daughter relationship, he stressed other familial relationships, especially that of father/son or brother/brother. For example, in his discussion of *Oedipus at Colonus*, Rank focuses on the brothers' hatred for the father, with only passing mention of the daughters (487–89; 523). But the play concludes with Oedipus and his daughters:

> But when he had his will in everything,
> And no desire was left unsatisfied,
> It thundered from the netherworld; the maids
> Shivered, and crouching at their father's knees
> Wept, beat their breast and uttered a long wail.
> He, as he heard their sudden bitter cry,
> Folded his arms about them both and said,
> "My children, ye will lose your sire today,
> For all of me has perished, and no more
> Have ye to bear your long, long, ministry;
> A heavy load, I know, and yet one word
> Wipes out all score of tribulations—*love*.
> And love from me ye had—from no man more;
> But now must live without me all your days."
> So clinging to each other sobbed and wept
> Father and daughters both, . . .[2]

The reader is free to interpret these lines as he may, and whether or not one wants to conclude that an Oedipus deprived of their mother turns to his daughters for more than moral support, the relationship of these three has been intense.

Perhaps the strongest literary affirmation of incest occurs in words spoken by the incestuous father in the Marquis de Sade's *Eugénie de Franval*:

"You mean to say that a lovely girl cannot tempt me because I am guilty of having sired her? That what ought to bind me more intimately to her should become the very reason for my removal from her? 'Tis because she resembles me, because she is flesh of my flesh, that is to say that she is the embodiment of all the motives upon which to base the most ardent love, that I should regard her with an icy eye? . . . Ah, what sophistry! . . . How totally absurd!" (394)

The eventual dénouement of this novel, however, does not bear out the father's early bravado. The incestuous father murders a prospective suitor and faking the renunciation of his daughter sleeps for a while with both mother and daughter. Told by her father to choose between her parents, Eugénie murders her mother, repents and dies. Her father's overwhelming guilt drives him to suicide. Sade had offered as an alternate title for the novel, *The Misfortunes of Incest* (373), and in spite of his moralistic conclusion, he was reimprisoned in the Bastille for life for its publication and that of *Justine*. Rank regards Sade's preoccupation with the incest theme as one more manifestation of the actual prevalence of incest in France during the eighteenth century (355).

Much English literature, both before and after Shakespeare, dealt in one way or another with fathers and daughters. An overview of these works reveals that some treat incest overtly, others covertly. In many others it exists only as an implied threat which is avoided through the actions of the participating characters. That most universally familiar fairy tale, *Cinderella*, existed in versions in which the heroine was fleeing an incestuous father. Alan Dundes makes a strong case for such a folktale as the basis for *King Lear*.[3] Triangular father/daughter/suitor relationships characterize Chaucer's *Troilus and Criseyde* (c. 1385), and at least two of the *Canterbury Tales* (c. 1386).[4]

One of the most widely transmitted plots of overt father-daughter incest occurs in the legend of King Apollonius of Tyre. "The material originally comes from a fourth-century A.D. Greek novel, of which a Latin translation exists. In the Middle Ages the story was translated into almost all languages and is found in a great number of manuscripts, editions, and reworkings: in one of these forms it earned a place in the *Gesta Romanorum* (no. 153)" (Rank, 304). Chaucer began his version of the legend with a witty disclaimer voiced by the Man of Law, who summarizes Chaucer's previous work which has not drawn on such sources as Apollonius (a jibe at Gower) since "Chaucer knew quite well what he was doing/And would not soil his sermons with narration/Of such unnatural abomination"[5] and that neither would he. The tale which follows is fraught with violence, and ends with the death of the suitor/husband and the return of Constance to her father. John Gower's version, *Confessio Amantis* (1390), served Shakespeare as a source for *Pericles* (c. 1609), and like its earlier sources treats father/daughter incest more blatantly than Shakespeare's version does. Cruder versions of the famous riddle in *Pericles* were also components of the earlier versions.

Although Rank focused on modern German literature, many other examples can be found in other European literature[6] and the English novel prior to Charles Dickens offers many variations on the father/daughter theme. Most of these do not depict overt incest but exhibit what Sandra Gilbert has dubbed "the submerged paradigm of father-daughter incest." Sandra Gilbert, noting the literary prevalence of the father/daughter theme in George Eliot's *Silas Marner* and Edith Wharton's *Summer* adds: "But, of course, countless other literary texts—both male- and female-authored—focus on the submerged paradigm of father-daughter incest that shapes the possibilities inscribed in these novels."[7]

William Congreve's only tragedy, *The Mourning Bride* (1697), depicts an enraged king who murders the suitor, then impersonates him, and is decapitated. More "submerged paradigms" can be found in Samuel Richardson's *Clarissa* (1747) which depicts both a father and a brother bent on marrying the daughter/sister to a man she detests. Henry Fielding's *Tom Jones* (1749) treats the same theme in a rollicking fashion, although Sophia Western, like Clarissa, at one point contemplates suicide. At least one critic has done a careful explication of Charlotte Bronte's *Jane Eyre* (1847) in father/daughter terms, and Jane Austen's *Emma* (1816) depicts an unusually strong father/daughter relationship, Emma's father being blatantly derisive of marriage, and Emma herself reluctant to leave home. Similar undercurrents are to be found in Austen's *Northanger Abbey* (1803), and Thackeray's *Vanity Fair* (1847).[8] With the paradigm not so submerged, Dylan Thomas wrote "The Burning Baby."[9] Almost a century separates two American examples which represent the extremes of implicit and explicit depiction of father/daughter incest: Nathaniel Hawthorne's "Rappaccini's Daughter" (1844), and F. Scott Fitzgerald's *Tender Is the Night* (1934), in which the appropriately modern punishment is the daughter's schizophrenia.

Although myth and legend have played an important role in the generation of father/daughter narratives, historical events have also had significant impact on both literature and literary criticism. Three hundred years separate two such historical sources: the sixteenth-century Italian tragedy of Beatrice Cenci and Freud's twentieth-century case history of Dora. Although these two narratives might seem at first glance to be strange bedfellows, they share many characteristics common to father/ daughter relationships as circumscribed by the strictures of a paternalistic society, their disparate historical periods lending added emphasis to this factor. They also share many of the key recurrent elements to be found in much of the literature.

Both young women were subject to autocratic fathers; Cenci was overtly abusive, Dora's father employed more subtle methods. Both mothers were physically present but absent as effective agents for change. Beatrice Cenci's stepmother too suffered under the abusive husband/father and is thus drawn into conspiring in his murder. Dora's mother had been discredited by Freud as having "housewife's psychosis," although he never met her, and had been usurped by her surrogate, Frau K., both as a mother/ companion for her daughter and a mistress for her husband.[10]

During the course of the action, Beatrice is confronted by a series of judgmental older men who ultimately put her to death. Dora is confronted by an equally united group of older men who not only deny her the validity of her perceptions but *tell* her what she is really feeling and thinking, and urge her sexual compliance with one of them. In contrast to the physical torture of Beatrice, Dora's torment is of a more subtle nature. Neither young woman has access to salvation through a viable suitor. Monsieur Guerra (also a father figure by virtue of age and authority) participates in Beatrice's father's destruction, but deserts her when he alone escapes the consequences. Dora also has failed to acquire a suitor of comparable age, and a liaison with her father's contemporary, Herr K., who has come to be repellent to her, is being urged by both her father and Freud. This follows the pattern that recurs throughout literature of the father who only approves of a suitor who is close to his own age and is unacceptable to the daughter; *Romeo and Juliet* is a classic example. Erickson summed up Dora's plight: "As a *woman*, Dora did not have a chance."[11]

Sources for the two narratives also share a record of objective unreliability regarding them. The Cenci story was originally transmitted in various Italian accounts (*relaziones*) that proliferated following the executions in 1599, augmented by a portrait long believed to have been painted of Beatrice Cenci by Guido Reni at the time of her execution. The widespread interest in the Dora case stems from the case history published by Freud in 1905. Both sources, for quite different reasons, are felt today to be somewhat unreliable. The recurrent question of reality versus fantasy, such a prominent feature of current incest discourse, enters into any consideration of the sources of inspiration for the various literary works and for the literary criticism.

Shelley's five-act play, *The Cenci* (1819), provides one of the most graphic examples in English literature of the fascination that historical narratives based on flawed father/daughter relationships have had for a broad spectrum of artists, illustrating the fine line between "influence" and intertextuality. Shelley's play had been preceded by a little-known Italian version by Pieracci in 1816.[12] The connection between the Italian *relaziones* and the various literary works based on the Cenci tragedy is complex and confusing, due both to variations in the sources and to opportunities for editing in translation.

Certain historically verifiable facts are common to all early accounts. Francesco Cenci, the wealthy father of Beatrice, from the age of fourteen on was repeatedly haled into court and forced to pay heavy fines to a series of popes for various crimes, including sodomy. He persecuted his family, virtually imprisoning his second wife Lucrezia (Beatrice's stepmother) and his daughter Beatrice. The two women, along with his sons Giacomo and Bernardo and a family friend "Monsignor" Guerra—not a cleric and possibly a suitor for Beatrice—collaborated to have him murdered. Guerra later escaped, but the four Cencis were arrested and compelled under torture to confess. All but Bernardo were executed on September 11, 1599, as decreed by Pope Clement VIII. Less than a century earlier, Pope Alexander VI had consorted with his own daughter, Lucretia.

Certain plot elements in the true story correspond to various literary versions of the father/daughter/suitor triad. The suitor as solution had been utilized by Beatrice's older sister who had petitioned the pope to arrange a marriage or place her in a convent so that she might escape the oppression of her father's house; the pope had complied and a marriage then took place. When Beatrice later also appealed to the pope for such a release, her father, threatened with losing his only remaining daughter, became enraged and thwarted her plans.[13]

In the final disposition of the case, Beatrice, who had participated in destroying her abusive father, was betrayed by a series of father-surrogates. One of the collaborators in the crime, her father/suitor, "Monsignor" Guerra, escaped. She was tried by another father figure, Farinacci, who evidently was as corrupt as her father had been. Her execution was ordered by the supreme father, the pope, who in effect refused to hear her defense.[14] During his lifetime, Cenci had lived under a series of permissive popes whose coffers had greatly benefited from his recurring infractions. Robert Browning refers to Clement VIII as "Pope Conniver at Francesco Cenci's guilt."[15]

Identification of the portrait as that of Beatrice remains uncertain and confusing, but responses to it by well-known literary figures constitute a unique record, especially in view of the fact that modern art authorities now pronounce the portrait to be neither by Guido Reni nor of Beatrice. Recently, art critics have also questioned Reni's identity as the creator of the well-known *Lot and His Daughters* in 1615–16.[16] The supposed picture of Beatrice generated thousands of words, both in recorded responses to it and in the number of literary creations triggered by it. Although Mary Shelley simply recorded in her *Journal* in 1819 that they had seen the portrait,[17] her husband told Trelawny that the picture "haunted" him,[18] elaborating on his reaction in the Preface to *The Cenci*, written that same year.[19]

Four years later, Stendhal (Henri Beyle) viewing the same portrait, echoed Shelley's impressions: "I was captivated by the portrait of Beatrice Cenci . . . at the palazzo Barberini. . . . The face has sweetness and beauty, the expression is most appealing and the eyes very large: they have the startled air of a person who has just been caught in the act of shedding large tears" (Stendhal, 173). Stendhal had met Shelley in 1818 and perhaps gave the Shelleys their copy of the *relazione* that Mary used for the translation she made for Shelley's use.[20] Stendhal's translation of manuscript no. 172 titled "The Cenci" appeared anonymously in *La Revue des Deux-Mondes* in July, 1837, and was later printed in *Chroniques Italiennes*. Shelley's play and the Stendhal translation agree in the basic components of the story. Rank focuses his brief discussion of the two artists on the shared hatred for their fathers which, he maintained, attracted them to the material. He refers to Shelley's intensely antagonistic relationship with his own father and with Harriet's father (327); the same could have been said of his relationship with Mary's father, William Godwin. Rank also points out that Stendahl left an unusually graphic account of his intense attachment to his mother in *Confessions of an Egoist* (27).

Although more widely recognized for her novel *Frankenstein* (1818), Mary Shelley wrote her own graphic novel about father/daughter incest, *Mathilda*, in 1819. The novelette treats the threat of incest much more explicitly than Shelley's play and culminates in the suicides of both father and daughter. Following Shelley's death in 1822, Mary entrusted her manuscript to friends who were returning to England, with instructions to give

Alleged portrait of Beatrice Cenci,
Galleria Nazionale d'Arte Antica
in Palazzo Barberini, Rome. For-
merly ascribed to Guido Reni. By
permission of the Ministry for Cultural and Environmental Affairs,
Florence, Italy.

it to her father, William Godwin, to see it through publication. Not surprisingly, her father pronounced it "disgusting and detestable," and made
no effort to get it published.[21] It was not published until 1959.

There is even the possibility that Shakespeare had read accounts of
the case, although the evidence is not overwhelming. In *The Tempest*,
Caliban plots to kill Prospero by knocking a nail into his head after he is
asleep.[22] This was the manner of Francesco Cenci's murder and it had
occurred twelve years prior to the writing of the play. A succession of other
works overtly based on the legend included Alexandre Dumas' account
in *Crimes Célèbres* (1839), Walter Savage Landor's five-act dialog (1850),
Guerazzi's novel (1853), "Cenciaja," a poem by Browning (1860), plays by
Artaud (1935) and Moravia (1942), and Frederick Prokosch's novel, *A Tale
for Midnight* (1956). Rank cites the tragedy by Arno Holz, *Sonnenfinsternis*
(1908), as being similar to the *Cenci* story (332). Steffan compares variations in this legend to those that evolve in the transmission of folktales,[23]
and surely the most interesting rationalization of incest by the father is the
argument made in some accounts that the offspring of incestuous relationships are guaranteed sainthood (De Sade, Dumas, Stendhal).

In 1844, less than 30 years after Shelley's and Stendhal's observations,
Charles Dickens, who wrote *Dombey and Son* in the years immediately
following his viewing of the Cenci portrait, described the picture in true
Dickensian fashion:

> She has turned suddenly toward you; and there is an expression in
> the eyes—although they are very tender and gentle—as if the wild-
> ness of a momentary terror, or distraction, had been struggled with
> and overcome, that instant; and nothing but a celestial hope, and
> a beautiful sorrow, and a desolate earthly helplessness remained.
> Some stories say that Guido painted it from memory, after having
> seen her, on her way to the scaffold. I am willing to believe that, as
> you see her on his canvas, so she turned towards him, in the crowd,
> from the first sight of the axe, and stamped upon his mind a look
> which he has stamped on mine as though I had stood beside him
> in the concourse.[24]

Two major American novelists, Herman Melville and Nathaniel Hawthorne, incorporated the portrait in their fiction. Toward the end of *Pierre*
(1852), as the three central characters tour an art gallery, Lucy pauses before "that sweetest, most touching, but most awful of all feminine heads—
The Cenci of Guido."[25] Hawthorne, who regarded it as "the saddest picture ever painted or conceived,"[26] named the daughter Beatrice and the

suitor Giacomo in "Rappaccini's Daughter" (1844). Recent Hawthorne criticism elaborates on the family dynamics reflected in Hawthorne's fiction, including the intense relationship with his mother and with his daughter Una: "Even more eerie is Hawthorne's own prefiguration of Una's fate in the life of the fictional daughter and prisoner Beatrice Rappaccini, a character created in the month of his daughter's birth. Beatrice is the creation, agent, and victim of the father with whom she lives in an exotic and cloistered garden."[27] Erlich notes of the fifteen-year-old Una's near-fatal illness in Rome that Hawthorne never recovered from the trauma of the experience.[28]

In an even more explicit tribute to the Cenci influence, Hawthorne discusses the Cenci portrait in the seventh chapter of *The Marble Faun* (1859), itself a variation on the legend as discussed by Carton: [The novel is] "dominated by treacherously intimate daughter-father relations, or by the collapse of relationship into two stark alternatives: utter filial submission to—and perhaps incestuous incorporation by—the father's imperial identity and symbolic—perhaps actual—patricide" (225).

When Miriam asks Hilda what gives the portrait "such a mysterious force," Hilda responds: "She knows that her sorrow is so strange and so immense that she ought to be solitary forever, both for the world's sake and for her own; and this is the reason we feel such a distance between Beatrice and ourselves, even when our eyes meet hers."[29] But Miriam offers a singularly modern, feminist response: "After all . . . if a woman had painted the original picture, there might have been something in it which we miss now. I have a great mind to undertake a copy myself and try to give it what it lacks" (56). One thing it evidently lacked was authenticity. Miriam too echoes the Cenci legend: "Miriam's origins are unknown, but in each of the various speculations about her she has 'fled from her paternal home' usually to escape an unsavory father or to avoid sexual domination by his representative" (Carton, 225). In both these Hawthorne works, the theme has to be "pieced together from hints."

Henry James, who certainly had seen the portrait in the course of his numerous visits to the Barberini Gallery in 1872,[30] might well have contended that a portrait actually done of Beatrice on the day of her execution would not have had the impact that the less-than-real object has had.[31] One can only speculate on the influence this portrait and its legend may have had on such Jamesian fathers as those in *Washington Square* (1878) and *The Portrait of a Lady* (1880).

Thus, Joyce's use of the final poignant lines of Shelley's powerful play in *Giacomo Joyce* (1913) became only one of many instances of the utilization of the tragedy by later writers. Although the correspondence between names in Joyce's use of "Giacomo" has been noted, the fact that Giacomo Cenci was executed for attempting to avenge his father's assaults on his sister and his mother has received less notice. The lines that Joyce selected are spoken by Beatrice in preparation for her execution. Each of the adapters of the Cenci story interpreted the evidence in his own way and Joyce was no exception. He describes Beatrice as "stainless of blood and violation."[32] Joyce later generated his own intertextuality by transferring material from *Giacomo* into his novels and his play.[33] When he interrupted his Italian exile to help open the first cinema in Dublin in December 1909 the initial bill included *The Tragic Story of Beatrice Cenci*. The reviewer found it "although very excellent, . . . hardly as exhilarating a subject as one would desire on the eve of the festive season."[34]

Corrado Ricci, an Italian art critic, museum curator, and historian, concluded his 1925 two-volume attempt to rectify the errors regarding both the portrait and the Italian sources on the trial, with these words: "The girl in the Barberini Gallery . . . who returns your gaze with so naive an indifference, her face neither illumined by joy nor shadowed by grief, is not Beatrice Cenci. She is the Samian sibyl. We say this for the benefit of historians and artists. For the great public we know well, the picture will remain to all eternity, Beatrice Cenci and none other" (287, 288). Copies still appear in Shelley texts. At least eight operas have been written based on the material, the first in 1863 and the most recent in 1951.[35] This combined with the recent opera version of "Rappaccini's Daughter" (1991) points up how often composers of operas are drawn to such material; operas display an almost infinite range of treatments of the father/daughter/ suitor triad, usually fraught with violence.[36]

Since the time of Freud's dramatic recanting of his seduction theory, the conflict between fantasy and reality has continued to be a prominent issue in contemporary discourse on incest and the Cenci story provides an interesting case in point. Although almost all of the artists who dealt with the legend directly assumed that incest had actually occurred, Ricci maintains that his research into Vatican records leaves this much in doubt, since Beatrice herself never seems to have pleaded this in her defense. By the same token, she may have felt that such an admission would only bring down additional wrath from her persecutors.[37]

An interesting parallel to the Cenci case is to be found in a more recent account of father/daughter relationships, Freud's widely publicized "Fragment of an Analysis of a Case of Hysteria" [Dora]. Since Freud undertook the case after abandoning his seduction theory, the question of possible incest was not a factor as it might have been a short time before. The focus on the forced sexual attentions of a father-surrogate, Herr K., encouraged by both her own father and Freud, has caught the attention of numerous literary critics and feminist theorists. Freud's three-month focus on Dora's case was begun in 1900 and his findings first published in 1905. As a written record, it vies with the Cenci legend as a paradigm of father/daughter relationships. Claire Kahane summarizes this: "*Dora* is thus no longer read as merely a case history or a fragment of an analysis of hysteria but as an urtext in the history of woman, a fragment of an increasingly heightened critical debate about the meaning of sexual difference and its effect on the representations of feminine desire."[38]

Freud's own evaluation of the cultural importance of the incest taboo undoubtedly colored his attitudes and his report of the case. Three years prior to meeting Dora and her father, Freud wrote to Fliess that "incest is antisocial—civilization consists in this progressive renunciation."[39] Thirty-three years later, the subject was still on his mind: "The tendency on the part of civilization to restrict sexual life is not less clear than its other tendency to expand the cultural unit. Its first, totemic phase already brings with it the prohibition against an incestuous choice of object, and this is perhaps the most drastic mutilation which man's erotic life has in all time experienced."[40]

Freud regarded his histories as narratives akin to fiction, and the close relationship is spelled out by Philip Rieff: "[T]he psychoanalytic case history crosses the barrier artificially erected between a literature of description and a literature of imagination. It matters little whether Freud's case histories are called science or art. Freud's interpretive science was itself, in practice, an art, aiming at a transformation of the life thus interpreted."[41] The key element that relates the two forms of narrative is, of course, selection of data. Freud did not record data until after his patient interviews had ended, allowing even greater leeway for selection and arrangement than would otherwise have occurred. Steven Marcus goes perhaps the furthest in his designation of the case history, which he finds comparable to Proust, as "indistinguishable from a systematic fictional creation." He concludes that by the end of the history, "Freud and not Dora has become the central character in the action."[42]

Although various sources have been cited for Freud's choice of the fictitious name for his patient, I am partial to Dickens's *David Copperfield*, his most autobiographical novel with its depiction of another Dora and her obsessive father. Freud's intensely personal involvement in this case is indicated in his own words to his friend, Wilhelm Fliess: "It has been a lively time, and I have a new patient, a girl of eighteen; the case has opened smoothly to my collection of picklocks." When the case was closed and the history written, he wrote that he "already miss[ed] a narcotic."[43] Freud's failure to comment on his own countertransference in this case has been widely discussed.

Provocative counterinterpretations of this controversial case continue to be published. As with the Cenci story, it has also triggered some literary creations such as Hélène Cixous' play, *Portrait de Dora* (1976). With the mother effectively removed for all practical purposes, Freud reports: "His daughter was most tenderly attached to him" (*SE*, 7:18), and later, "Dora was by that time in the first bloom of youth—a girl of intelligent and engaging looks" (*SE*, 7:23). She was sixteen, Freud forty-four when they first met. The absence of the mother in this case illustrates Paula Cohen's assessment of fiction: "Daughters in novels before James either didn't have mothers or had mothers who were discredited by male authority and hence rendered already open to daughterly replacement."[44] Dora's mother had been "discredited" and neglected by both husband and daughter; this was further reinforced by Freud's neglect of her as a participant in the case history.

The ramifications of Freud's identification, both with Dora's father and with the rejected Herr K., give this analysis a tone not to be found in the other case histories. Freud himself suggests this sort of reading: "At the beginning it was clear that I was replacing her father in her imagination, which was not unlikely, in view of the difference between our ages" (*SE*, 7:118). But when Dora decided to terminate her treatment, Freud carried the transference further: "In this way the transference took me unawares, and, because of the unknown quantity in me which reminded Dora of Herr K., she took her revenge on me as she wanted to take her revenge on him, and deserted me as she believed herself to have been deceived and deserted by him" (*SE*, 7:119). Our knowledge of how Freud sided with Herr K. in this analysis indicates that Dora was entitled to "revenge" on all three father figures. Willbern suggests that Freud's own speculation that perhaps he should have persisted anyhow, showing a more personal interest, "discloses the potential rapist in the therapist."[45]

In addition to the controversy the Dora case has provoked, Freud has also become increasingly involved as the center of heated controversy in recent years over the reversal of his early belief in the seduction theory which had attributed neurosis to early sexual violations of his patients by a male member of their families: "I no longer believe in my *neurotica* [theory of the neuroses]" (Freud to Fliess 264, September 21, 1897). Feminist critics in particular have castigated him and devalued his work in this regard. Herman rejected the reasons he gave for his abandonment of his theory as inadequate, taking him to task for initially indicting uncles instead of fathers as the culprits in the histories of Rosalia and Katharina (9). Although the cases were reported in 1886, Freud did not disclose the true identity of the culprits until 1924. But considering the shocking nature of his disclosure, the substitution of "uncles" would not have been that much more palatable for his audience.

Freud eventually admitted that in some cases an actual infraction had occurred. The mistake of reducing the question to one of either/or lies at the heart of much of the difficulty, both for current critics and originally for Freud himself. The tempering of such a view was suggested by Freud in 1917: "You must not suppose, however, that sexual abuse of a child by its nearest male relatives belongs entirely to the realm of phantasy."[46] Peter Gay also urges the more moderate view: "What Freud repudiated was the seduction theory as a general explanation of how all neuroses originate."[47]

The chronology of Freud's promulgation of the "seduction theory" in 1896 and his retraction less than a year later sheds light on Freud's handling of this case. In 1896, Freud had publicly committed himself to the seduction theory. In May 1897, he had his erotic dream regarding his nine-year-old daughter, Mathilde. By September 1897, he renounced the theory. Had he encountered Dora a few years earlier, he would have assumed that she had been sexually assaulted by her father as the cause of what he diagnosed as her hysteria. Instead, the onus was placed on Dora vis-à-vis Herr K.'s attempt to kiss her when she was fourteen: "I should without question consider a person hysterical in whom an occasion for sexual excitement elicited feelings that were preponderantly or exclusively unpleasurable" (SE, 7:28). Freud did not seem to understand the potential trauma in her reaction to Herr K.'s advances as elucidated by others:

> But intercourse is only half the story. . . . Any number of acts may be committed which frequently are at least as traumatic to the victim as full intercourse. Neither does the offender have necessarily to be the father—anyone in a parental position, such as a stepfather, may cause exactly the same kind of damage to the victim as an actual father.[48]

Although many critics have cited Freud's singular attitudes and preconceived notions regarding the expected erotic responses of fourteen-year-old and sixteen-year-old girls, it should also be noted that his oldest daughter Mathilde was fourteen when he first met Dora, who was sixteen. The first sexual approach to Dora had been made by Herr K. when she was only fourteen and one can only wonder whether Freud would have foisted the same sort of judgments on his own daughter under those circumstances.

It is difficult not to judge Freud in terms of our present knowledge augmented by the feminist vantage point that has now been attained. Many of his critics believe that the Oedipus complex and the seduction theory are mutually exclusive, and while this is not the time or place for such discussion, I do not agree. This seems comparable to me to the old joke that being paranoid did not preclude someone's being out to get you. A strong oedipal attachment does not preclude a violation of a young person's trust.

The controversy between reality and fantasy continues to rage in many areas, including present-day court cases involving child molestation revealed through repressed memories brought to the surface, based on the assumption that certain symptoms can only be explained by the fact that certain violations took place in the past. The truth probably lies somewhere in between, and the difficulties of accurately distinguishing between fantasy and reality in an individual's testimony regarding childhood incidents can never be fully resolved; the circumstances of how the repressed memories are released must always be carefully examined.

The scholarly interest that both Rank (1884–1939) and Freud (1856–1939) brought to bear on father/daughter relationships can be put into some context by the family dynamics of both men. Much has been written about Freud's relationships with his daughters and it is important to note: "During the years between conceiving and abandoning the seduction theory, Freud was engaged in self-analysis, in which he discovered, through dreams, his own incestuous wishes toward his daughter Mathilde."[49] Freud managed with some insight and irony to suggest that the dream was the fulfillment of his wish to provide a *"Pater* as the originator of neurosis."[50] Freud also had a very special relationship with his daughter Anna (whom he called "Antigone"), who followed in his professional footsteps, nursed him through his final illness, and never married. Anna's lifelong attachment to her father genuinely concerned him for many years.

Otto Rank was twenty-one to Freud's forty-nine when they met in 1905. He was eleven years older than Anna Freud and seems to have been Freud's preference as a husband for his daughter. This did not materialize, but Rank and the woman he married had one child, a daughter. Rank had selected his pen name based on a character in Ibsen's A *Doll's*

House.[51] Late in his life, he was involved for a substantial period of time both as therapist and as lover with Anaïs Nin who was almost twenty years younger than he. Nin had begun her now famous diaries at the age of eleven "to charm and seduce" her Don Juan father, who had deserted the family, into rejoining them. Fresh from her eventual sexual encounter with her father, she met Rank for the first time in 1933. He asked to read the diary and then insisted she drop writing in it during his analysis; she complied for three and a half years.[52] In her diary, Nin acknowledges that she had been seeking her father in all the other men with whom she had been sexually involved, including Rank.[53]

The psychobiographical data on Shakespeare, Dickens, James, Conrad, and Joyce is frequently as dramatic as that on Freud and Rank and in some of these artists, the connections will seem abundantly clear, in others less obvious. In addition, the four novelists are intricately related intertextually to Shakespeare (Fleissner, Gillon, Harbage, Schutte, Cheng), and to each other. Joseph Conrad provided some of his own documentation. The harsh years that he spent as a boy in Siberian exile with his father, Apollo Korzeniowski, were passed in large part by his father's translating both Shakespeare and Dickens into Polish. Conrad relates in *A Personal Record:* "It is extraordinary how well Mrs. Nickleby could chatter disconnectedly in Polish and the sinister Ralph could rage in that language." But he also adds: "My first acquaintance was (or were) the 'Two Gentlemen of Verona,' and that in the very MS. of my father's translation."[54]

Henry James relates his first emotional encounter with Charles Dickens. The family thought the young James had gone to bed, as a cousin began reading *David Copperfield* aloud to the assembled members. But Henry had sneaked back into the room and hidden until "the tense chord snapped under the strain of the Murdstones and the elders assembled in the room became aware of a loud sobbing."[55] When he was twenty-four, James met Dickens briefly in Boston in 1867.[56] He later wrote a critical essay on Dickens, and his essay on *The Tempest* provides interesting commentary on his own work.[57]

Since the Joyce corpus has been widely acknowledged as a repository of all previous literature, his relationship to his four predecessors has already received elaboration.[58] By thematically utilizing Shakespeare in the "Scylla and Charybdis" chapter of *Ulysses*, Joyce moves back through the intervening artists to link up with the great precursor of them all. Atherton lists references to various writers in *Finnegans Wake:* Shakespeare, 29; Dickens, 7; James, 2.[59] There may be more, and I discovered a number of Conrad references in *Ulysses* and at least one in the *Wake.*[60]

It is important to note here that the shared recurrence of themes and patterns throughout the works of these writers should not necessarily be attributed to direct, overt influence, but rather to shared psychological predispositions, which attracted them to each other's work to begin with. Rank emphasizes this point: "Most important, we believe we have demonstrated that the writer, like the myth-maker, deals with given material not through external borrowing or assimilation, but from a deep psychic need, insistently demanding release" (571). That this "deep psychic need" should turn out to be a widely shared one comes as no surprise and fits more readily with theories of intertextuality.

The incest theme, as it relates to fathers and daughters in the following chapters, will be considered in its broadest terms, rarely as actual occurrence, frequently as what Herman has defined as "covert incest": "For every girl who has been involved in an incestuous relationship, there are considerably more who have grown up in a covertly incestuous family. . . . overt incest represents only the furthest point on a continuum" (110). All literature treating conflict within the father/daughter/suitor triad can be considered to have the incest theme as its subtext. The relationships and attitudes of both father and daughter prior to resolution are related to the threat of incest or its avoidance. Boose maintains that "The potent impulse of paternal retention/possession has always been the defining and problematic nucleus within the exchange patterns that have struggled to contain it."[61] In fiction, the father/daughter relationship, whether openly or covertly incestuous, is always one major, underlying motive for the action. Freud's principle of overdetermination applies in this instance. While in certain narratives the implied incest threat seems to be the only source of motivation for the action, there are usually others; sometimes it is one of many.

A survey of Shakespeare's prolific corpus reveals three basic patterns of resolution of the father/daughter/suitor triangle: (1) the father reluctantly relinquishes the daughter, usually in submission to an outside authority, (2) the father retains the daughter for himself, or (3) the father assumes an active role in procuring a suitor to resolve the potential incest threat—the "Tempest" schema. In order to view the development of the theme as it was influenced by the various stages in the artist's development, I have focused on an early, a middle, and a late work of each writer. The "Tempest" schema applied in this survey complements Rank's exposition of the "Carlos" schema which entails the stepson's passion for the stepmother, and the "Phaedra" schema which entails the stepmother's love for the unreceptive stepson (118). "The Tempest" schema differs from the "Carlos" and "Phaedra" schemas in that rather than defining an uncontrollable, destructive passion, it represents the positive resolution of a potentially destructive situation.

Otto Rank's view of developing patterns in the corpus of any writer is based on his general premise that for each individual artist, repression ("dampening") of the incest theme increases throughout the sequence of the author's work.[62] "These works illustrate the incest complex from its impetuous appearance in puberty, through the stage of fear of retribution, to the clear skies of the father perspective" (148). This corresponds to my analysis of an early, a middle, and a late work being tied primarily to the artist's chronological maturation process. In early works, it is probable that the artist, either concurrently with his writing or in the recent past functioned as a suitor himself, thus identifying with the suitor in the narrative. In a middle work, especially when the father of daughters, he can identify with the possessive father, a "stage of fear of retribution." In a late work, he would be expected to evolve into a mature father capable of renunciation. I thus view Rank's linear progress of repression over time as arising from an age-related shifting viewpoint. There is a loose correspondence here to Erikson's description of life's stages of development. But unlike Rank's and Erikson's sense of a linear progression, my ultimate findings rather indicate that this progression is deceptively conclusive and that movement is really cyclical.

Any selection of specific works from a writer's corpus as a basis for conclusions involves a basic flaw. As many artists have indicated, the only fully valid judgments are to be made from a reading of the entire body of work. However, this is not always practical and I selected works by each writer to fit certain requirements of my own. This sometimes becomes a slippery matter, especially in situations such as that of Henry James, who disavowed his actual first novel and put forth a second one as the first, immediately raising questions about the content of each. James also left two unfinished novels in contrast to Dickens and Conrad, raising similar questions.

Within the recognized limitations of such choices, one proceeds to such conclusions as seem reasonable, trying to avoid Joyce's "sequentiality of improbable possibles."[63] With a focus on each artist's three successive works, two central questions arise: "Are the patterns among the various artists similar or dissimilar?" and "What apparent relationship is to be found between these patterns and each artist's individual psychobiographical data?" Maisch reaffirms the importance of the latter factor: "If one analyses the life and works of great writers from a psychoanalytical point of view, as for example Rank (1912) tries to do, then one discovers increasingly manifold connections between individual experience, life history, and the literary working over of the incest motif" (15).

In considering the incest theme in the literary works to follow, I neither offer them in support of Freudian theory, nor offer Freudian theory in support of my reading of the literature. Rather, the relationship between the two can be viewed as a reciprocal juxtaposition of theme and theory. Freud and Rank pioneered in the explication of this interplay. The recurrence of the incest theme throughout a large body of literature also offers interesting evidence for Freud's theory of the "compulsion to repeat" which he believed overrode the pleasure principle and was related both to dreams and to the play of children.[64]

A perusal of any artist's recurrent need to produce art corroborates its compulsive nature and many artists have attested to this. Rank elaborates:

Through dramatic creativity this psychic conflict is only temporarily resolved. (The playwright is continually driven to compose more works based on internally related themes that inspire and grip him and that become uninteresting to him only through the process of composition.) (187)

But since each artist's handling of the theme has a different resolution in each work, the compulsion to repeat applies to the preoccupation with the incest theme itself, rather than to its resolution; the handling of the theme is repetitive, its resolution is cyclical. Autonomous renunciation, as illustrated in the "Tempest" works of the five artists is, after all, a fantasy of total control. Or as Joyce expressed it, "Abnegation is Adaptation" (*FW*, 306). The threat of loss is removed through voluntary renunciation; what is given up can never again be taken away.

Shakespeare's *Tempest* and Joyce's *Ulysses* were followed by final, finished works that portray the aging mother/wife as yielding autonomy to a daughter or a daughter-figure—*Henry VIII* and *Finnegans Wake*. But the closure suggested by the penultimate "Tempest" works of Dickens, James, and Conrad is undercut by final, unfinished works all of which portend a cyclical return to the father's possession of the daughter—Dickens's *The Mystery of Edwin Drood*, James's *The Ivory Tower*, and Conrad's *Suspense*. This suggests that the artist's attempt to resolve his desire for union with a lost object is never finally achieved. Henry James, however, compounded the problem with the novel he was working on when he died, *The Sense of the Past*, illustrating the tenuousness of such conclusions.

Thou simular of virtue/
That art incestuous.
William Shakespeare, *King Lear*

2

The Triangle in
William Shakespeare

Although variations on the father/daughter theme are central to at least twenty-one of Shakespeare's plays (Boose 1982, 325), the focus here is on four of the plays that illustrate basic patterns of resolution of the incest-threat for the father and the daughter through marriage to a suitor. These patterns will then serve as the basis for analysis of an early, a middle, and a late work by Charles Dickens, Henry James, Joseph Conrad, and James Joyce.

Of all the writers under consideration, the least amount of intimate detail is known about Shakespeare's family relationships. This has only served to stimulate endless speculation, usually based on the correlation between known historical facts found in public records and the sequence and content of the various plays. In this way critics have found grounds for conjectures regarding the man himself.

Born in 1564, the bard was eighteen when he was precipitously married to a woman eight years his senior. "But special circumstances attended this match. The groom was a minor, and his lady, pregnant."[1] By the age of twenty he had three children but for most of the ensuing years, except for yearly visits to Stratford, Shakespeare lived and worked in London.[2] Hamnet, the only son, died at the age of eleven when his father was thirty-two—six years before the publication of *Hamlet*. His oldest daughter, Susanna, was married when she was twenty-four and her father was forty-three—one year after *King Lear*. Her daughter, Elizabeth, was born the following year (1608), the same year that Shakespeare's mother died and that *Pericles* was published. Hamnet's twin, Judith, married at thirty-one when Shakespeare was fifty-two—the year of his death—1616. This was five years after he wrote *The Winter's Tale* and *The Tempest* and three years after *Henry VIII*.

Shakespeare spent most of his final years, 1614–16, in Stratford, returning to London from time to time for short periods. In 1613, Susanna had brought suit against John Lane for defamation for having accused her of adultery and consequent gonorrhea; she was exonerated and he was excommunicated.[3] Judith's marriage to Richard Quiney in February, 1616, was followed soon after by a legal scandal involving her new husband's adultery; both the illegitimate infant and the mother had died. Suit was brought against Quiney on March 26, Judith already pregnant with their first child. Schoenbaum conjectures that the resulting stress may have precipitated Shakespeare's death two months later on April 23 (292). Certainly having both daughters involved in unsavory lawsuits must have been a burden to their aging father. When he died, he left his wife the now notorious "second-best bed," with the bulk of his estate going to Susanna, her husband, and their heirs, while also making provision for Judith.

Otto Rank was one of the pioneers in tying the artist's life to the work and Joyce followed in his footsteps with Stephen Dedalus's elaborate discourse in the library. Both writers speculated on the implications of Shakespeare's having played the Ghost in *Hamlet*: "This suggests that at the time Shakespeare identified more closely with the role of the father. This conception gains in significance given that this role is generally said to have been Shakespeare's best performance" (Rank, 186). Jean Kimball has presented substantial evidence that Rank's work was available to and utilized by Joyce.[4]

Stephen Dedalus waxes poetic on the subject:

A player comes on. . . . It is the ghost, the king, a king and no king, and the player is Shakespeare who has studied *Hamlet* all the years of his life which were not vanity in order to play the part of the spectre. . . . To a son he speaks, the son of his soul, the prince, young Hamlet and to the son of his body, Hamnet Shakespeare, who has died in Stratford that his namesake may live for ever.

Is it possible that that player Shakespeare, a ghost by absence, and in the vesture of buried Denmark, a ghost by death, speaking his own words to his own son's name (had Hamnet Shakespeare lived he would have been prince Hamlet's twin) is it possible, I want to know, or probable that he did not draw or foresee the logical conclusion of those premises: you are the dispossessed son: I am the murdered father: your mother is the guilty queen. Ann Shakespeare, born Hathaway? (*U*, 9.164–80)

Stephen then elaborates on the potential damage to the male ego of loss of sexual initiative, perhaps telling us more about Joyce than it does about Shakespeare: "Belief in himself has been untimely killed. He was overborne in a cornfield first (a ryefield, I should say) and he will never be a victor in his own eyes after nor play victoriously the game of laugh and lie down" (*U*, 9.455–58). One of Joyce's listeners had raised the question which still plagues critics and critics of critics: "But this prying into the family life of a great man" (*U*, 9.181).

In addition to a lack of detail about his life, Shakespeare's corpus is distinguished by uncertainty regarding the exact sequence of his works; much of the dating remains speculative. Nevertheless, his prolific output resulted in an interesting chronological proximity for many of the plays. Although I have selected a play from his earlier years, *A Midsummer Night's Dream* (1596), one from his middle period, *King Lear* (1606), and two from his later period, *Pericles* (1609) and *The Tempest* (1611) for more intense focus, certain other plays are pertinent by virtue of their chronological proximity and the light this throws on their variations in treatment of the incest theme.

Shakespeare followed his first play in 1592 when he was twenty-eight with the writing of *Love's Labour's Lost* in 1593, in which the father's death imposes a period of enforced mourning before the marriages of his daughter and her friends can take place. In 1594, Shakespeare wrote three plays embodying a broad spectrum of treatments of the incest theme: *Titus Andronicus*, *Romeo and Juliet*, and *A Midsummer Night's Dream*. *Titus Andronicus*, the least popular of Shakespeare's works, concludes with the father's slaying of his daughter, who has been sexually violated by others. The other two plays offer diametrically opposed resolutions. Susanna was only eleven when these plays were written, still very young, but old enough to cause her father to view himself as father of a maturing daughter. She was close to Mathilde's age when Freud had his erotic dream about her.

Romeo and Juliet (1594), while based ostensibly on the Montague/Capulet opposition, encompasses several components of the father/daughter theme. Capulet's preferred suitor for his daughter is closer to his double than the young Romeo, selected by the fourteen-year-old Juliet. Although her father is at first disposed to let her postpone any action until she is sixteen, he agrees to allow Count Paris to woo her and ultimately seems caught up in that frantic haste to get the daughter safely married off that characterizes other father/daughter plots—especially Shakespeare's. This dramatizes the father's necessity for a resolution of his own incestuous impulses through immediate marriage.

Juliet is shocked at the urgency: "I wonder at this haste, that I must wed/ Ere he that should be husband comes to woo."[5] As Juliet's resistance becomes clear to her parents, the incestuous implications become evident in her father's violent reaction:

Hang thee, young baggage! Disobedient wretch!
I tell thee what—get thee to church a Thursday
Or never after look me in the face.
Speak not, reply not, do not answer me!
My fingers itch. Wife, we scarce thought us blest
That God had lent us but this only child;
But now I see this one is one too much,
And that we have a curse in having her.
Out on her, hilding! (3.5.161–169)

As her father continues his tirade, Juliet concludes: "If all else fail, myself have power to die" (3.5.244), foreshadowing her father's later poignant realization: "Death is my son-in-law; Death is my heir" (4.5.38). The actions of the father, both in his haste to marry off the newly nubile daughter, and in his insistence on choosing a man he favors and she disdains, are prime factors in the rapid movement toward a tragic dénouement.

The contrast between *Romeo and Juliet* and *A Midsummer Night's Dream* nicely illustrates the skirting of potential violence that is always a component when the suitor and the daughter are opposed by a possessive father. The tension in the latter play is established at the outset by the refusal of Hermia's father, Egeus, to allow her to marry Lysander, while making it clear that he wishes her to marry Demetrius instead. The father's autonomy, as established by Athenian law, is summed up by Egeus: "And what is mine, mine love shall render him. / And she is mine, and all my right of her / I do estate unto Demetrius."[6] Theseus, the supreme authority figure, has indicated that the penalty for disobedience to this injunction is either death or lifelong celibacy in a convent. There are no apparent age or attribute distinctions between suitors in this play, and one is free to infer that the restrictions are related to the father's own repressed motives. After listing the attributes they share in common, Hermia's favored suitor makes clear the single distinction between himself and Demetrius, "I am beloved of beauteous Hermia" (1.1.99–104).

Herein lies the rub. It is frequently one aspect of the incest motif that the father so involved can cope with the daughter's marriage only when her object-choice is a man other than the one she finds sexually attractive. The implication here is that although the father accepts the fact that he cannot retain her, he can only tolerate renunciation with the knowledge that she will not be happy or sexually satisfied. There is also a sadistic streak in the father's forcing marriage on an unwilling daughter in the name of authority.

In A Midsummer Night's Dream, the bulk of the action takes place in the forest, with the pairs of lovers ultimately happily aligned; every Jack has his Jill. The parodied production of Pyramus and Thisbe, the original of which foreshadows the bloody end of Romeo and Juliet, parallels the differences between the thwarted love of Hermia and Lysander and that of the scions of Capulet and Montague. This raises the crucial question of wherein lies the difference. Does Egeus differ from Capulet in his resolution of the dilemma? The difference lies in the avoidance of violence effected by the intervention of Theseus: "Egeus, I will overbear your will" (4.1.178); we never hear from Egeus again. Theseus can thus be viewed as a "good" father who by his imposed renunciation fosters love and prevents the bloodshed that occurs in Pyramus and Thisbe and Romeo and Juliet. What is more important is that Theseus contravenes Athenian law and takes power into his own hands. He thus serves as a successful contrast to the Prince of Verona who tries to put a stop to the violence and death but fails. This play then can serve as a prototype for other narratives in which the father renounces the daughter, but only after renunciation is imposed by an outside authority; sometimes it is the daughter who intervenes.

With The Two Gentlemen of Verona (1593), Shakespeare effected an important transition from the father's threat to impose his own choice of a friend and contemporary as his daughter's groom, to his voluntary relinquishment of control in favor of the daughter's choice. But by 1602 the productions of Hamlet and Othello exemplified a return to a dénouement of violence and destruction. Although *Hamlet* has been scrutinized much more extensively regarding the mother/father/son triad, in the Polonius/Ophelia/Hamlet triangle the suitor inadvertently destroys the father as a prelude to the ultimate destruction of the other two members of the triangle. But Polonius had already deterred his daughter from responding to Hamlet on the grounds of protecting her and it is her father's murder that precipitates her madness. "In Polonius is embodied the disdained and derided elderly father who wants to keep his daughters for himself" (Rank, 181).

The primacy of the father/daughter theme in *Othello* is readily apparent and not surprisingly it is Iago's language that insinuates the idea of incest into the play. Dr. Robert Fliess points out: "Othello, much older than Desdemona, constitutes a kind of father to her in the special sense of a forbidden love relation, one surrounded with taboos."[7] Brabantio sums up for all these Shakespearean fathers the solution to the incest-threat that the suitor represents: "I here do give thee that with all my heart / Which, but thou hast already, with my heart / I would keep from thee."[8] Although the father's ambivalence remains, the situation has been taken out of his hands.

Since Shakespeare wrote his first play at twenty-eight, a representative play of his middle period can be found in *King Lear* (1606), written when he was forty-two, Susanna was twenty-three, and Judith was twenty-one. Neither daughter had yet married, but since Susanna did marry in 1607, it is likely that the event was anticipated. Kay cites Susanna's epitaph which praised her as "witty above her sex" and "wise to salvation," concluding that she thus resembled her father (329).

One critic found the father/daughter theme so central to this play that he coined the term "Lear complex," the complex that focuses on the "neglected" adult to define the attachment of the older member of the oedipal twosome.[9] In spite of a wide variety of interpretations of Lear's initial decision to divide his kingdom, the most immediate result will be to force his periodic presence on his daughters, and Cordelia, whom "He always loved . . . most,"[10] is the only one left unmarried. The Fool tells Lear: "[T]hou madst thy daughters thy mothers" (1.4.168–69).[11] Cordelia's declaration of independence precipitates her father's wrath and provokes him into banishing his youngest:

Happily, when I shall wed,
That lord whose hand must take my plight shall carry
Half my love with him, half my care and duty.

Sure I shall never marry like my sisters,
To love my father all. (1.1.99–103)

Although the Fool had told Kent that "this fellow has banish'd two on's daughters, / and did the third a blessing against his will" (1.4.100,101), toward the end of the play, Cordelia returns to England to come to the aid of her father. And a short time later, her suitor/husband is bereft and alone as Lear joins his daughter in death. The originator of the "Lear complex" outlines briefly what has ensued: Lear "reaches the depths of human despair and endurance until he finds his peace in death as a 'smug bridegroom' in blessed union with his youngest daughter as the bride" (59). Lear's words at the height of the storm have suggested his sense of his guilt:

> Tremble thou wretch,
> That hast within thee undivulged crimes
> Unwhipped of justice. Hide thee, thou bloody hand,
> Thou perjured, and *thou simular of virtue*
> *That art incestuous.* . . . I am a man
> More sinned against than sinning. (3.2.51–59, emphasis mine)

During this period, Shakespeare created many examples of the violence and destruction lying at the heart of the incest theme. Ophelia ends as a suicide, her father having been murdered by the suitor. Desdemona, an innocent victim, is murdered. As Cordelia and her father lie dead, only the suitor remains when the violence has spun itself out. Earlier versions of the play did not entail a tragic finale, nor did the folktales which served as its base end tragically (Dundes, 234–35). *King Leir*, performed in 1590, depicted a reconciliation between Leir and Cordelia (Kay, 313).

In those plays that end in the destruction of both father and daughter and frequently of suitor, the violence is precipitated by the refusal of the father to renounce the daughter. But Shakespeare also wrote a number of plays in which the father's renunciation of the daughter to a suitor avoids the potential violence and destruction. Focus on the theme of renunciation in these plays also provides guidelines for analysis of the theme in subsequent chapters. Joyce attributed this transformation to the birth of Shakespeare's granddaughter in 1608: "Marina, Stephen said, a child of storm, Miranda, a wonder, Perdita, that which was lost. What was lost is given back to him: his daughter's child" (*U*, 9.421–24).

Pericles (1609), the first of the late renunciatory series, embodies an array of plot possibilities in the father/daughter incest theme, establishing the basic motif in the opening story of Antiochus and his daughter who are living in incest. Although there are other literary examples of overt incest such as Shelley's *The Cenci* and Mary Shelley's *Mathilda*, this is one of the few in which the incest is sustained with apparent complacency on the part of both participants, as divulged early in the play by Gower:

This king unto him took a peer,
Who died and left a female heir,
So buxom, blithe, and full of face
As heaven had lent her all his grace;
With whom the father liking took
And her to incest did provoke.
Bad child; worse father! to entice his own
By custom what they did begin
Was with long use accounted no sin. (1 Chorus 21–30)

By whom was it accounted no sin? Certainly by the participants, and probably by the king's subjects also. And this father does not enjoin celibacy upon his suitor/rivals who fail to guess the riddle, their heads are ranged for all to see—a classic castration symbol.

Pericles guesses that the riddle spells an incestuous relationship and his life is immediately endangered. But a more crucial factor is involved, both in Pericles' guessing of the riddle and in the effect that this has on his subsequent behavior. His intuitive response to the riddle marks him as an early "secret sharer" since the proclivities of Antiochus are his own. We are never told precisely what ideas are aroused in Pericles by the riddle which is stated in the daughter's voice:

I am no viper, yet I feed
On mother's flesh which did me breed.
I sought a husband, in which labour
I found that kindness in a father.
He's father, son, and husband mild;
I mother, wife, and yet his child:
How they may be, and yet in two,
As you will live, resolve it you. (1.1.65–72)

This disclosure makes Pericles "pale to read it" (1.1.76), and he evades making a direct answer to the king with: "Few love to hear the sins they love to act" (1.1.93), concluding with an oblique incest reference: "All love the womb that their first being bred. / Then give my tongue like leave to love my head" (1.1.107–08). Does knowledge of the relationship between

Antiochus and his daughter perhaps suggest to Pericles his own love of the "womb that first their being bred" since the father/daughter attachment can operate as a reversal of the mother/son? Ostensibly to flee possible death at the hands of Antiochus, Pericles leaves Tyre and is soon again the third party in another father/daughter/suitor triangle.

King Simonides is the complete antithesis of Antiochus. On his daughter's birthday (always significant in the incest motif narrative), he is parading before her a series of knights for her selection; in the array, Pericles seems an unlikely choice due to his recent shipwreck. He becomes, however, the chosen love-object of Thaisa and she uses the subterfuge of total withdrawal for one year to rid herself of all other suitors. Simonides weighs his own autonomy against his daughter's:

> She tells me here, she'll wed the stranger knight,
> Or never more to view nor day nor light.
> 'Tis well, mistress; your choice agrees with mine;
> I like that well: nay, how absolute she's in't,
> Not minding whether I dislike or no!
> Well, I do commend her choice,
> And will no longer have it be delayed.
> Soft, here he comes: I must dissemble it. (2.5.16–23)

Again, there is that sense of urgency on the part of the father to see the daughter safely in the arms of the suitor once the decision to renounce has been made. But Shakespeare's fathers are sometimes good psychologists and also realize that what comes too easily may not prove very attractive. Obstacles enhance desire, but when agreement is finally reached, there is again that sense of urgency: "It pleaseth me so well that I will see you wed; / And then, with what haste you can, get you to bed" (2.5.91–92).

Before this marriage takes place, the audience has learned that Antiochus and his daughter have been destroyed in a terrible death. Although Simonides has "dissembled" his opposition to the marriage, it also reflects his true ambivalence toward this usurper of his fatherly rights. The marriage is short-lived (just short of nine months) since Thaisa ostensibly perishes in childbirth and is buried at sea to be resuscitated on land five hours later, unbeknown to Pericles. Subsequently, Pericles deposits his daughter with another pair of surrogate parents. Cleon, the father, is fond of his foster daughter whom he has "trained / In music's letters" (4 Chorus 7, 8).

Comprising another plot variation on the theme, the true daughter of Cleon and Dionyza is quite outshone by the foster daughter, and the mother plans Marina's murder. In this oedipal plot, the second daughter is a double for the mother and it is really the usurpation of the mother by the daughter that leads to Dionyza's decision to have her murdered—by yet another father figure, Leonine. This is a fairly rare literary instance in which there is open conflict between the mother and daughter for the father, in this case displaced onto a daughter surrogate. Leonine, reluctantly faced with Marina's murder, is saved from action by her abduction by pirates who sell her to a brothel owner, thus setting up the fourth oedipal configuration. The confrontation between Cleon and Dionyza, followed by the supposed murder, reinforces the oedipal reading that was added to the Gower version by Shakespeare.[12]

The Pander/Bawd/Boult (father/mother/brother) triangle is perhaps one of the least recurrent paradigms in terms of future literary patterns. It is significant that Shakespeare added a character not in the Gower version: "[I]n the brothel scenes he has no female Bawd, only a pandar and a servant." Shakespeare also "cuts to a minimum" the story of Antiochus's incest.[13] But possibly the most interesting change made by Shakespeare in the Gower materials was the more prominent role given to Marina (xvii). In this plot variation, the daughter's sexuality becomes a commercial commodity for the father who, in a sense, acts as her pimp. The father figure in this "family" is simply called "Pandar," but he is not Chaucer's benign, lovable Pandarus. The "mother" allies herself with the father to exploit the daughter. Marina's stubborn refusal to submit culminates in a further incestuous elaboration, as the surrogate mother suggests to the surrogate brother that he deprive her of her virginity, thus paving the way for her future exploitation: "Boult, take her away; use her at thy pleasure. / Crack the glass of her virginity, and make the rest malleable" (4.6.141–43). But Marina manages to escape the brothel due to her ability to gain the respect of a perceptive Lysimachus who then refrains from using her as a prostitute. In effect, a father-surrogate saves Marina and eventually marries her with her own father's blessing. In Gower, this character never enters the brothel (xv).

As Pericles is reunited with his daughter, but is still unaware of her identity, the function of the daughter as a double of the mother is made clear: "My dearest wife / Was like this maid, and such a one / My daughter might have been" (5.1.106–08). A short time later he tells her: "thou look'st / Like one I lov'd indeed" (5.1.124–25). Pericles and Marina are here placed in the position described by Masters in which separated relatives, when reunited, are more prone to incest (5). Marina calls up immediately the earlier love-object, and one might surmise that if Pericles doesn't find out who she really is, a sexual involvement is imminent. The transfer of paternal desire from mother to daughter is embodied in Marina's words to her father: "Thaisa was my mother, who did end / The minute I began" (5.1.210, 211). Again, Joyce comments: "'*My dearest wife,*' Pericles says, '*was like this maid.*' Will any man love the daughter if he has not loved the mother?" (*U*, 9.423–24). Joyce echoes this with "Molly. Milly. Same thing watered down" (*U*, 6.87). The Chinese box metaphor also holds since Joyce's daughter was an adolescent while he was writing *Ulysses.*

The function of the father/daughter relationship as a reversal of the mother/son is succinctly stated in the words of Pericles to the daughter he now recognizes: "O, come hither, / Thou that beget'st him that did thee beget" (5.1.194–95). As in some of the later literature, there is an element of ambiguity in the suitor in this play, since Lysimachus, as governor, is really a father-surrogate who has first encountered the undefiled Marina in the brothel. The transfer of the daughter to this suitor is very low-key compared to other plays as Pericles says: "You shall prevail, / Were it to woo my daughter; for it seems / You have been noble towards her" (5.1.259–61). In an ironic parody of the series of suitors in other plays, such as *The Merchant of Venice,* and of the competition arranged by Simonides in which Pericles was chosen, Marina has been besieged by "suitors" in the brothel, but has successfully fended them off. Lysimachus, the sole authority-figure who visits the brothel, has played the "good" father by not exerting his authority. As in the other plays, age is significant. Marina "Was nurs'd with Cleon, who at fourteen years / He sought to murder" (5.3.8,9).

At this point, not only is the incest-threat resolved by marriage and by restoration of the mother to the father; the couples are to be permanently separated as rulers of two kingdoms due to the death of Thaisa's father. Lest there be any doubt that this dénouement is above all the resolution of the incest threat, the Epilogue returns to Gower and to the original incest-plot in the play:

> In Antiochus and his daughter you have heard
> Of monstrous lust the due and just reward;
> In Pericles, his queen, and daughter, seen,
> Although assailed with fortune fierce and keen,
> Virtue preserved from fell destruction's blast,
> Led on by heaven, and crowned with joy at last. (Epilogue 1–6)

What "virtue preserved" has meant for Pericles is more subtly stated, but I feel that it is quite clearly his refusal to succumb to the fatal "crime" of Antiochus, the understanding of which first made him so uneasy and nearly cost him his life. The play can then be read as both an allegorical and an archetypal resolution of the father/daughter incest-threat with a full range of possible solutions set out in a series of related plots. The incestuous attraction that Marina holds for her father is much more explicit in the Gower version.

The cluster of plays that began with *Pericles* (1608) and ended with *The Tempest* (1611) all deal with the father/daughter theme. One critic points out that "critical opinion is at last recognizing that the same ideas, preoccupations, situations, devices, and themes inform Shakespeare's comedies from the very earliest to the latest."[14] *The Winter's Tale* (1611), while reversing the tragic resolution of *Othello*, is also an extrapolation of one of the plots from *Pericles*. Although the causal factors are different, the same components are present: the disappearance of both mother and daughter immediately following the daughter's birth, reunion with both when the daughter reaches puberty, resolution in the reunions of father/mother and daughter/suitor. The recurrent exile theme is embodied both in Hermione's simulated death and in Perdita's removal by ship. In contrast to Shakespeare's transformation of a nontragic Leir into a tragic one, the incest theme in *The Winter's Tale* reverses the earlier presentation in Robert Greene's *Pandosto* (1588), in which the theme is more explicitly stated: "[T]he queen dies, and the king, despite the happy reunion with his daughter, commits suicide in a fit of melancholy."[15] In Shakespeare's version, Hermione only seems to die and Leontes survives his period of penance to be reunited with his wife. It should be noted that Leontes has arranged to urge Florizel's suit to Polixenes while still unaware of the identity of the girl. The joy has become a loss, and "Perdita" becomes an oxymoron, summed up by Paulina: "Our Perdita is found"[16].

In *The Winter's Tale*, then, the basic resolution occurs with the father momentarily attracted to the nubile daughter who is a double of the mother, but the incest-threat is contained by the restoration of the mother and the simultaneous availability of a suitor for the daughter. The oedipal configuration is again stabilized and equilibrium restored—until next time. Joyce summarizes: "There can be no reconciliation . . . if there has not been a sundering" (*U*, 9.397–98).

Shakespeare begins *The Tempest* with a recurrent narrative companion to the incest theme in several other plays and in some of the novels—the tempest. Although in both *Pericles* and *The Winter's Tale*, Shakespeare introduces such ambiguous and unnatural actions as Thaisa's burial and recovery from the sea and Hermione's retrieval from a statue, in *The Tempest*, he further abandons the semblance of reality by introducing Ariel and presenting the tempest as a contrivance of the father himself. Since these final plays all depend on unrealistic devices—mothers who survive presumed death to be ultimately reunited with the renunciatory father at the end of the play, or contrivances such as Ariel—suggests that Shakespeare needed to resort to extraordinary dramatic measures to effect a nonviolent resolution of the incest-threat for the father.

The total autonomy represented by Prospero is an essential aspect of the resolution of the incest-threat by the father. Very early in the course of the action we are told three things: that the storm has done "no harm,"[17] that Prospero is in control, and that what has happened has some as yet undisclosed connection with Miranda, his daughter:

> I have done nothing but in care of thee,
> Of thee my dear one, thee my daughter, who
> Art ignorant of what thou art, naught knowing
> Of whence I am! nor that I am more better
> Than Prospero, master of a full poor cell,
> And thy no greater father. (1.1.16–21)

Again, the recurrent components of the father/daughter/suitor theme occur: Miranda and her father have been exiled by themselves since she was three and they have been on the island for twelve years, until she has attained the magic age of fifteen (1.2.54). Although as the play opens, Prospero is about to divulge to Miranda that he is indeed the usurped Duke of Milan, he has had other fatherly authority roles: "and here / Have I, thy schoolmaster, made thee more profit / Than other princess' can, that have more time / For vainer hours, and tutors not so careful" (1.2.171–74). And Miranda asks her father his "reason / For raising this sea-storm?" (1.2.176–77).

Although the machinations of Prospero will effect the resumption of control of his dukedom, the primary solution the tempest brings is that of a suitor for the daughter in the person of Ferdinand. The disclosure of a parallel father/daughter subplot sheds light on the importance of the solution to the incest-threat contained in the main plot. The shipwrecked group is returning from a wedding which has all the elements of the incest theme, with exile in this instance serving as an additional means of resolution, as described by Gonzalo: "Methinks our garments are now as fresh as when we put them on first in Afric, at the marriage of the King's fair daughter Claribel to the King of Tunis" (2.1.66–68).

But Claribel's father is having second thoughts: "Would I had never / Married my daughter there! for, coming thence, / My son is lost; and, in my rate, she too, / Who is so far from Italy removed / I ne'er again shall see her" (2.1.103–07). The designation of this marriage as a form of banishment becomes clearer as Sebastian reminds Alonso that he has only himself to blame:

SEBASTIAN. Sir, you may thank yourself for this great loss,
That would not bless our Europe with your daughter,
But rather loose her to an African,
Where she, at least, is banish'd from your eye,
Who hath cause to wet the grief on't.
ALONSO. Prithee peace.
SEBASTIAN. You were kneel'd to and importun'd otherwise,
By all of us; and the fair soul herself
Weigh'd, between loathness and obedience, at
Which end o' th' beam should bow. We have lost your son,
I fear, for ever.
* * *
The fault's your own.
ALONSO. So is the dear'st o' th' loss. (2.1.118–32)

The greater loss has been that of Alonso's daughter, who torn "between loathness and obedience" has been banished to Africa. Prospero, isolated on an island with his daughter and that projection of his own potential, uninhibited sexual impulses, Caliban, creates a "tempest" which produces a suitor for his daughter. It is the onset of Caliban's desire to possess Miranda sexually (which we may assume to have coincided with her menarche) that has totally altered Prospero's attitude toward Caliban:

PROSPERO. Thou most lying slave,
Whom stripes may move, not kindness! I have us'd thee
Filth as thou art, with human care, and lodg'd thee
In mine own cell, till thou didst seek to violate
The honour of my child.
CALIBAN. O ho, O ho! would't had been done!
Thou didst prevent me; I had peopled else
This isle with Calibans. (1.2.346–53)

Not only is the appearance of a suitor contrived, but the actual attraction between Ferdinand and Miranda is manipulated through the magic of Ariel:

MIRANDA. I might call him

A thing divine; for nothing natural
I ever saw so noble.
PROSPERO. [Aside] It goes on, I see,
As my soul prompts it. Spirit, fine spirit, I'll free thee
Within two days for this. (1.2.420–23)

This aspect of Ferdinand's immediate attraction to Miranda is again commented upon:

PROSPERO. [Aside] The Duke of Milan
And his more braver daughter could control thee,
If now 'twere fit to do't. At the first sight
They have chang'd eyes. Delicate Ariel,
I'll set thee free for this. (1.2.442–45)

But Prospero, like Simonides, feels he must put artificial barriers in the way in order to enhance the romance:

PROSPERO. [Aside] They are both in either's pow'rs: but this
swift business
I must uneasy make, lest too light winning
Make the prize light. (1.2.452–54)

Prospero proceeds to accuse Ferdinand of being a spy and a traitor, and as Miranda pleads for gentle treatment of her newfound love, her father's language burgeons with phallic imagery: "Put thy sword up, traitor, / Who mak'st a show but dar'st not strike, thy conscience / is so possess'd with guilt: come, from thy ward, / For I can here disarm thee with this stick / And make thy weapon drop" (1.2.472–76). Like Simonides, Prospero is able to give vent to his very real ambivalence toward his daughter's suitor, and his deep awareness of the sexual implications are voiced when he says of Ferdinand: "To th' most of men this is a Caliban" (1.2.482).

Prospero enjoins upon Ferdinand a "trial" in which he must remove thousands of logs and pile them up in another place. The logs serve as a sexual symbol of the transition from Prospero to Ferdinand as well as from the unbound sexual impulses of Caliban, whose duties the prince is performing. As the unseen Prospero watches and listens to the two lovers, he indicates his acceptance of the match in another aside: "Fair encounter / Of two most rare affections! Heavens rain grace / On that which breeds between 'em! (3.1.74,76). Prospero's musings as he hears the two promise to marry and watches them exit is fully ambiguous, again suggesting his deep ambivalence:

So glad of this as they I cannot be,
Who are surpris'd with all; but my rejoicing
At nothing can be more. I'll to my book. (3.1.92–94)

The father acknowledges his limited joy in the event, but "rejoicing / At nothing can be more," can either indicate that nothing would make him happier, or that nothing will ever make him happy again.

After telling Ariel that he is about to "visit / Young Ferdinand,—whom they suppose is drown'd,— / And his and mine lov'd darling" (3.3.91–93), Prospero turns his daughter over to the suitor with strict injunctions about the forms which must be adhered to:

Then, as my gift, and thine own acquisition
Worthily purchas'd, take my daughter: but
If thou dost break her virgin-knot before
All sanctimonious ceremonies may
With full and holy rite be ministr'd,
No sweet aspersion shall the heavens let fall
To make this contract grow; but barren hate,
Sour-ey'd disdain, and discord shall bestrew
The union of your bed with weeds so loathly
That you shall hate it both: therefore take heed,
As Hymen's lamps shall light you. (4.1.13–23)

But Prospero is an anxious, worried father indeed, and further instructs them, as though no assurance Ferdinand can give him can allay his fears:

Look thou be true; do not give dalliance
Too much the rein: the strongest oaths are straw
To th' fire in' th' blood: be more abstemious,
Or else, good night your vow! (4.1.51–54)

One can only conclude that he knows whereof he speaks. His abdication of any possible sexual inclination is again symbolically expressed: "I'll break my staff, / Bury it certain fadoms in the earth, / And deeper than did ever plummet sound / I'll drown my book" (5.1.54–57).

That Prospero has deliberately instigated the tempest to produce a suitor as soon as his daughter has reached puberty, and that renunciation has been a traumatic experience, is made clear in his exchange with Alonso who still believes his son lost. Again the ambiguity of "oozy bed" suggests the father/son rivalry already explored in The Winter's Tale:

PROSPERO. Than you may call to comfort you, for I
Have lost my daughter.
ALONSO. A daughter?
O heavens, that they were living both in Naples,
The King and Queen there! that they were, I wish
Myself were mudded in that oozy bed
Where my son lies. When did you lose your daughter?
PROSPERO. In this last tempest. (5.1.147–53)

That this play is characterized by the condensation typical of dreams is
pointed up by the fact that Ferdinand and Miranda have only known each
other for three hours (5.1.186). Prospero's Epilogue, regarded as the artist's
renunciation of his art, is again fraught with meanings that can refer back
to the incest theme:

And my ending is despair
Unless I be reliev'd by prayer,
Which pierces so, that it assaults
Mercy itself, and frees all faults.
As you from crimes would pardon'd be,
Let your indulgence set me free. (Epilogue, 15–20)

Lear too has spoken of "undivulged crimes" and "virtue / That art incestuous" (3.2.52–55). The widely varied critical interpretations of the
Epilogue omit the view of it as a statement of the guilt over incest wishes
and fantasies, and the acceptance of the resolution of that guilt. Ariel
(superego), Caliban (id), and Prospero (ego), in which the first two are
contained, are reunited at the end, and Prospero is once more a unified
whole: "What strength I have's my own, / Which is most faint" (Epilogue,
2,3).

The tempest itself has served as a metaphor for sexuality that, like all
violent action, has a life of its own, once it has been set in motion. Ella
Sharpe comments: "Prospero and Lear are alike, and different. In Prospero omnipotence becomes benign. Prospero's storm saves, Lear's destroys."[18] Lear renounces his daughter to the suitor, but reluctantly and
filled with rage, instigating a chain of violence as he sends her into exile.
Prospero too renounces the daughter to a suitor, but with control and
love, albeit also reluctantly. Claribel's father's renunciation has been
voluntary and although the tragic dénouement is avoided, one can only
speculate on Claribel's plight, both as victim of her father's incestuous
impulses and her own submission to his will. Desdemona was at least a
willing participant in her marriage.

Shakespeare's *Tempest*, written toward the end of his life, is a condensation of the renunciation of the daughter by the father, involving his own control in the production of a suitor. Bernard J. Paris tells us: "*The Tempest* is one of only two Shakespearean plays whose plot, as far as we know, is entirely the author's invention. It is, more than any other play, a fantasy of Shakespeare's."[19] The novelists' "Tempests," all written toward the end of their careers, include Dickens's *Our Mutual Friend*, James's *The Golden Bowl*, Conrad's *The Rover*, and Joyce's *Ulysses*. The broad spectrum of possibilities in the development of this model will be seen in the ensuing discussion of these novels.

3

The Triangle in
Charles Dickens

The relationship between psychobiographical data and the recurrent fa-
ther/daughter theme is particularly explicit for Charles Dickens (1812–
70). The early trauma of his relegation to the blacking factory at the age
of twelve, which entailed his own banishment from the oedipal circle
at home,[1] occurred at the outset of a life punctuated by a series of unhappy or unsatisfactory relationships with women. Mollie Hardwick sums
this up:

> His strange, deep idealistic love for Mary Hogarth—the cause of
> years of haunting sorrow to him—his early passion for Maria Bead-
> nell, the "Dora" who rejected her "David" and left a scar on his
> mind and whose deterioration in middle-age caused Dickens such
> cruel disillusion; and worst of all his terrible incompatibility with
> his wife. . . . All these were to culminate in that 13-year relationship
> with Ellen Ternan—a "disappointing partnership," . . . for Ellen's
> youth could not bring back Dickens's own lost boyhood, and she

was obviously never able to give him the ideal love he longed for, or to satisfy that feeling of "something wanting" in his life, which always haunted him.[2]

The circumstances of Mary Hogarth's death were indeed traumatic. Dickens attended one of his own plays, a satire on marriage, in the company of his wife and her sister, Mary, who later that evening suddenly became ill and died the next day aged eighteen. Dickens had become very attached to her as the third member of the triangle that formed the family of his early marriage and requested that he be buried next to her. In later life, when accused of having an affair with Ellen Ternan, he was outraged, protesting that he regarded her as one of his own daughters. Dickens was forty-five when he met the eighteen-year-old Nelly, who was one year younger than his daughter Mary. However, the historical evidence for an affair is substantial.[3] The situation was compounded by the "unhappy first marriage of his younger daughter and the rejection of all acceptable suitors by the other."[4]

The life of Charles Dickens offers an unusual number of examples of the search for that first love-object that is paralleled in so many of his works. His feeling of "something wanting" was also recorded by many other artists, including Henrik Ibsen and Joseph Conrad. Dickens seems to have accompanied his active writing career by a continual "acting out" of the father/daughter/suitor drama, in one form or another. He is also distinguished by his treatment of the theme in a number of early pieces, commented upon by Morton Zabel: "The stories may be said to define or isolate the germs and sources of his greater achievements."[5] Several short pieces from *Sketches by Boz* (1836) illustrate Zabel's point, and one of them includes a passage to delight Freudians.[6]

Another story, "The Misplaced Attachment of Mr. John Dounce,"[7] sums up the transference of the father's attachment from the absent mother to a daughter or a daughter-substitute. This story preceded *Pickwick Papers*, and encompasses its central theme of the father's struggle to renounce the daughter and cope with the threatening alternatives of solitude or solace with an older woman. A sampling of these early stories makes clear Dickens's lifelong preoccupation with the father/daughter relationship. While the emphasis here will be on *Pickwick Papers, David Copperfield, Bleak House*, and *Our Mutual Friend*, other novels also reveal the pervasiveness of the theme throughout the Dickens canon.[8]

Dombey and Son (1848) is especially significant because it illustrates a less frequently depicted defense on the part of the father against the incest threat: his open hostility and rejection of the maturing daughter. Critics have long been aware of this: "The title kept a bigger secret than it disclosed."[9] The ambivalence inherent in the incest-theme is summed up: "In regard to Florence, the deepening of his resentment into hate is overtly linked with her transition from girl to young woman."[10] Herman documents this aspect of clinical cases: "A number of the seductive fathers who were not habitually violent became violent during their daughters' adolescence. Others, perhaps in order to avoid becoming violent and paranoid, completely withdrew from their daughter when they began showing sexual interest in boys their own age. They reacted to their daughters' emerging sexuality either with an attempt to establish total control or with total rejection" (117). Years prior to Dickens and Herman, Mary Shelley had graphically developed this aspect of the complex in *Mathilda*.

Although Dickens first planned the destruction of the suitor, Walter Gay, he later changed his mind (Butt and Tillotson, 98–99), an important alteration in terms of triangular resolution. This novel ends with the reconciliation of the father, daughter, and suitor—a suitor who has suffered a near-fatal exile by water.

Pickwick Papers (1837), Dickens's first novel, interweaves his earlier short story form with the picaresque novel he so admired in Smollett and Fielding. The interpolated tales are related to the main narrative through the father/daughter/suitor relationship. Ironically, in his introduction to the novel, Dickens apologized for the lack of a unifying theme: "I could perhaps wish now that these chapters were strung together on a stronger thread of general interest,"[11] evidently oblivious to the thread of oedipal configurations strung not only between chapters but linking chapters and interpolated tales. The seemingly artless and haphazard narrative structure conceals an intricate, interrelated series of incidents, each composed of father/daughter/son, or father/daughter/suitor—sometimes in combination. The novel depicts a series of lovely young women and Dickens himself suggested the connection between the writing of the novel and his personal life: "Having written for the most part in the society of a very dear young friend [Mary Hogarth] who is now no more, they are connected in the author's mind at once with the happiest period of his life, and with its saddest and most severe affliction."[12] Perhaps it was this background that resulted in its juxtaposition of the interpolated tales against the many triangular configurations in the novel. Sylvia Bank Manning comments: "The brightness of the world of *Pickwick Papers* allows hardly a need for struggle against darker forces. This may be due at least in part to the compression and isolation of evil into the interpolated tales."[13]

The interpolated tales deal with a variety of family configurations, one of the most explicit in terms of fathers and daughters being "In Which the Old Man Launches Forth Into His Favourite Theme, and Relates a Story About a Queer Client" (298). This tale shifts most of the action to the young husband's revenge on the father who has contributed to the destruction of his own daughter and her child by imprisoning him: "[F]rom that hour, he devoted himself to revenge her death and that of his child" (307). As this story is concluded, Mr. Pickwick leaves the room, and the narrative returns to his lighthearted adventures. The only evidence of the impact of this tale on Mr. Pickwick lies in his unobtrusively acting as a low-key, romantic father figure throughout the novel, bringing about a series of happy dénouements in father/suitor or father/son conflicts in contrast to the tragedy of the interpolated tales.

Pickwick's ambiguous role vacillates between leering older gentleman and benevolent father and is ironically suggested in Mr. Phunky's inquiry of the young Mr. Winkle: "'Has his behavior, when females have been in the case, always been that of a man, who, having attained a pretty advanced period of life, content with his own occupations and amusements, treats them only as a father might his daughters?' 'Not the least doubt of it,' replied Mr. Winkle, in the fulness of his heart. 'That is—yes—oh yes—certainly'" (515). Mr. Winkle is obviously not at all certain and Pickwick assumes the seeming innocence of the benign father figure in explaining to Winkle his plan to "protect" Arabella:

> "In affording you this interview the young lady has taken a natural, perhaps, but still a very imprudent step. If I am present at the meeting, a mutual friend, who is old enough to be the father of both parties, the voice of calumny can never be raised against her hereafter."
>
> Mr. Pickwick's eyes lightened with honest exultation at his own foresight, as he spoke thus. Mr. Winkle was touched by this little trait of his delicate respect for the young protégée of his friend, and took his hand with a feeling of regard, akin to veneration. (591, 592)

But Pickwick's voyeuristic proclivities assert themselves as he and Winkle set out on the expedition and Mr. Pickwick "with many smiles and various other indications of great self-satisfaction" produces a dark lantern, and by climbing on the backs of Sam and Mr. Winkle, manages "to bring his spectacles just above the level of the coping" (594). As the men groan under his weight, Pickwick looks over the wall at Arabella and the gentle leers become less subtle: "I merely wished you to know, my dear, that I should not have allowed my young friend to see you in this clandestine way, if the situation in which you are placed, has left him any alternative; and lest the impropriety of this step should cause you any uneasiness, my love, it may be a satisfaction to you, to know that i am present. That's all, my dear" (595).

Pickwick's reassurances end abruptly when he is dropped to the ground and Sam speculates that "his heart must ha' been born five-and-twenty year arter his body, at least!" (595). Mr. Winkle's romantic interlude with Arabella is brought to an abrupt end by Mr. Pickwick's "false alarm" (597). This only serves as a delaying action, however, since ultimately Pickwick has to cope with the surprise announcement that Arabella has become Mrs. Winkle:

> Mr. Pickwick returned no verbal response to this appeal; but he took off his spectacles in great haste, and seizing both the young lady's hands in his, kissed her a great number of times—perhaps a greater number than was absolutely necessary—and then, still re- taining one of her hands, told Mr. Winkle he was an audacious young dog, and bade him get up. (709)

Indicative of Pickwick's transition from possessiveness to renunciation, "he surveyed Arabella's face with a look of as much pride and exultation as if she had been his daughter" (709). He has managed to pull back from a potentially lecherous father to a benign one, but his ambivalence remains regarding the marriage: "Mind, I do not say I should have prevented it, if I *had* known that it was intended" (723). He still has doubts.

Pickwick then pleads with the elder Mr. Winkle to give his blessing to the union, thus hoping to neutralize the father/son rivalry. He is at first unsuccessful with this Dickensian Montague and tells Arabella, as he looks at her pretty face, "I am sure . . . he can have very little idea of the pleasure he denies himself" (791). But this is hardly incipient tragedy, since Pickwick offers himself as an alternate father to the couple and is amply rewarded when Arabella throws "her arms around his neck . . . kissing him affectionately" (792). Has Pickwick silently learned his lesson from the "Tale of the Queer Client"? Pickwick's contemporary, Wardle, reenters the picture to declare Pickwick's own unvoiced hopes regarding Arabella: "I had a great idea of marrying her myself one of these odd days" (807); Wardle's own daughters are the same age. And Pickwick is finally successful in reconciling the elder Winkle to the marriage of his son and

Arabella, a reconciliation that culminates in Winkle's "Kiss me, my love. You *are* a very charming little daughter-in-law, after all!" (847).

Prompted by the secret marriage of young Winkle and her friend, Arabella, Wardle's daughter, Bella, tells her father of her sister Emily's wishes to marry Snodgrass, although Wardle had been urging another match. Wardle then sums up the father/daughter attachment that makes release to the suitor so poignantly painful: "Both my girls are pictures of their dear mother, and as I grow old I like to sit with only them by me; for their voices and looks carry me back to the happiest period of my life, and make me, for the moment, as young as I used to be then, though not quite so light-hearted" (808). Wardle is obdurate in his opposition to the match and the girls plot the elopement of Emily and Snodgrass in the event that her father remains "cruel" (815). However, he becomes reconciled to the match as the chapter ends.

Pickwick continues to act as an archetypal good father as he extends his matchmaking to Sam and Mary, influencing old Mr. Weller who "had been much struck with Mary's appearance, having; in fact, bestowed several very unfatherly winks upon her, already" (841). Again, the ambivalence and covert jealousy in the father/son/heroine triangle is apparent.

Mr. Pickwick's silent renunciation of the young women to their suitors comes full circle when he is "much troubled at first, by the numerous applications made to him by Mr. Snodgrass, Mr. Winkle, and Mr. Trundle, to act as god-father to their offspring; but he has become used to it now, and officiates as a matter of course" (855). This novel encompasses a number of real fathers (Wardle, Weller, Winkle), with Pickwick replacing each briefly as surrogate father for a daughter or for a suitor. Once Pickwick, as proxy, has accepted renunciation, the true fathers fall into line, accepting with good, though reluctant, grace their usurpation by the young suitors.

As counterpoint to the appealing young women characters, Pickwick's (and Dickens's?) disdain for older, motherly figures surfaces throughout the novel. As early illustrated in John Dounce's story, following the renunciation of daughters, Dickens's fathers are faced with the reluctant return to a disdained mother or mother-figure. This undercurrent of antipathy toward older women runs throughout the Dickens canon illustrated in the breach of promise suit brought against Pickwick by Mrs. Bardell, which serves as a leitmotif through most of the novel, even forcing Pickwick's imprisonment for a time. Unlike Dounce, who succumbs to an unhappy compromise with an older woman, Pickwick always feels deeply threatened by them: "The truth is, that the old lady's evidently increasing admiration, was Mr. Pickwick's principle [sic] inducement for going away. He thought of Mrs. Bardell; and every glance of the old lady's eyes threw him into a cold perspiration" (726).

Pickwick chooses isolation instead, mitigated by his function as godfather to innumerable little Snodgrasses, Winkles, Trundles, and Wellers. Since he has indeed played a "godlike" role in their lives, this is appropriate. His decision parallels that made by the Bagman's uncle: "He remained staunch to the great oath he had sworn to the beautiful young lady: refusing several eligible landladies on her account, and dying a bachelor at last" (746). It is not difficult to assume that this expressed antipathy for older women throughout his fiction stemmed in part from Dickens's lifelong bitterness regarding his mother's efforts to return him to work in the hated blacking factory after his father had rescued him from it.

Pickwick and presumably the other fathers in the novel accept what Erik Erikson later defined as the eighth stage of life: "Ego Integrity vs. Despair."

> Potency, performance, and adaptability decline, but if vigor of mind combines with the *gift of responsible renunciation*, some old people can envisage human problems in their entirety (which is what "integrity" means) and can represent to the coming generation a living example of the "closure" of a style of life. (emphasis mine)[14]

The correspondence with Dickens's final description of Pickwick is striking:

> Mr. Pickwick is somewhat infirm now; but he retains all his former juvenility of spirit, and may still be frequently seen, contemplating the pictures in the Dulwich Gallery, or enjoying a walk about the pleasant neighbourhood on a fine day. He is known by all the poor people about, who never fail to take their hats off, as he passes, with great respect. The children idolise him, and so indeed does the whole neighbourhood. Every year, he repairs to a large family merry-making at Mr. Wardle's. (855)

In the years following *Pickwick Papers*, Dickens created many variations on the father/daughter theme and about thirteen years later wrote *David Copperfield*, which he declared to be his most autobiographical novel. As such, it is a rewarding hunting ground for variations on the father/daughter/suitor configuration as a version of the oedipal triangle. Like Pericles,

David participates in a series of triangles—in most of them as the suitor set off against an unusually symbiotic father and daughter. The Edenic garden figures prominently throughout the novel and first occurs as the background for David's earliest oedipal confrontation. Born after his father's death, he had for a number of years been his mother's sole charge, but he is now displaced by a new and hostile father due to his mother's remarriage to a stern man who functions more as a father to them both. The transfer takes place in the garden and constitutes a graphic displacement of the oedipal configuration onto a father-surrogate:

> a coach drove up to the garden-gate, and he went out to receive the visitor. My mother followed him. I was timidly following her, when she turned round at the parlour-door, . . . and taking me in her embrace as she had been used to do, whispered me to love my new father and be obedient to him. She did this hurriedly and secretly, as if it were wrong, but tenderly, and, putting out her hand behind her, held mine in it, until we came near to where he was standing in the garden, where she let mine go, and drew hers through his arm.[15]

David's oedipal battle with his stepfather is fought out with all of the anger and rage that in a primary triangle would have been repressed, or at least subdued, and David is exiled from his home at an early age. With his idealized and submissive mother helpless in the hands of the Murdstones, David is banished by a "bad" father and mother as Dickens himself felt he had been when, under the pressure of the family's straitened circumstances, he was sent at the age of twelve to work in the blacking factory. And even after his father had succeeded in withdrawing him from this hated situation, his mother recommended that he be sent back, resulting in a bitterness from which he never recovered: "I never afterwards forgot, I never shall forget, that my mother was warm for my being sent back" (Johnson, 659). In his view, she evidently preferred remaining with his father while exiling her son.

Some years later, in his first adult role as member of the triangle, he is invited to move into the home of Mr. Wickfield and his daughter Agnes based on the father's plea that it will make things "wholesome" for all of them (238). Agnes and her father have also lived to themselves for many years due to her mother's death at the time of her birth. As with Shakespeare's plots, most of Dickens's fathers and daughters are bereft of the third member of the family who might have prevented their isolation from becoming a problem. Mr. Wickfield is a heavy wine drinker and the

strength of his attachment for his daughter has distinctly incestuous overtones (225).

A parallel father/daughter pair appears at the same time: Dr. Strong
who is sixty-two and his young wife, Annie, who is twenty and is mistaken
by David for the doctor's daughter. "It was very pleasant to see the Doctor
with his pretty young wife. He had a fatherly, benignant way of showing
his fondness for her which seemed in itself to express a good man. I often
saw them walking in the garden where the peaches were" (244). Annie's
young suitor had been banished to India through the combined efforts of
the two fathers. David attends Dr. Strong's school, but lives with Agnes
and her father although he does not become a suitor for Agnes until a
number of years later.

In the intervening time, David functions as suitor in the triangle with
Mr. Spenlow and his daughter Dora, who becomes his first wife. David,
who works in a legal office with Mr. Spenlow (a widower), is brought
home just as Dora has returned from her stint away at school in Paris to be
reunited with her father. Seemingly unaware that Dora represents exactly
the same childlike qualities his deceased mother had displayed, he falls in
love with her immediately and totally: "I loved Dora Spenlow to distrac-
tion" (394). After dinner, as one of their dinner companions discusses gar-
dening, David's attention is diverted since he "was wandering in a garden
of Eden all the while, with Dora" (396).

The following morning David has his first encounter with her alone in
the garden. David never sees Dora and her father together in this garden,
and Mr. Spenlow has taken the precaution of bringing David's old enemy,
Miss Murdstone, into the household as a "protector," effecting a déjà vu
for David. Dora protests to David, "Who wants a protector?" (399), and
in her innocence, would only see this woman as a protector against the
suitor, rather than against her own father; Miss Murdstone is prepared to
be both. Eventually, the couple become engaged, agreeing to keep it a
secret from Dora's father and shift their meetings to the public garden.

Ultimately, David is confronted by an outraged Mr. Spenlow and Miss
Murdstone, who has turned David's letters to Dora over to her father.
Since Miss Murdstone had complied in her brother's appropriation of
David's mother and David's subsequent ejection, he is faced with the repetition of his confrontation with Murdstone over his mother, for whom
Dora is a childlike replica. But this time David does not back down; he
refuses to take back the letters, and Mr. Spenlow, on his way home to
confront Dora with the evidence, dies suddenly and inexplicably, thus
imposing an ineradicable burden of guilt on both young people. Although

the marriage eventually takes place, Dora, presumably deprived of the opportunity of working through her attachment to her father in a natural way, succumbs swiftly to this burden of remorse and also dies.

David, once again solitary, eventually returns to Agnes and her father. Since he and Agnes had long ago fostered a brother/sister relationship, that incest-barrier must now be broken down before the marriage can take place. The garden functions again in this resolution of the triangle. David finds on his return that Mr. Wickfield has given up his drinking. That the incest threat is held in abeyance is symbolized by the displacement of the garden which serves to remove the father from the house: "When I returned, Mr. Wickfield had come home from a garden he had, a couple of miles or so out of town, where he now employed himself almost every day. . . . We sat down to dinner . . . and he seemed but the shadow of his handsome picture on the wall" (835). Renunciation has taken its toll.

Following dinner, Mr. Wickfield reiterates his sense of guilt over bygone days: "My part in them . . . has much matter for regret—for deep regret, and deep contrition. . . . But I would not cancel it, if it were in my power" (835). He then refers to his love for his daughter as a "diseased love" (836) and relates that his wife had died soon after Agnes's birth because of her grief over her father's failure to forgive her marriage. The cycle has been perpetuated; fixated daughters do not make successful transitions to suitors.

This seemingly endless chain of nonrelinquishing fathers is broken with David's happy marriage to Agnes following the defeat of the "bad" suitor, Uriah Heap. And in a singular case in Dickens's novels, the fixated father simply disappears. The wedding takes place, but there is no further mention of Mr. Wickfield in the novel. The wedding guests consist of two couples: in one of these we find the only suitor in the novel to whom the daughter has been willingly relinquished (Traddles and Sophie); this daughter, however, ends up providing a home for her sisters—her father's other daughters, removing them from her father's house. The only other couple at the wedding are Dr. Strong and Annie—the father who had never relinquished.

In this novel, a tempest functions in the final resolution of another triangle in which David had served as friend to Emily and her uncle. In a violent storm at sea, the good suitor (Ham) attempts to save the life of the bad suitor (Steerforth), who has already seduced and abandoned Emily, who was Ham's fiancée. Both suitors drown in the chapter titled "Tempest." But Dickens has reversed Shakespeare's tempest, since the destruction of the two suitors results in the return of the daughter Emily to her surrogate father—her uncle (790). The father/uncle retains the daughter/niece and they live out their lives in exile in the American colonies, with Emily repeatedly refusing any suitors.

Dickens had, in fact, been prevented from marrying an early and intensely loved young lady by the girl's father, and in the person of David the artist/creator, he reverses this unhappy situation and wins the daughter from two successive fathers, killing off the first one and simply removing the second one from the narrative.

Just three years after completing *David Copperfield* with its happy conclusion for the hero and at least one heroine, Dickens published what is regarded by most critics as his darkest novel, *Bleak House* (1853). In *Bleak House*, however, good and evil are so intricately interwoven that Esther's comment, "The fog is very dense indeed!"[16] becomes a metaphorical statement for the world of the novel. In this story, Dickens, through the device of the double narrator, creates the illusion of giving the reader all the information, when there are really significant gaps. Crucial judgments can only be made by a skeptical reader willing to see irony where none seems intended. The novel contains three central father/daughter/suitor configurations: Lord and Lady Dedlock and her dead suitor, Captain Hawdon; John Jarndyce/Ada/Richard; and John Jarndyce/Alan Woodcourt/Esther Summerson.

The oedipal triangle that revolves around Lady Dedlock as both daughter and mother is almost classic in its simplicity, entailing both a "good" and a "bad" surrogate father—Dedlock, her husband, and Tulkinghorn, his lawyer. The unfortunate suitor is, of course, Esther's father, Captain Hawdon, who ends his life as the nameless one, Nemo the law-copier. But "he had been young, hopeful, and handsome" (312), and we know from Lady Dedlock's reaction to his death that he had also been loved. At the time of his death, he was living in abject poverty and using opium, and the question remains unanswered as to the possibility of his working as law-copier having to do with information which he was seeking regarding the Jarndyce estate. Bucket informs Snagsby after Hawdon's death that "there seems to be a doubt whether this dead person wasn't entitled to a little property, and whether this female hasn't been up to some games respecting that property" (319). Hawdon was forty-five at the time of his death (159). George Rouncewell feels a great loyalty to Captain Hawdon, and it is only when he is blackmailed that he consents to give a handwriting sample to Tulkinghorn.

Esther, the product of the out-of-wedlock union between Lady Dedlock and Hawdon, had been raised by her mother's sister, who had never told the mother that her child had survived. Lady Dedlock is viewed by others as more like Lord Dedlock's daughter than his wife: "Though my Lord *is* a little aged for my Lady, says Madame the hostess of the Golden Ape, and though he might be her amiable father, one can see at a glance that they love each other" (169). Lady Dedlock is separated from the suitor to whom she had once been engaged, is married to a "good" father-surrogate, and persecuted by a "bad" father-surrogate. In terms of the oedipal configuration, Tulkinghorn can be viewed as pursuing the truth of the daughter's sexual transgression with the suitor and ultimately destroying her. His views on marriage are made explicit: "My experience teaches me, Lady Dedlock, that most of the people I know would do far better to leave marriage alone. It is at the bottom of three fourths of their troubles. So I thought when Sir Leicester married, and so I always have thought since" (587).

While Tulkinghorn is ruthless in his pursuit of Lady Dedlock's secret, following the divulgence of her past, Sir Leicester has only compassion: "Therefore I desire to say, and call you all to witness . . . that I am on unaltered terms with Lady Dedlock. That I assert no cause whatever of complaint against her, that I have ever had the strongest affection for her, and that I retain it undiminished" (796). Ultimately, Dedlock's compassion cannot save his Lady from destruction by the irate Tulkinghorn, who is also destroyed in the process.

In *Bleak House*, Dickens presents a galaxy of fathers, good and bad (including those parodies: Skimpole, Turveydrop, and Smallweed), but the daughter-figures, Esther and Ada, are quietly pursued by one of the most unobtrusive surrogate fathers in all literature, John Jarndyce. The recurrent motif of "Jarndyce and Jarndyce" suggests the two aspects of his character: the Jarndyce seen through Esther's eyes and the Jarndyce that can only be pieced together from scattered hints. There is a further doubling in this novel in the concept of "suitor," for it serves both in its legal and in its romantic connotations—pointing up the inextricable ties between love and material interests. Richard is both a suitor in Chancery and a suitor for Ada's hand in marriage. John, although ostensibly neither one, is in reality both. In order to assess his function in the novel, these two aspects of Jarndyce as father and suitor are inextricably linked and prove mutually enlightening. The narrator alludes to the double role: "Westminster Hall itself is a shady solitude where nightingales might sing, and a tenderer class of suitors than is usually found there, walk" (270).

Critical discourse has almost unanimously accepted John Jarndyce on the basis of Esther's assessment. George Gissing, still respected as an important Dickensian, commented: "In John Jarndyce I can detect no vulgarity; he appears to me compact of good sense, honour, and gentle feeling . . . Impossible not to like and respect Mr. Jarndyce."[17] Among the more skeptical was George Bernard Shaw who said, "Jarndyce, a violently good man, keeps on doing generous things, yet ends by practicing a heartlessly cruel and indelicate deception on Esther Summerson for the sake of giving her a pleasantly melodramatic surprise."[18]

There has been little critical questioning of the function of John Jarndyce in his economic world in spite of the fact that John's predecessor in Bleak House, then called "The Peaks" (111), was Tom Jarndyce, who "in despair blew his brains out at a coffee-house in Chancery Lane" (20). The narrator raises the central question: "How many people out of the suit Jarndyce and Jarndyce has stretched forth its unwholesome hand to spoil and corrupt would be a very wide question" and "no man's nature has been made better by it" (21).

Although no participants have received money in the case which has dragged on for years in Chancery, John Jarndyce's expenditures are substantial. When Mr. Kenge makes John's offer to educate Esther, the costs in the case are "from *six-ty* to *seven-ty thousand pounds!*" (36), and at the time of Richard's death, the entire estate has been wiped out in court costs. Nevertheless, John Jarndyce maintains a large house with gardens and servants (107), supports Miss Flite (211), Skimpole, and presumably his wife and twelve children (83, 602, 605, 606), educates Esther from the time she is fourteen until she comes to live with him at twenty, at which time he also supports Ada and Richard. He maintains quarters in London to which they all repair at frequent intervals, and he also takes them on extensive visits to Boythorn's country place. John ultimately hires Charley as maid to Esther and provides support for the two children she has been caring for (345).

John, who has totally corrupted Skimpole (a physician manqué), says at one point: "He is in a child's sleep by this time, I suppose; it's time I should take my *craftier head to my more worldly pillow*" (95, emphasis mine). Esther prefers not to interpret the unexplained incongruities in her guardian's associations: "Any seeming inconsistencies in Mr. Skimpole or in Mrs. Jellyby I could not be able to reconcile, having so little experience or practical knowledge" (95). Esther is fully capable of comprehending the hypocrisy in both these individuals, but refuses to question their relationship to her guardian.

Esther's special naiveté seems to suit John perfectly, since when she tells him that she is not clever, "He did not seem at all disappointed; quite the contrary. He told me with a smile all over his face, that he knew me very well indeed and that I was quite clever enough for him" (112). My reading of John is that he would indeed be grateful for a "housekeeper" who was not clever—at least not clever enough to wonder where the housekeeping money was coming from. Another questionable aspect of John's financial affairs is his association with the "philanthropists"; Dickens's attitude toward them is well known, but Kenge reports to Esther: "Mr. Jarndyce, who is desirous to aid any work that is considered likely to be a good work and who is much sought after by philanthropists, has, I believe, a very high opinion of Mrs. Jellyby" (50). But it is obvious throughout the novel that this high opinion is not shared by her creator—nor by Esther herself. Consequently, this association not only raises doubts about Jarndyce, but again raises the question of the source of his income—one possibility is usury. Although Humphrey House does not group Jarndyce with Dickens's other usurious characters, he delineates this novelist's position:

> Beneath his hatred of people like Ralph Nickleby, Gride and Quilp is the ancient moral feeling that usury is wrong because it enables people to make money without having to work for it, and that the power conferred by money earned in this way is the more hateful for its illegitimacy. Dickens was very careful, even when he was detaching his benevolent rich men from the immediate economic struggle, to insist that they *had*, at least in the past, worked for what they spent so generously.[19]

But it is virtually impossible to detach John Jarndyce from the immediate economic struggle since that is what the novel is all about and the notorious case carries his name—twice. There is never any indication in *Bleak House* that John Jarndyce at any time, past or present, has worked to earn the money he is so generously spending. In fact, when he inherited Bleak House itself, it was in a state of decay and had to be repaired and renovated. He also eventually helps set Woodcourt up in practice and buys another Bleak House, fully furnished, for the newlyweds.

The important point here is that there is an unnamed usurer in the background throughout the novel, and the blackest note in this black novel may well be that the usurer is the ostensibly "good" man. The authentically good men in the novel are the most obvious victims, namely Richard Carstone and George Rouncewell, not to mention the dead Captain Hawdon. Although such reprehensible characters as Vholes, Tulkinghorn, and Smallweed are openly and avariciously involved in lending money, the real culprit is "Smallweed's friend in the city" (308) who "is not to be depended on" and although George speculates that his name begins with a D—this may stand for Devil as described by Dickens, in an early description of white-collar crime:

> For howsoever bad the devil can be in fustian or smockfrock (and he can be very bad in both), he is a more designing, callous, and intolerable devil when he sticks a pin in his shirt-front, calls himself a gentleman, backs a card or colour, plays a game or so of billiards, and knows a little about bills and promissory notes than in any other form he wears. (373)

There are veiled references throughout the novel to possible links between John and the shadier characters. Esther observes: "It was Mr. Rook. He seemed unable to detach himself from Mr. Jarndyce. If he had been linked to him, he could hardly have attended him more closely" (213). And again: "During the whole of our inspection . . . he kept close to Mr. Jarndyce and sometimes detained him under one pretence or other until we had passed on, as if he were tormented by an inclination to enter upon some secret subject which he could not make up his mind to approach" (214). But Guppy, who has tracked down Esther's resemblance to Lady Dedlock and reports to Tulkinghorn, also pays an allowance to Miss Flite and her rent to Krook (291). The relationship between Vholes and John is also suspect, as is pointed up by Esther's observations:

> A more complete contrast than my guardian and Mr. Vholes I suppose there could not be. I found them looking at one another across the table, the one so open and the other so close, the one so broad and upright and the other so narrow and stooping, the one giving out what he had to say in such a rich ringing voice and the other keeping it in such a cold-blooded, gasping, fish-like manner that I thought I never had seen two people so unmatched. (620)

But in this novel, Dickens uses Esther herself to point out the inherent fallacies in the appearance/reality dichotomy when she is externally disfigured by smallpox. While the function of Jarndyce as Chancery suitor is heavily veiled (Richard has accused Esther of being "blind," 531), his role as father/suitor for the surrogate daughter, Ada, is not much more explicit. Although John's marriage proposal is made to Esther, there is evidence that she has been educated and prepared to come to Bleak House as "mother" to Ada. Esther's highly controlled preparation is begun at the death of her godmother when she is told, "the scheme of your pursuits has been arranged in exact accordance with the wishes of your guardian, Mr. Jarndyce" (40). When she is twenty, an official letter secures her services as "an elgble compn" for "a Ward of the Ct," who is, of course, Ada, then seventeen. Although Ada has never seen her cousin John, her mother had told her "of the noble generosity of his character, which she has said was to be trusted above all earthly things; and Ada trusted it" (58). It is perhaps not irrelevant that shortly before this comment, Esther had been telling the Jellyby children the story of Little Red Riding Hood (55), another story of misplaced trust.

Upon their first arrival, John greets the girls warmly with "Ada, my love, Esther, my dear," and Esther describes him:

> The gentleman who said these words in a clear, bright, hospitable voice had one of his arms round Ada's waist and the other round mine, and kissed us both in a fatherly way, and bore us across the hall into a ruddy little room, all in a glow with a blazing fire. Here he kissed us again, and opening his arms, made us sit down side by side on a sofa ready drawn out near the hearth. (78)

Esther estimates his age as "nearer sixty than fifty," and Ada is described by Skimpole: "She is like the morning . . . with that golden hair, those blue eyes, and that fresh bloom on her cheek, she is like the summer morning" and during this adulation, Esther notices Mr. Jarndyce "standing near us, with his hands behind him, and an attentive smile on his face" (87).

Esther makes perhaps her first mistake as she concludes that John hopes for an eventual match between Richard and Ada, and also surmises that John might really be her father (96). But John himself hints at the ambiguities in the relationship: "I hear of a good little orphan girl without a protector, and I take it into my head to be that protector. She grows up, and more than justifies my good opinion, and I remain her guardian and her friend. What is there in all this?" (109). What is there indeed? It is significant that Esther is shortly being called by a variety of "mother" names: "This was the beginning of my being called Old Woman, and Little Old Woman, and Cobweb, and Mrs. Shipton, and Mother Hubbard, and Dame Durden, and so many names of that sort that *my own name soon became quite lost among them*" (112, emphasis mine).

After Richard has abandoned medicine and decided to try his hand at the law, Ada and John discuss it in an intimate scene recorded by Esther. John repeatedly calls Ada "my love," and she talks to him "with her hand upon his shoulder, where she had put it in bidding him good night" (246). Both declare their affection and faith in Richard to be undiminished, and then Ada places both hands on John's shoulders:

"I think," said my guardian, thoughtfully regarding her, "I think it must be somewhere written that the virtues of the mothers shall occasionally be visited on the children, as well as the sins of the father. Good night, my rosebud. Good night, little woman. Pleasant slumbers! Happy dreams!"

This was the first time I ever saw him follow Ada with his eyes with something of a shadow on their benevolent expression. I well remembered the look with which he had contemplated her and Richard when she was singing in the firelight . . . but his glance was changed, and even the silent look of confidence in me which now followed it once more was not quite so hopeful and untroubled as it had originally been. (247)

Following this encounter, Esther is "low-spirited," and cannot sleep, but is not sure why. She comes upon John, also sleepless, worn and weary, and when she inquires whether he is troubled, he replies that it is nothing she "would readily understand" (248). He then tells her of her aunt's request that he care for her if anything should happen, and Esther calls him "the guardian who is a father to her!": "At the word father, I saw his former trouble come into his face. He subdued it as before, and it was gone in an instant; but it had been there and it had come so swiftly upon my words that I felt as if they had given him a shock" (250).

The ambiguities in John's reaction to "father" are never fully explained and can only be speculated upon. Perhaps John really is Ada's father; her mother had spoken of him with tears in her eyes, and we are given no information regarding Ada's background. When Richard loses interest in the law and is about to embark for Ireland and an army career, John intervenes and insists the engagement be broken off, much to Richard's consternation (349). Although the narrator never comments directly on Jarndyce, Richard gets Vholes to admit that his own (Richard's) financial interests are not identical to John's (560).

In spite of the fact that Esther and John have established a relationship in which she sees him as a father while he seems to see her as Ada's mother, immediately following her disclosure that she is Lady Dedlock's daughter, he proposes marriage, saying he "has long had something in his thoughts" (614). He proposes by letter and, among other things, exerts subtle pressure by telling her "to remember that I owed him nothing" (616). Esther's reaction is gratitude—and tears:

> Still I cried very much, not only in the fullness of my heart after reading the letter, not only in the strangeness of the prospect—for it was strange though I had expected the contents—but as if something for which there was no name or distinct idea were indefinitely lost to me. I was very happy, very thankful, very hopeful; but I cried very much. (617)

But it is Esther's revelation of her parentage that precipitates the proposal. Are financial considerations operative here? Significantly, after two weeks have elapsed without John's mentioning the proposal, Esther feels compelled to accept, but decides not to tell Ada (619).

Woodcourt returns, the hero of a shipwreck (survivor of a tempest), but still poor, and in response to Esther's request, agrees to befriend and help Richard. Although the actions taken by John at this point seem on the surface to be altruistic, they also are highly manipulative. Since Esther has been going into London each day to care for Caddy, he suggests that they all move to London and that Woodcourt be called in on the case. This not only leaves John and Ada together a great deal of the time; it also throws Esther and Woodcourt together. Even after John has been informed of the secret marriage between Richard and Ada, he takes no positive step toward the marriage he has proposed for himself, and Esther is puzzled by his procrastination:

> The letter had made no difference between us except that the seat by his side had come to be mine; it made none now. He turned his old bright fatherly look upon me, laid his hand on my hand in his old way, and said again, "She will succeed my dear. Nevertheless, Bleak House is thinning fast, O little woman!"
>
> I was sorry presently that this was all we said about that. I was rather disappointed. I feared I might not quite have been all I had meant to be since the letter and the answer. (704)

While John's proposal had been precipitated by Esther's disclosure of her parentage, John is obviously in no hurry to conclude the arrangements, and there are several possible reasons. Ada has just turned twenty-one and Richard is in bad shape, emotionally and physically. Is John playing a waiting game, and if so, what is he waiting for? Richard is already heavily in debt and Ada's funds have been eaten away. Following Lady Dedlock's death, John resumes his manipulation of events as he brings Mrs. Woodcourt into the house during Esther's illness. After her recovery from smallpox, he tells Esther of his decision to remain in London: "I have a scheme to develop, little woman. I propose to remain here, perhaps for six months, perhaps for a longer time—as it may be. Quite to settle here for a while, in short." This, of course, means that he must sustain the expense of two households. Esther realizes that he is happy at the prospect of leaving Bleak House, and he reminds her: "It is a long way from Ada, my dear, and Ada stands much in need of you." When Esther commends him for his usual consideration of herself and Ada, John comes as close as anyone in the novel to an accurate appraisal of his situation:

> Not so *disinterested* either, my dear, if you mean to extol me for that virtue, since if you were generally on the road, you could be seldom with me. And besides, I wish to hear as much and as often of Ada as I can in this condition of estrangement from poor Rick. Not of her alone, but of him too, poor fellow. (815, 816, emphasis mine)

Obviously hearing more of "poor Rick" is an afterthought. Lady Dedlock, during her previous introduction to Ada, had observed to John: "You will lose the *disinterested* part of your Don Quixote character . . . if you only redress the wrongs of beauty like this" (267, emphasis mine). But the real question is whether John was ever disinterested—the evidence seems to indicate that he was not. If John is following the pattern of the destructive father, he is doing so in a subtle manner. If he is behind the usury in the novel, he is also indirectly contributing to Richard's slow deterioration. The nature of the responsibility involved here is voiced by Skimpole: "If it is blameable in Skimpole to take the note, it is blameable in Bucket to offer the note—much more blameable in Bucket to offer the note, because he is the knowing man" (832). A short time before, Skimpole had defined Richard's relationship to himself: "Parallel case, exactly!" (829). When Esther, years later, looking into the published diary left by Skimpole (the sometime artist), reads the judgment, "Jarndyce, in common with most other men I have known, is the incarnation of selfishness," she refrains from comment (833). Is this in fact, authorial comment? Only Richard and Skimpole, the two dependent borrowers in the novel, are unequivocally condemnatory of John Jarndyce.

John's machinations with regard to Woodcourt and Esther (which so incensed Shaw) continue and his failure to meet Esther results in Woodcourt's opportunity to make his own proposal. It is regretfully declined by

Esther because of her prior commitment: "I learned in a moment that what I had thought was pity and compassion was devoted, generous, faithful love. Oh, too late to know it now, too late, too late. That was the first ungrateful thought I had. Too late" (835). She goes to bed in the dark to avoid the sight of her own tears.

The lack of urgency on John's part in the matter of the marriage, plus Esther's statement that "He had never altered his old manner" (839) strongly suggests a lack of sexual interest on John's part. He also continues to use those no-names, "Dame Durden" and "Dame Trot," with which he had denied her identity as a woman from the time she took over the housekeeping keys. And it is finally Esther who pushes toward the fulfillment of the marriage letter, setting the date on which John shall become "more enviable than any other man in the world" (840), set for a month hence.

John's excuse for not acting is that he has had only Rick on his mind (840), but immediately following the setting of the wedding date, Smallweed and Bucket appear with a newly discovered will (which had been partially burned), which reduces John's financial interest while increasing Richard's and Ada's (845). The will is to be read "next term," that is, the following month. Esther begins her wedding preparations with constraint: "I did it all so quietly because I was not quite free from my old apprehension that Ada would be rather sorry and because my guardian was so quiet himself" (855). The relationship between the two "suitor" roles is made clear as Esther relates: "I understood that my marriage would not take place until after the term-time we had been told to look forward to" (856). Material interests are paramount.

Suddenly invited by her guardian to go into Yorkshire to approve Woodcourt's house, Esther is overcome with sobs but (as Shaw reminds us) is allowed to go through the night without being told that John is about to set her free. This indicates either a total unawareness of her feelings or a veiled sadism. When John finally tells her that she is to be Woodcourt's wife in a new Bleak House, he says, "I am your guardian and your father now. Rest confidently here" (859).

It is perhaps important that for John, father and guardian are two distinct things; when he takes Ada in to live with him following Richard's death, he insists that she no longer call him "cousin," but "guardian" (878). Esther says, "He was her guardian henceforth, and the boy's; and he had an old association with the name. So she called him guardian, and has called him guardian ever since. The children know him by no other name. I say the children; I have two little daughters" (878).

The reader is easily seduced into seeing John's yielding up of Esther as a selfless renunciation, until it is noted that he ends up in possession of Ada and her child by Richard, who has died after the collapse of the suit. Although Richard succumbs finally to declaring John a "good" man on his deathbed, Esther unwittingly is perhaps closer to the truth: "My guardian, the picture of a good man" (871). As Richard is dying, Esther observes John's responses without passing judgment when John says to him:

> "And you will come there too, I hope, Rick. I am a solitary man now, you know, and it will be a charity to come to me. A charity to come to me, my love!" he repeated to Ada as he gently passed his hand over her golden hair and put a lock of it to his lips. (I think he vowed within himself to cherish her if she were left alone.) (872)

As Richard realizes that he has been a dreamer, John says, "What am I but another dreamer, Rick?" (872). During the meeting in the park at Chesney Wold, when Lady Dedlock first met the girls and John there, she inquired about Richard, "Is the young gentleman disposed of whom you wrote to Sir Leicester?" John replies, "I hope so" (267). Poor Richard is permanently "disposed of" by the end of the novel.

After the birth of Ada's fatherless baby, John says to her: "When you and *my boy* are strong enough to do it, come and take possession of your home" (emphasis mine), and we are told that this surrogate "to Ada and her pretty boy . . . is the fondest father" (878). There is never the slightest hint that Esther sees Ada's fate as less than satisfactory, but we are never told how Ada feels. Esther's continued reluctance to tell Ada of her commitment to marry John is never explained. Dorothy Van Ghent responded to Edmund Wilson's observations that Dickens generally failed to "get the good and bad together in one character," with the comment: "[I]n Dickens's nervous world, one simplex is superimposed upon or is continuous with another, and together they form the complex of good-in-evil or of evil-in-good."[20]

Although many critics join Esther in her misreading of John Jarndyce, he may be Dickens's consummate achievement of "the complex of good-in-evil or of evil-in-good." He is the father who has either destroyed the suitor or passively complied in that destruction and then retained the daughter, not by the overtly violent means of an Antiochus, but by the subtle means of a victim of the irrational world of Chancery. John himself has pointed to his own duplicity: "Ah, Dame Trot, Dame Trot . . . what shall we find reasonable in Jarndyce and Jarndyce! Unreason and injustice at the top, unreason and injustice at the bottom, unreason and injustice from beginning to end—if it ever had an end—how should poor Rick, always hovering near it, pluck reason out of it?" (816). The novel ends with a domestic situation that provides a classic example of what Herman dubbed "covert incest," with a dilution of the theme in the involvement of surrogates.

If *Bleak House* obliquely reflects the blackness of *King Lear* or *Othello*, *Our Mutual Friend* (1865) is Dickens's *Tempest*. But it also contains variations on the father/daughter theme that suggest comparison with *Pericles*. The novel opens with Lizzie Hexam and her father, Gaffer, "On the Look Out" for bodies in the river. In spite of the horror of the work her father forces her to do, Lizzie has a genuine tenderness for him. Lizzie's father does not survive, however, either to protect her from suitors, or to give her up to one, and Lizzie becomes the haunted prey of those bitter rivals, Bradley Headstone and Eugene Wayburn, a rivalry that ends violently in the destruction of one suitor and the near-destruction of the other. The father of another subordinate father/daughter pair is likewise destroyed in the same drama, Pleasant's father, Rogue Riderhood, engaged in the same unsavory calling as Gaffer Hexam. Pleasant's suitor, Mr. Venus, is engaged in the even more bizarre occupation of "Preserver of Animals and Birds," and "Articulator of Human Bones." But in this case it is not the father who stands in the way of the match, but the daughter herself who protests: "I do not wish . . . to regard myself, nor yet to be regarded, in that boney light."[21]

Jenny Wren, the doll's dressmaker, and her incurably alcoholic father are one of Dickens's more famous reversed parent/child pairs. Jenny, small and crippled, is vitriolic in her assessment of this human wreck: "He's enough to break his mother's heart, is this boy . . . I wish I had never brought him up. He'd be sharper than a serpent's tooth, if he wasn't as dull as ditch water. Look at him. There's a pretty object for a parent's eyes!" (595). But Jenny also has a "good" father in Riah, her "second father" (881), and is eventually married to her suitor, Sloppy.

A more complex father/daughter/suitor configuration occurs with the Podsnaps and their surrogates, the Lammles, the latter of whom come close to the Pandar/Bawd of *Pericles*. Certainly one of the most flagrantly bitter marriages in literature, the Lammles are mutually disillusioned to find that neither one has any money when each was counting on the other having a great deal. The conspiracy by the Lammles to recoup their losses by pairing Miss Podsnap with one of the least prepossessing suitors ever created, Fascination Fledgeby, fails.

The central oedipal configuration in the novel consists of Bella Wilfer, her father, and John Harmon. But the enactment of the oedipal plot is temporarily transferred to surrogate parents, the Boffins, with Mr. Boffin in the Prospero role. There is one important difference between the two sets of parents, however, since Bella's true mother is in effect "absent," as one of Dickens's humorous/obnoxious mother-wives. Like Dora's mother in Freud's case history, she has been discredited and obliterated as a person with any power. Consequently, her husband has developed an unusually close relationship with his daughter, "a girl of about nineteen, with an exceedingly pretty figure and face, but with an impatient and petulant expression both in her face and in her shoulders" (77). The father/daughter/suitor triangle is set up almost immediately, since unbeknown to the Wilfers, the new boarder is really Rokesmith/Handford/Harmon—the young man thought drowned, who had been designated Bella's suitor by his father's will: "A dark gentleman. Thirty at the utmost. An expressive, one might say handsome face. A very bad manner. In the last degree constrained, reserved, diffident, troubled" (81).

Since Bella's family is very poor, she goes to live with the Boffins who have inherited the supposedly dead Harmon's wealth, while the living Harmon is unwittingly hired as Boffin's secretary. Bella's transference to the Boffins represents her father's initial renunciation, since the implicit hope is that she will find a wealthy suitor. It is also significant that the Boffins represent one of the few instances in Dickens of a happily married, older couple, whose compatibility has been maintained through compromise.

> Mrs Boffin, as I've mentioned, is a highflyer at Fashion; at present I'm not. I don't go higher than comfort, and comfort of the sort that I'm equal to the enjoyment of. . . . So Mrs Boffin, she keeps up her part of the room, in her way; I keep up my part of the room in mine. In consequence of which we have at once, Sociability (I should go melancholy mad without Mrs Boffin), Fashion and Comfort. (100)

Since Bella has been deprived of her marriage to the wealthy John Harmon by his supposed drowning, the Boffins seek to make restitution by bringing her to live with them "to brisk her up, and brisk her about, and give her a change" (153). The suitor thus becomes a factor in the households of both fathers, and the daughter moves back and forth between the worlds of genteel poverty and inherited wealth. It is this aspect of the situation that leads to the transformation of Boffin into a Prospero, a reading that throws a light on much of the confusion over that character's seemingly incongruous change of heart. James Kincaid summed up the consensus: "Nearly all critics have felt either that Boffin ought not to have changed or that, once changed, he should have stayed changed."[22]

Bella is a very mercenary young lady, and although she really loves John, she feels she cannot allow herself the luxury of marrying a poor man and Boffin sets out to show her the absurdity of her position by carrying it to extremes:

> "But I think it's very creditable in you, at your age, to be so well up
> with the pace of the world, and to know what to go in for. You are
> right. Go in for money, my love. Money's the article. You'll make
> money of your good looks, and of the money Mrs Boffin and me
> will have the pleasure of settling upon you, and you'll live and die
> rich. That's the state to live and die in!" said Mr Boffin, in an unc-
> tuous manner. "R—r—rich!" (526)

In a marvelous travesty of Don Quixote, Boffin reads only the lives of misers: "Bella very clearly noticed, that, as he pursued the acquisition of those dismal records with the ardour of Don Quixote for his books of chivalry, he began to spend his money with a more sparing hand" (529).

But Boffin's attachment to Bella is also made quite clear, and his feigned ill treatment of John parallels that of Simonides toward Pericles and Prospero toward Ferdinand. While ostensibly serving another purpose, it gives the father a chance to vent his very real hostility toward the prospective suitor. Mrs. Boffin tells Bella: "He is so much attached to you, whatever he says, that your own father has not a truer interest in you and can hardly like you better than he does" (527). But in the interests of showing Bella the true nature of greed by exaggerating it, Boffin allows himself to assume the role of father-as-pander: "Give me a kiss, my dear child, in saying Good Night, and let me confirm what my old lady tells you. I am very fond of you, my dear, and I am entirely of your mind, and you and I will take care that you shall be rich. These good looks of yours . . . are worth money, and you shall make money of 'em" (527).

But Bella begins to have misgivings, and outraged by Boffin's treatment of John, abandons her false, mercenary goals, and marries for love, following which John acknowledges his true identity and inheritance—"Harmony" is restored. One other aspect of the father/daughter/suitor theme in *Our Mutual Friend* is worth noting—Bella's wedding. This too is unusual, both for Dickens and for fiction in general. It serves to emphasize the romantic possibilities in the renunciation by the father in favor of the suitor.

On the morning of the secret wedding, Bella and her father have a sentimental breakfast together before departing "aboard an early steamboat for Greenwich" (731). The awful mother is left out of the wedding entirely—only father, daughter, and suitor are present, and the transference is symbolized in the dinner which follows:

> But, the marriage dinner was the crowning success, for what had the bride and bridegroom plotted to do, but to have and to hold that dinner in the very room of the very hotel where Pa and the lovely woman had once dined together! Bella sat between Pa and John, and divided her attentions pretty equally, but felt it necessary . . . to remind Pa that she was *his* lovely woman no longer.
>
> "I am well aware of it, my dear," returned the cherub, "and I resign you willingly."
>
> "Willingly, sir? You ought to be brokenhearted."
>
> "So I should be, my dear, if I thought that I was going to lose you."
>
> "But you know you are not; don't you, poor dear Pa? . . . Look here, Pa!" Bella put her finger on her own lip, and then on Pa's, and then on her own lip again, and then on her husband's. "Now we are a partnership of three, dear Pa." (734–35)

Although Bella is in the same relative position as Cordelia, her father is no Lear and manages to view his renunciation to her suitor from a positive vantage point. While the wedding involves only Bella, John, and her real father, a later dénouement with the surrogate parents vindicates Boffin's duplicity. There is also a brief reference to the potential jealousy on the part of the mother toward the usurping daughter: "'From the first, you was always a special favourite of Noddy's,' said Mrs Boffin, shaking her head. 'O you were! And if I had been inclined to be jealous, I don't know what I mightn't have done to you. But as I wasn't—why, my beauty,' with a hearty laugh and an embrace, 'I made you a special favourite of my own too'" (843–44).

The pairing-off that marks the end of this novel is a skewed variation on Shakespeare's late comedies. The romantic father/daughter/suitor threesome gathered for the wedding dinner excludes the mother whose "absence" presumably has intensified Wilfer's attachment to his daughter and made his renunciation more dramatic. But Dickens saw fit to temporarily remove the triangle to a set of surrogate parents, the Boffins, thus defusing some of the intensity that might have occurred within the primary triangle. Boffin has emulated Pickwick in facilitating the father's renunciation.

Since I maintain that Dickens's final, unfinished novel suggests a return to fatherly retention, it is worth noting a short piece of fiction which marks the transition between *Our Mutual Friend* and the unfinished *Mystery of Edwin Drood.* "George Silverman's Explanation" (1868) treats the same theme as the two novels but reverts stylistically to the early stories and the interpolated tales.[23]

The tale involves surrogates in the persons of the tutor, George, and his pupil, Adelina. George, a clergyman, falls deeply in love with his young wealthy pupil, who has been placed in his charge by her mother. Although she reciprocates his love, he painfully matches her with another young pupil. The incestuous implications, due to the age difference and the fact that her mother entrusted her to his care, can be inferred. Silverman carries renunciation to a painful extreme by performing the wedding ceremony himself. At the age of sixty (he was thirty at the time of the renunciation), he pens his "explanation." The story condenses the theme of fatherly renunciation—a theme that Dickens was to reverse in *Edwin Drood.*

Dickens paralleled Shakespeare in the creation of multiple variations on the father/daughter/suitor theme. Steven Marcus characterizes Dickens's imagination as "preeminently Shakespearean,"[24] borne out by Dickens's appraisal of a performance of *King Lear*: "From his rash denunciation of the gentle daughter who can only love him and be silent, to his falling dead beside her, unbound from the rack of this tough world, a more affecting, truthful, and tremendous picture never surely was presented on the stage."[25] While Dickens has seen fit to avoid repetition of Lear's "rash" actions in his fiction, he profoundly understood them.

Everything's terrible, cara—
in the heart of man.
Henry James, *The Golden Bowl*

4

The Triangle in
Henry James

A preponderant number of Henry James's works deal with fathers and daughters, beginning with his first novel, *Watch and Ward* (1871), through a middle work, *The Portrait of a Lady* (1880), and culminating in the complex *The Golden Bowl* (1904). Henry James (1843–1916) differs biographically from the other four artists in that he never married and had no children. However, Leon Edel notes the psychobiographical links in James's life:

> But in the close-knit family constellation he created in *The Golden Bowl* James was dealing with the deepest webs of his own inner world—his father's having had in the house not only his wife Mary Walsh, Henry's mother, but her sister Catherine, the loyal Aunt Kate. There had always been triangles in James's life.[1]

In addition, although there is every indication that he never intended to marry, throughout his life Henry James formed close relationships with various women, some of whom probably were disappointed that no further commitment ever materialized. His affection for and support of his semi-invalid sister Alice, who also lived in London for a number of years, is well documented. Several of the women he was fondest of died traumatic deaths, the first being his cousin, Minny Temple, who died of tuberculosis at the age of twenty-four. His much admired friend, Clover Hooper, the wife of Henry Adams, committed suicide hard on the heels of her father's death. In later years, one of his closest women friends and novelist colleagues, Constance Fenimore Woolson, committed suicide, some thought due to her unresolved relationship with James. This deeply affected him and was probably reflected in "The Beast in the Jungle." Strong attachments for several young men friends greatly enriched his later years. A comparison of the variations in his handling of the father/daughter/suitor triads in his fiction as compared with the other writers should prove useful in the evaluation of psychobiographical factors in general.[2]

The James corpus, like those of both Shakespeare and Dickens, entails some of the almost infinite plot possibilities in the father/daughter/suitor configuration. *The American* (1877), *Washington Square* (1878), *The Bostonians* (1886), *What Maisie Knew* (1897), and *The Wings of the Dove* (1902), to name only a few, present wide variations on the theme. Most of these deal with actual fathers and daughters, and *What Maisie Knew* represented an important element in James's development of the father/daughter theme. This novel is perhaps one of literature's best examples of the distancing of the oedipal triangle onto surrogates. Through the process of divorce and a succession of realignments, the oedipal conflict is gradually transferred as each parent remarries and their new mates become a pair, always with Maisie as the third member of the triangle. James is thus able to treat situations more explicitly that might have proved too threatening in terms of Maisie and her actual parents. But the narrative also foreshadows the assumption of autonomy on the part of the daughter, which culminates in *The Golden Bowl*. In a final confrontation, Maisie reluctantly renounces Sir Claude when she learns she cannot have him to herself.

Among the authors here under consideration, Henry James is unique in terms of what we deem to be his first novel. Although he published the serialized version of *Watch and Ward* in 1871 and *Roderick Hudson* in 1875, he didn't publish the heavily revised first novel in book form until 1878. In his respective introductions to the two novels, Leon Edel refers to each as James's first.[3] But James himself seems to have relegated the earlier novel into limbo; it was left out of the Macmillan Edition of his works in 1883, and later omitted from the definitive New York edition. Leon Edel, discussing *Watch and Ward* summarized "the original fantasy":

> We need not go into the original fantasy—it would take us far afield; I mean that of the young man who, rejected by the woman he loves, . . . dreams up a marriage with a wife he will raise from childhood, one who is almost, by his having adopted her, a kinswoman. (14)

"Kinswoman" suggests a delicacy which avoids the harsh realities of implied incest in the relationship between guardian and ward in this novel, previously explored by Dickens in *Bleak House*. In *Watch and Ward*, the theme is worked out between a daughter and a surrogate father who has indirectly eliminated Nora's real father by withholding needed financial aid and precipitating his suicide. James's changes in this novel between serialization and bound book constituted a significant toning down and muting of the sexual passages.[4] There are highly erotic overtones in the description of Nora's father just prior to his suicide: "Suddenly he called her. . . . and he bade her get out of bed and come to him. She trembled, but she obeyed. On reaching the threshold of his room she saw the gas turned low, and her father standing in his shirt against the door at the other end. He ordered her to stop where she was. Suddenly she heard a loud report and felt beside her cheek the wind of a bullet."[5]

The sexual overtones in this passage suggest a paradigmatic reading of the father of the motherless child who is approaching puberty, and sees the only possible solution to the incest-threat as death for one or both. Nora's father is referred to by her cousin as "more sinned against than sinning" (60), with its echoes of *King Lear*. With Nora's true father eliminated, Roger Lawrence steps in immediately and begins to mold her to his own design, expecting later to switch from father to lover with "the child,—the little forlorn, precocious, potential woman" (16). The blurring and blending of the two kinds of love are then elaborated:

> She stared for a moment, without moving, and then left the sofa and came slowly towards him. She was tall for her years. She laid her hand on the arm of his chair and he took it. . . . "Do you remember my taking you last night in my arms?" It was his fancy that, for an answer, she faintly blushed. He laid his hand on her head and smoothed away her thick disordered hair. She submitted to his consoling touch with a plaintive docility. He put his arm round her

waist. An irresistible sense of her childish sweetness, of her tender feminine promise, stole softly into his pulses. A dozen caressing questions rose to his lips. Had she been to school? Could she read and write? Was she musical? . . . Lawrence felt the tears rising to his eyes; he felt in his heart the tumult of a new emotion. Was it the inexpugnable instinct of paternity? Was it the restless ghost of his buried hope? (16)

The "restless ghost of his buried hope" suggests both the earlier mother/son attachment and Roger's need for a restoration of lost autonomy following Miss Morton's refusal of his offer of marriage. The "mother" is also handled obliquely in *Watch and Ward* since the once-loved lady later becomes the widow, Mrs. Keith, who serves as surrogate mother for Nora during Roger's later courtship. His transfer of affection immediately following his rejection by Miss Morton is replete with sexual implications:

He thought of his angry vow the night before to live only for himself and turn the key on his heart. . . . Before twenty-four hours had elapsed a child's fingers were fumbling with the key. . . . Was he to believe, then, that he could not live without love, and that he must take it where he found it? . . . But there was love and love! He could be a protector, a father, a brother. What was the child before him but a tragic embodiment of the misery of isolation, a warning of his own blank future? "God forbid!" he cried. And as he did so, he drew her towards him and kissed her. (16–17)

Although Nora's real mother was already absent before the novel began, a series of surrogate mothers hover throughout the novel (Lucinda Brown, Teresa, Mrs. Keith, Miss Sands), all of whom either are not viable sexual alternatives, or are rejected by Roger. The "exile" motif functions several times, both for the father and for the daughter. The first trip is taken by Roger, who summarizes exile as a potential enhancement of the familiar:

Then as he seemed to taste, in advance, the bitterness of disappointment, casting about him angrily for some means of appeal: "I ought to go away and stay away for years and never write at all. . . . I ought to convert myself into a beneficient shadow, a vague tutelary name. Then I ought to come back in glory, fragrant with exotic perfumes and shod with shoes of mystery! (47, 48)

Nora returns as a "beauty" from her year in Rome with Mrs. Keith (116), to finally confront Roger who has been seriously ill: "Roger leaned back in his chair, watching her, . . . offering her this and that; in a word, falling in love. . . . The flower of her beauty had bloomed in a night, that of his passion in a day" (144).

The watching of the ward until a suitable maturity is reached is thus summarized. In addition, three fundamental aspects of the relationship between patriarchal autonomy and sexuality that are embodied in the father/daughter relationship are also included in *Watch and Ward*: the control maintained by the father in the development of the young girl as a future wife, the element of gratitude as it operates to force the daughter's compliance, and the relationship with a younger woman as rejuvenating and restorative of lost potency. Roger writes to Mrs. Keith: "Perhaps six years hence, she will be *grateful enough* not to refuse me as you did" (34, emphasis mine). His ultimate intentions are also reflected in his decision as to what Nora should call him: "At the outset he decided instinctively against 'papa'" and she begins calling him "Roger" (26).

The hope of rejuvenation which characterizes the father/daughter relationship is made clear as Nora puts on long dresses and arranges her hair as a young lady: "He was now thirty-three; he fancied he was growing stout. Bald, corpulent, middle-aged,—at this rate he should soon be shelved! He was seized with a mad desire to win back the lost graces of youth" (49). Nora is at this point fifteen and Roger cuts off his whiskers in order to seem more youthful. Nora begins at this point to see their living together as "strange," and asks, "Is there any secret in all that you have done for me?" (52).

The potential for the miscarriage of Roger's "scheme" is embodied in Nora's encounters with two suitors: her cousin, Fenton, and Roger's cousin, Hubert. Both are depicted as possessing a virility that Roger lacks, but hopes to restore through his conquest of Nora. One of the most erotic passages in the novel occurs as Roger coldly contemplates a possible sexual encounter between Nora and a suitor as a kind of whetting of her sexual appetite for him, a factor that makes it difficult to accept Edel's assessment of the novel: "It is the utter innocence of this story which, in a way, endears it to us. *Lolita*, for all its verbal delicacies, is written in full awareness of its theme. *Watch and Ward* is naïve from beginning to end." But Edel has just pointed out that James was twenty-eight when he wrote this novel.[6]

Roger caught himself wondering whether, at the worst, a little precursory love-making would do any harm. The ground might be gently tickled to receive his own sowing; the petals of the young girl's nature, playfully forced apart, would leave the golden heart of the flower but the more accessible to his own vertical rays. (58)

Following her rejection of Roger's offer of marriage, Nora reacts as might be expected to an old letter from him to Mrs. Keith: "Nora took the letter; it was old and crumpled, the ink faded. She glanced at the date, — that of her first school year. In a moment she had read to the closing sentence. 'It will be my own fault if I have not a perfect wife.' In a moment more its heavy meaning overwhelmed her; . . . Nora dropped the letter and stood staring, open-mouthed, pale as death, with her poor young face blank with horror" (153). Nora moves almost immediately into a self-imposed exile in the city where she goes to seek the two absent suitors, and on the train she reflects significantly that "she was once more her father's daughter" (157).

It is in the resolution of *Watch and Ward* that James diverges most widely from the other four writers. Reversing the more common role of the suitor as a means of resolution of the incest-threat, Fenton and Hubert both prove unsuitable. Nora, thrown back upon her own resources, meets Roger coming "down the bright vista of the street" (195), and she is filled with "the full realisation of being. Yes, she was in the secret of the universe, and the secret of the universe was, that Roger was the only man in it who had a heart" (195–96).

James unites the father and daughter in spite of hints of incest throughout the novel. By making Roger a surrogate father, he was able to deal with incest and not deal with it at the same time. He was able to resolve the dilemma in an idyllic manner, free from a sense of guilt, an important part of the resolution being the patent unsuitability of the two suitors. Roger, winning by default, has his cake and eats it too, but Mrs. Keith, the surrogate mother, comments in the final lines of the novel: "The fact is, Nora is under a very peculiar obligation to me!" (197). By not marrying Roger years before, she has opened the way for the lengthy preparation of his ward as a wife. Unlike the resolution of *The Winter's Tale* and *Pericles*, the younger suitors are dismissed, the father and daughter are united, and the surrogate mother remains alone, although "Mrs. Keith and Mrs. Lawrence are very good friends" (197).

In *Roderick Hudson*, as in *Watch and Ward*, the parent/child roles involve surrogates, and there are two overlapping triangles: Cavaliere/Mrs. Light/Christina and Rowland/Mary/Roderick. In spite of no sharp age difference between Rowland and Roderick, Rowland assumes the father role through acting as mentor of the younger man's career and through his subsequent vigilance regarding Roderick's associations with both Christina and Mary. He is commandeered for a similar function by Mrs. Light and the Cavaliere who ask him to persuade Christina to marry the Prince, an assignment he declines.

But Rowland himself is interested in Mary, although he believes that his suit is hopeless in view of her feelings for Roderick, while also knowing that Roderick has no intention of marrying her. Rowland subsequently destroys the suitor by telling him the truth about his egotism, driving him to go out into the "tempest" (517) in which he dies—a shocking and unexpected dénouement for Rowland. The bereft Mary remains with her mother, and Rowland presumably carries his unrequited love to his grave. The juxtaposition of the conclusion of this novel against that of the earlier one suggests that the incestuous implications of the first novel proved too unsettling for James, and that he almost immediately reversed himself with a more palatable conclusion, later designating that as his first novel.

Another of Henry James's complex variations on the father/daughter theme occurs in *The Portrait of a Lady* (1880), in which two father/daughter pairs are intricately and inextricably related, with triangles overlapping. As the novel opens, Isabel's father has been dead a year, and the positive nature of their intimate attachment is made clear: "It was a great felicity to have been his daughter."[7] But the relationship with this handsome, "deplorably convivial" man, who had taken his three motherless girls to Europe three times by the time Isabel was fourteen and "squandered a substantial fortune" (39, 40), is not one-sided. Isabel is the only one of the three girls who has not married, and she had been his favorite: "In his last days his general willingness to take leave of a world in which the difficulty of doing as one liked appeared to increase as one grew older had been sensibly modified by the pain of separation from his clever, his superior, his remarkable girl" (40). Although Isabel carries "within herself a great fund of life" (41), she rejects the suitor, Caspar Goodwood, following her father's death. Although "he was the finest young man she had ever seen," she "felt no eagerness to receive him" (42). We might rename the novel *Portrait of a Fixated Lady*.

Thus, the first father/daughter/suitor triangle is controlled by one member who is dead. Isabel leaves for Europe with her aunt since "she had a desire to leave the past behind her and, as she said to herself, to begin afresh" (39). But she is fleeing a relationship with a young, virile man at the same time that she is returning to that part of the world where she had spent time with her father. Isabel defines her own fixation when Ralph Touchett tells her that she wants to "drain the cup of experience," and she replies, "No, I don't wish to touch the cup of experience. It's a poisoned drink!" (132).

During Isabel's stay with her uncle and his family in England, she rejects another masculine, compassionate male, Lord Warburton, who says to Isabel, "I don't think your uncle likes me" (75). When her uncle dies, leaving her a substantial sum of money, Isabel says, "He liked me too much" (188). Her reflections concerning men indicate why she has rejected two viable suitors: "[S]he held . . . that it was perfectly possible to be happy without the society of a more or less coarse-minded person of another sex. . . . Few of the men she saw seemed worth a ruinous expenditure" (55).

Isabel's rejection of two suitors is a prelude to her encounter with Gilbert Osmond, who has "no career, no name, no position, no fortune, no past, no future, no anything," and is "very indolent" (169). The contrast with the two previous suitors is important, and the similarities to Isabel's father significant. Gilbert seems to pose very little sexual threat; indeed he has no inclination to marry at all except for his financial needs and the pressure from Madame Merle, the mother of his child. Isabel's initial attraction to him is couched in the imagery of a father/daughter relationship, rather than in that which would suggest a lover: "She had carried away an image . . . of a quiet, clever, sensitive, distinguished man, strolling on a moss-grown terrace . . . and holding by the hand a little girl. . . . It spoke of . . . an old sorrow that sometimes ached today" (232).

The "old sorrow" suggests Isabel's own sorrow for her father, of whom the sight of Osmond with his daughter reminds her. She not only sees him as a father, but he has made explicit to her his need for autonomy: "There were two or three people in the world I envied—the Emperor of Russia, for instance, and the Sultan of Turkey! There were even moments when I envied the Pope of Rome—for the consideration he enjoys" (223). There is a substantial discrepancy between the Osmond Isabel sees before her marriage, and the man with whom she has to deal afterwards: "[H]er imagination supplied the human element which she was sure had not been wanting" (223). The "human element" had been a component of her father's character, but this aspect of Osmond remains a quality only in Isabel's imagination; Osmond is forty, Isabel twenty-three. The traditional plot in which the financially helpless young girl is forced into marriage with the man old enough to be her father because of her financial need is reversed. Isabel, enriched through the "kindness" of her uncle, ties herself to a man who resembles her own father in having been a profligate, reduced to penury. He too needs "saving."

Isabel's relationship with Gilbert Osmond soon evolves into a role as mother to replace his daughter Pansy's absent mother, Madame Merle. Pansy has just returned from her exile in a convent until reaching womanhood, at which time she has returned home. Although Madame Merle is alive, her presence in the home is not feasible and she manipulates Isabel to fulfill that role. While this is ostensibly for financial reasons and for Isabel's benefit, it is also implicitly for the protection of Pansy. In view of Osmond's heightened paternal interest following his prolonged separation from his daughter, this seems prudent.

Pansy, whose name suggests docility, is repeatedly described as "impregnated with the idea of submission, which was due to any one who took the tone of authority; and she was a passive spectator of the operation of her fate" (199). Her father's proclivities for "the tone of authority" make his daughter a natural victim. During a preliminary interview between Isabel and Gilbert, his behavior toward Pansy is sensual: "He presently sat down on the other side of his daughter, who had shyly brushed Isabel's fingers with her own; but he ended by drawing her out of her chair and making her stand between his knees, leaning against him while he passed his arm around her slimness" (216).

The Gilbert/Pansy relationship develops into probably one of the most common versions of the father/daughter theme, especially in the English novel, although it occurs several times in Shakespeare. The lack of material wealth is stated as a reason by Osmond in his rejection of Pansy's suitor, Rosier, in spite of the fact that Warburton, an older suitor approved of by her father, is impressed with that wealth. Rosier's offer to sell off his collection does nothing to change Osmond's attitude, illustrating the speciousness of the objection.

Pansy's genuine affection for and submissiveness to her father, countered by her love for Rosier, tear her apart. Before falling in love, she had stated to Isabel: "At any rate I am too young to think about it yet, and I don't care for any gentleman; I mean for any but him. If he were not my papa I should like to marry him; I would rather be his daughter than the wife of—of some strange person" (263). No one is better equipped to understand this than Isabel, but she is powerless to interfere.

Osmond's ultimate violence in committing Pansy to the convent is reminiscent of the father's cruelty in Shelley's *The Cenci*. His daughter's reaction to such treatment has been predicted earlier: "[S]he could be felt as an easy victim of fate. She would have no will, no power to resist, no sense of her own importance; she would be easily mystified, easily crushed" (262). Death or the convent were the alternatives offered to the daughter of Egeus, but Pansy has no good Duke Theseus to intervene on her behalf. When cowed into submission by her enforced "exile," she tells Isabel that she now understands that she must never displease her father, saying: "I'll do anything—I'll do anything," and Isabel "saw the poor girl had been vanquished" (454).

Pansy and Isabel are the obverse sides of the father/daughter coin. Pansy has been able to free herself from her attachment for her father and to relate with love to Rosier, but she is frustrated by a domineering father who is unable to renounce her in order that she may marry the man she loves. Isabel, on the other hand, is paralyzed by an unresolved attachment for her dead father and is unable to relate to a young suitor in a mature, sexual relationship. The real irony lies in Isabel's return to a father who is himself the victim of an excessive attachment for his daughter. Each character is entrapped in his or her own private, psychologically determined nightmare, from which there seems no possibility of awakening at the end of *The Portrait of a Lady*. James had commented on this novel: "The obvious criticism of course will be . . . that I have not seen the heroine to the end of her situation" (487). This may apply to what occurs, but not to what is implied. Isabel's final action is the return of the daughter to the father, and given her particular psychological predisposition, she has no real alternative.

Madame Merle summarizes with appropriate pessimism the individual's power to change, a view shared by both Freud and Sartre: "Changing the form of one's mission's almost as difficult as changing the shape of one's nose: there they are, each, in the middle of one's face and one's character—one has to begin too far back" (232).

Abandoning his extensive use of surrogates in his last completed novel, *The Golden Bowl* (1904), Henry James chose as his subjects an actual father/daughter pair, Adam and Maggie Verver. Leon Edel comments on the pervasive father/daughter theme in this novel when he cites the notes made by James twelve years prior to the actual writing:

> At that time the other element in the plot, the "incestuous" element of the father and daughter, did not constitute a difficulty. The Victorian daughter was expected to be devoted to the father; she was expected to sacrifice her own interests. From the days of *Washington Square*, James had written stories of "dutiful" daughters in various stages of revolt. Or of daughters so "fixated" on their fathers that they ruin the paternal chances of remarrying. (Edel, *Master*, 210, 211)

Interestingly enough, Edel does not note what this daughterly "fixation" does to the daughter's chances of marrying. James also had relationships in his daily life which may have added to his interest in the subject matter of *The Golden Bowl*. For a prolonged period while living in Italy, he had been intimate with the Boott family, an unusually attached father/daughter pair. James went horseback riding with Lizzie Boott every day during this period. When the forty-year-old Lizzie Boott did marry her art teacher, Duveneck, letters from James make it clear that he considered the suitor an interloper and identified with her father in his loss: "Nevertheless life with her father had gone on as before and Duveneck had seemed to James very much a third party" (Edel, *Master*, 211). When Lizzie died in 1888, although Alice thought it a suicide, James thought it was a result of her "family responsibility" (Lewis, 426).

 The Golden Bowl also depicts an intense, longtime father/daughter relationship but the reader is plunged into the novel in media res and, for the time being, lacks essential information concerning the lives of the characters prior to the beginning of the narrative. The involuted and fragmented narrative has embedded within it a precise sequence which James offers little help in establishing. *The Golden Bowl*, with its complex dual narrative structure, is distinguished more than most novels by critical lack of agreement over what actually occurs.

 This novel can be read as an ironic inversion of the incest theme in *Pericles*. The island is Great Britain and the novel begins with a quasi-incestuous situation that is more subtle than that of Antiochus and his daughter. That "little old-time union"[8] has already characterized the Ververs' life together prior to the procurement of a suitor in the person of the Prince. The acquisition of the suitor is facilitated by the separation of a pair of lovers unable to marry due to dire financial straits. One of the pair, Maggie's former schoolmate Charlotte Stant, is bribed into an exile in America to leave "the field free" (53); her lover, the Prince, is then manipulated by the wealthy Ververs into a marriage which will serve as a cover for the actual father/daughter relationship. Charlotte returns just in time for the wedding, completing the quadrangle that sets the stage for the fusion of incest and adultery that distinguishes this novel.

 The Ververs represent an unusually intimate father and daughter isolated together by the mother's death when Maggie was ten. Adam, a wealthy art connoisseur and collector, during his first trip to Europe, "read into his career, in one single magnificent night, the immense meaning it had waited for" (98) and when he returns to Italy with his thirteen-year-old daughter, he has developed a "passion for perfection at any price" (102). Maggie defines three ways of loving:

> When you love only a little you're naturally not jealous—or are only jealous also a little, so that it doesn't matter. But when you love in a deeper and intenser way, then you are, in the same proportion, jealous; . . . When, however, you love in the most abysmal and unutterable way of all—why then you're beyond everything, and nothing can pull you down. (473–74)

She then tells her father, "Nothing can pull *you* down" (475). The sketchy information about the Ververs' life prior to the wedding comes toward the end of the novel when Adam recalls "the feelings we used to have" and "Maggie appeared to wish to plead for them a little, in tender retrospect—*as if they had been also respectable*" (470, emphasis mine). Maggie's description of "the real old days" with her father is redolent of the nostalgia of lovers.

The factors involved in the Ververs' selection of mates is made quite clear. Maggie has chosen the Prince, a descendant of the licentious Borgia Pope Alexander VI, who probably fathered his daughter's child, the "Roman Infante."[9] Taylor supports this: "The court of this Pope was the scene of licence which could scarcely be credited, if it were not recorded in the annals of the papal historian Burchard, whose evidence is unimpeachable" (141). James himself commented: "my sense of the sinister too, of that vague after-taste of evil things that lurks so often, for a suspicious sensibility, wherever the terrible game of the life of the Renaissance was played as the Italians played it."[10]

After signing the marriage agreement, the Prince feels unmanned since the moment "had something of the grimness of a crunched key in the strongest lock that could be made" (2), suggesting simultaneous castration and imprisonment. Maggie tells the Prince unequivocally that it was not his "particular self," but his unsavory background that determined his selection: "It was the generations behind you, the follies and the crimes, the plunder and the waste—the wicked Pope, the monster most of all, whom so many of the volumes in your family library are all about. . . . Where, therefore . . . without your archives, infamies, would you have been?" (6). This is an explicit statement of Maggie's cynical basis for the choice of the Prince and is most frequently not taken into account in critical readings of the novel. In an interesting and provocative reading, Lynda Zwinger states: "Mr. Verver does not say No to the impoverished suitor, as he might have done in another story of a rich daughter falling in love with a charming penniless title, and thus his daughter is not required to choose between lover and father."[11] This is absolutely true; there is no father/suitor rivalry in this novel because the Ververs have made this choice together.

It is possible that only someone with the combination of the Prince's sinister history and precarious financial position could be counted on to preserve the discretion required by the Ververs' lifestyle. When the Prince asks if he might be sent to America, Maggie tells him, "only if we have to come to it. There are things that father puts away" (8). The Prince is to function as "one of the little pieces" to be unpacked "at the hotels . . . and put out with the family photographs and the new magazines" (9).

The Prince wonders what would happen if he asked Fanny, "what *was* morally speaking, behind their veil?" suspecting that it was not what they expected him to do as much as to *be* (15, 16). This suggests that Adam, bent on "perfection at any price," had decided to perpetuate his line through his daughter—a common prerogative for royalty in various eras, with the marriage arranged as a screen for the incest. This is reinforced by the Prince's passive abdication of the role of father to the Principino: "Maggie and her father had . . . converted the precious creature into a link between a mamma and a grandpapa. . . . They had no occasion to talk of what the Prince might be or might do for his son—the sum of service, *in his absence*, so completely filled itself out" (110, emphasis mine). The child is the "heir-apparent" and his Italian designation endlessly amuses his grandfather (103).

The Prince may also have been selected for his physical characteristics for we learn of Adam that "since the birth of his grandson, . . . there was henceforth only one ground in all the world, he felt, on which the question of appearance would ever really again count for him. He cared that a work of art of price should 'look like' the master to whom it might perhaps be deceitfully attributed; but he had ceased on the whole to know any matter of the rest of life by its looks" (103). It is important that the Principino resemble the Prince. Following the reestablishment of the family on their English estate, the Ververs drift into their old intimacy and Fanny and various houseguests are provided to divert the Prince; Maggie thinks she might have waited to marry (118).

Two years later, Adam's marriage to his daughter's schoolmate, Charlotte, is precipitated by factors which are hardly less calculating than those for his daughter to the Prince had been. Maggie manipulates her father into inviting the impoverished Charlotte, in spite of his protests that he has always thought of her as a "little girl" (133). Subsequent developments make it likely that Maggie has brought her back to occupy the Prince.

Adam, who is only forty-seven, proposes to Charlotte, pending his daughter's approval. Charlotte protests that the factors involved are "not quite enough to marry me for" (157) and Adam admits to himself that "he might have been her father" (155), explaining that he is doing it "to help Maggie" (147). Rank has described this situation: "For the father, the second marriage substitutes a young spouse for the daughter" (309). The "doubling" of Charlotte and Maggie in this novel is an unusual component of such narratives.

Echoing primitive incest taboos, Charlotte is apprehensive about the Prince's acceptance of her as his "stepmother" (164), but her ultimate consent is precipitated by the Prince's telegram which Charlotte believes would have "dished" the marriage had Adam read it: "*A la guerre comme à la guerre then. . . . We must lead our lives as we see them; but I am charmed with your courage and almost surprised at my own*" (205). The ambiguous message ["War justifies the means"] gives Charlotte sufficient impetus to face the problems of renewed proximity to her former lover.[12] Two years after this second marriage, the shift in the equilibrium of the two couples is publicly confirmed by the appearance of the Prince and Charlotte together at a Ball that Maggie has left precipitously to return to her father who has remained at home, a home which now provides a wing for Maggie and the child and to which she has moved her clothing (266).

Charlotte's defensive stance indicates that she views the relationship as, in effect, incestuous. She and the Prince have been forced together since "Maggie thinks more, on the whole, of fathers than of husbands" (180). Charlotte's observations are corroborated by the Prince's perception that "he had been living these four or five years, on Mr. Verver's services. . . . He relieved him of all anxiety about his married life in the same manner in which he relieved him on the score of his bank account" (206). The novel's most objective observer, Bob Assingham, regards all of life as "a matter of pecuniary arrangement" (46).

In their imposed isolation, the Prince, who views himself as living "in so grim a joke, so idiotic a masquerade" (208), and Charlotte resume their affair. On the day of this decision, Charlotte returns three times to her home where Maggie and her father are now ensconced, letting herself into the house with a latch key which she rarely uses; the implications are unmistakable. The question of the consummation of Charlotte's own marriage is put to rest by her assurance to the Prince that she and Adam will never have a child through no "fault" of her own, but that "it would have taken more than ten children of mine . . . to keep our *sposi* apart" (217). Charlotte perceives the Ververs' relationship as "extraordinary beyond words. It makes such a relation for us as, I verily believe, was never before in the world thrust upon two well-meaning creatures. Haven't we therefore to take things as we find them?" (214) adding, "I know as I haven't known before the way they feel" (215). They agree that the Ververs are "extraordinarily happy," that "it doesn't matter, really that one doesn't understand," and that they must be protected (219). Maggie and her father constitute a "pair so together, as undivided by the marriage of each" (229).

The weekend at Matcham, declined by Adam and Maggie, marks the crisis which terminates the tenuous equilibrium maintained by the two couples, triggering James's establishment of the dual narrative structure that ostensibly refers to the affair between Charlotte and the Prince, while simultaneously revealing information regarding the relationship between the Ververs. James, in his preface, states that the reader's greatest pleasure "waits but on a direct *reading out of the addressed appeal*" (xxii, emphasis mine). The addressed appeal to be read *out* in *The Golden Bowl* is adultery, which in any event would never have been viewed by either James or his contemporaries as "Evil—with a very big E" (273).

James's awareness of incest as a possible topic for fiction was indicated in an 1890 letter to Howells in which he reported that a young woman in Paris "had asked me what I thought of *incest* as a subject for a novel—adding that it had against it that it was getting, in families, so terribly common."[13] Even Leon Edel acknowledged that James "had heard not only of desire but of incest under the elms," and that the village street and lonely farm "borrowed for dignity, a shade of the darkness of Cenci-drama, of monstrous legend, of old Greek tragedy, and thus helped themselves out for the story-seeker more patient almost of anything than of flatness" (Edel, *Master*, 252).

The obfuscation inherent in the dual narrative structure is augmented by various rhetorical devices: contradictory narrators, the omission of antecedents for pronouns, statements qualified by "almost," characters who either withhold information or lie to each other, dialogue only imagined by the listener, statements made about a third character but initially misunderstood as applying to someone else, and by James's extensive use of puns and double entendres such as "issue," "intercourse," "service," and "conception." The proliferation of involuted language, in conjunction with the complexity and density of the novel itself, are out of proportion to the theme of adultery, especially an adultery precipitated by the behavior of the "offended" parties. In the preface to *The Turn of the Screw*, James wrote: "Make him [the reader] *think* the evil, make him think it for himself and you are released from *weak specifications*."[14] Few would deny that *The Golden Bowl* lacks weak specifications of incest; the burden is shifted to the reader.

If we assume that the rearrangement of the couples has been satisfactory to all, there is only one factor that could disturb it—Maggie's again becoming pregnant. Immediately following the Matcham weekend during which Charlotte and the Prince flaunt convention by staying after other guests have left, Maggie returns home to seduce her husband, whom she hasn't seen for five days, administering "to her husband the first surprise to which she had ever treated him" (294). "She wanted him to understand . . . that she was going to be *with* him again . . . as she doubtless hadn't been since the 'funny' changes" (306, emphasis James's). She is aware of the abruptness of her unprecedented approach. "Amerigo never complained . . . any more than Charlotte did; but she seemed to see tonight . . . that their business of social representation, conceived as they conceived it, *beyond any conception of her own* . . . was an affair of living always in harness" (303, emphasis mine). Of a subsequent encounter we learn that "It made, *for any issue,* the third time since his return that he had drawn her to his breast" (307, emphasis mine). Maggie is making it plausible that the Prince might be the father of the child she already expects—probably an unexpected event.

Maggie manipulates the rearrangement of the couples while declining to provide them with a "reasonable reason" (311). She begins to insistently deflect attention from her own predicament by focusing on her supposedly new knowledge of the adultery between her husband and her father's wife, but she is concerned "absolutely, with no secret but her own" (322). "Amerigo and Charlotte were arranged together, but she—to confine the matter only to herself—was arranged apart" (318). Maggie views herself as "the scapegoat of old . . . charged with the sins of the people" (453) and toward the novel's close, following an encounter with the local priest, resolves that "some day in some happier season, she would confess to him that she hadn't confessed" (499). If adultery were the only infraction, there would be nothing for her to confess. Maggie's view of herself as "scapegoat" is apt since by becoming pregnant only she would provide physical evidence of the group's "sins."

The imagery becomes more explicit when at a social function Maggie "was passed about, all tenderly and expertly, like a dressed doll held, in the right manner, by its firmly-stuffed middle, for the account she could give.

She might have been made to give it by pressure of her stomach" (323). The "wonderful reunion of the couples" following Adam's and Charlotte's wedding trip "was now bearing, for Mrs. Verver's stepdaughter at least, such remarkable fruit" (387). The event on which the action now pivots isolates Maggie and is "the proof of her misadventure," "the secret of her own fermentation" (391), and the grounds for telling Charlotte that her anxiety "rests quite on a misconception" (465). When speaking to Fanny of what she senses as the Prince's pity, Fanny inquires if it isn't "for the state you've let yourself get into?" (372).

Having created a facade behind which she can bear her father's child, Maggie forces Charlotte back with her father, and ultimately manipulates the pair into exile in America. Her final confrontation with her father further reinforces this: "I never went into anything, and you see I don't; I've continued to adore you—but what's that from a decent daughter to such a father? what but a question of convenient arrangement, our having two houses, three houses, instead of one . . . and my making it easy for you to see the child?" (479).

There is, in the final encounter between Maggie and Adam, a sense of resolution for Maggie of her obsessive attachment to her father and a transfer to her husband. Equally important is Maggie's assumption of autonomy as she engineers the realignment of the couples. Having learned from Fanny that her father and Charlotte are going, she comes upon him sitting by the sleeping child's crib and steals away silently "*as if once more renewing her total submission*" (505, emphasis mine). She seems reconciled to what she has come to see as her "wrong" (291) culminating as she faces her father in the park in "an embrace that august and almost stern, produced for its intimacy, no revulsion and broke into no inconsequence of tears" (483). The implication here is that this had not always been true of past embraces. Critical appraisal of Maggie's role in this drama runs the full gamut.[15]

The poignant separation of the two couples signifies the resolution of both the incestuous situation: "Lost to each other—father and I" (523) and the adultery. Incest and adultery are uniquely fused in this novel since once all parties are married, the affair between Charlotte and the Prince is also incestuous since she is his mother-in-law, and the incest between Maggie and her father is also adultery by virtue of their respective marriages. This blurring of boundaries is amplified by the fact that Adam's wife is also a daughter-double and the oedipal intricacies of the quadrilateral relationship are further amplified by Maggie's jealousy of Charlotte vis-à-vis her father rather than her husband.

Time is an intrinsic factor in the dual narrative with April/Eastertime signifying both the weekend at Matcham, identified by Maggie as the beginning of her knowledge of the affair, and also of her awareness of her own condition. Names of months appear lowercase as double entendres giving clues to this passage of time: "an embrace that *august*," "the *march* of their intercourse" and so on. As Maggie awaits her husband's return, her "consciousness of a recent change in her life" is "a few days old" (290) and has taken "a month to arrive" (341). When the Prince quizzes her as to Fanny's role, Maggie replies, "She has gained me time; and that, these three months has been everything." She then identifies that time as "counting from the night you came home so late from Matcham. . . . For that was the beginning of my being sure. Before it I had been sufficiently in doubt" (424).

Maggie conflates her knowledge of the affair and her knowledge of her pregnancy, shifting the guilt onto the adulterers and deflecting their attention away from the real issue. It seems probable that Maggie feigns knowledge of the adultery, when in fact she had arranged it. In addition, she struggles to keep both facts from her father.

The Ververs' abandoned physical relationship is suggested toward the end of August: "The cups were still there on the table, but turned upside down; and nothing was left for the companions but to confirm that the wine had been good" (490). Maggie is still living in one of her father's houses "where more of his *waiting* treasures than ever were provisionally ranged," and Adam continues to "review his possessions and verify their *condition*" (491, emphasis mine). And "if something dreadful hadn't happened there wouldn't, for either of them, be these dreadful things to do" (478). Maggie forestalls accusations of incest by attacking first with accusations of adultery, and the financial dependence of the Prince and Charlotte guarantees the success of such genteel blackmail.

As the novel ends, Maggie and her father overtly employ a dual narrative that provides a corollary for the covert dual narrative. Maggie, rejecting the suggestion that she and the Prince return to Fawns following Adam's departure, protests that she couldn't without Charlotte, "an allusion to what she didn't and couldn't say," realizing that she has offered "a bold but substantial substitute" (544). Contemplating her father's wedding gift, a Florentine painting (probably a Madonna), they agree that "it's all right. He had applied the question to the great fact of the picture, as she had spoken for the picture in reply, but it was as if their words for an instant afterwards symbolised another truth" (542). The nature of the other truth is veiled in Maggie's reflection "that in leaving the thing behind him, held as in her clasping arms, he was doing the most possible toward leaving her a part of his palpable self" suggestive of an unborn child rather than of a work of art.

James too has offered "a bold but substantial substitute" that symbolizes "another truth" and once the reader recognizes a dual narrative structure that refers to adultery and incest simultaneously—to the discovery of the adultery as a screen for the discovery of the pregnancy—the question of the relationship between them becomes paramount; the dual narrative is raised to the level of metaphor. Legalized marriage has always functioned as one safeguard against incest. The Catholic religion, ironically that of the Prince and Maggie, has traditionally enforced severe injunctions against marriage between kin, at times extending as far as the seventh degree. Adultery evades legal guarantees against incest, and the uneasiness occasioned by incest is also, to some extent, characteristic of the anxiety produced by adultery; historically, their punishments have been similar. Henry James, treating the two simultaneously, removes boundaries and offers a linguistic metaphor for civilized society's unspoken merging of the two infractions.

This novel entails a double double bind—first for the reader confronted with the manifest and latent content of the complex text, and second for James's characters. Freud maintained that "the prohibition against an incestuous choice of object . . . is perhaps the most drastic mutilation which man's erotic life has in all time experienced" (*SE*, 21:104). But he also maintained that "An obstacle is required in order to heighten libido."[16] In *The Golden Bowl*, James creates sympathy for all four members of the doomed foursome. Unlike many of his earlier works, rather than being about failed relationships, this novel entails two pairs of star-crossed lovers forced to separate. Their plight illustrates the quandary of civilized man caught between desires intensified by prohibitions and the machinations necessary to circumvent them. This delicate equilibrium is maintained by balancing the Verver wealth against the poverty of their mates. But once one of their number begins to exhibit an outward sign of their shared duplicity, the only solution becomes the dissolution of the "happy arrangement."

Finally, the dual narrative can be extended to include the political ramifications of the novel and to undercut the view that the American/European dichotomy represents the new and untarnished as opposed to the old and decayed. The original Adam's children had to be the offspring of incestuous relations. But the Prince is Amerigo "the name . . . of the pushing man who followed, across the sea, in the wake of Columbus and succeeded, where Columbus had failed, in becoming godfather, or name-father, to the new Continent" (55). The Prince's ancestor, Alexander VI, ascended the papal throne in 1492, the year that Columbus discovered the new world. By the end of the nineteenth century, the American Ververs, having achieved the corruption of Renaissance Italy, return to that country to exploit one of its citizens who had vainly hoped to "*make* something different" (10). Early in the novel, the Prince has told Maggie: "[I]t's you who are not of this age. You're a creature of a braver and finer one, and the *cinquecento*, at its most golden hour, wouldn't have been ashamed of you" (8). The correspondence between the two civilizations is stated at the outset:

> The Prince had always liked his London, when it had come to him; he was one of the modern Romans who find by the Thames a more convincing image of the truth of the ancient state than any they have left by the Tiber. Brought up on the legend of the City to which the world paid tribute, he recognised in the present London much more than in contemporary Rome the real dimension of such a case. (1)

This suggests a cyclical (and cynical) view of history summed up in the Prince's words to Maggie: "Everything's terrible, *cara*—in the heart of man" (535). James seems to be denying the possibilities for humanity's improvement; man's mode of operation in modern London is still akin to "the truth of the ancient state." The ancient state is both physical and moral—the *cinquecento* at its worst. But the ancient state also implies a regression to the animal world that existed before men imposed order through laws and restrictions. *The Golden Bowl* is singular as a "Tempest" version since the daughter both procures her own suitor and orchestrates the final renunciation by the father.

A sentiment unexpected like an
intruder and cruel like an enemy.
Joseph Conrad, *The Rover*

5

The Triangle in
Joseph Conrad

Joseph Conrad (1857–1924) failed to acknowledge in his own work the
pervasiveness of the father/daughter theme, in spite of the fact that he had
cited it as being of paramount interest to him. This was evident in the
report of a 1921 conversation with Conrad in Corsica by the French playwright of psychoanalytic bent, H.-R. Lenormand:

> One day while we were watching the daughter of his friend P pass
> by, a girl eighteen years old whose distracted eyes and wild appear-
> ance made me think of the ostracized recluse Alice in "A Smile of
> Fortune," he said to me, "My whole life, I've been obsessed by the
> relationship of father to daughter." We talked about *Almayer's Folly.*
> "It's a book I wrote when I was thirty-six, without any aim. I had no
> idea I would become a man of letters. I wrote it in a single burst of
> inspiration and as if in spite of myself." I asked him if he had not
> had some intention of suggesting that Almayer's eclipse and fall
> were to be attributed to an unconscious feeling of the exile for his

daughter, an incestuous passion hidden behind a paternal affection. He protested against the existence of such an emotion in his
hero. When I pointed out to him the passages which had led me
to that interpretation . . . Conrad was silent, obviously annoyed;
then he changed the subject.[1]

Two years after writing this first novel "comme malgré moi," at the
age of thirty-eight, Conrad married a twenty-three-year-old woman, thus
formally abandoning the possibility of a more intimate relationship with
Marguerite Poradowska, then forty-nine. Bernard Meyer comments:
"While Marguerite was called 'Aunt,' placing her in the psychological
position of a parent, Jessie was so young that she was occasionally taken for
Conrad's daughter — to his great annoyance."[2] But Jessie Conrad was soon
transformed, both emotionally and physically, into a mother-figure.

Joseph Conrad's early family relationships were certainly the most tem-
pestuous of any of the artists under consideration. As a child, he spent a
great deal of time alone with his mother, especially during the six-month
period when his father was in jail.[3] When he was only four the family was
exiled to Siberia because of his father's political activity against the Rus-
sians. His mother died there when he was eight leaving him isolated with
a father whose grief was never assuaged and who also died when Conrad
was twelve. We can only speculate as to whether Conrad blamed his
father's political activity for the loss of his mother. In any event, such
abortive and traumatic early family relationships leave their mark. Leaving Poland to go to sea at sixteen, Conrad's early life continued to be
marked by traumatic events, including a suicide attempt in Marseilles in
early 1878, aged twenty-one. During these years he was also engaged in
gunrunning activities in the Mediterranean and was constantly being ad-
monished by his uncle in letters from Poland to be more prudent in his
expenditures.[4]

But Conrad also had his share of frustrated early attachments to young
ladies. After his return from Africa and the publication of *Almayer's Folly*,
Conrad became enamored of Emilie Briquel, but his marriage proposal
was rejected by her family on the grounds that she was too young; she was
twenty to Conrad's thirty-eight. He then proposed to Jessie Conrad at the
time of the announcement of Emilie's engagement to another. This had
constituted Conrad's third romance in a year (Najder, 189, 194). An "unhappy love affair is bitterly described in the discarded rough draft of the
beginning of *Arrow of Gold*" (Najder, 32).

Not unexpectedly then, the father/daughter theme occurs with notable
regularity throughout the Conrad canon, in both shorter works and longer

ones. Although the focus here will be on *Almayer's Folly* (1895), *Chance* (1913), and *The Rover* (1923), it is important to consider the theme briefly as it occurs in *Lord Jim* (1899). This novel illustrates the way in which the incest theme can subtly function as an important factor in the narrative, providing motivation for actions that are otherwise puzzling. Although most critical attention has been paid to Jim's history and his inner compulsions, his eventual destruction is partially precipitated by his wife Jewel's stepfather, Cornelius. There is also the strong possibility that Stein, who has orchestrated the action from afar, is really Jewel's father. Marlow brings this to our attention by denying it:

> I can only guess that once before Patusan had been used as a grave for some sin, transgression, or misfortune. It is impossible to suspect Stein. The only woman that had ever existed for him was the Malay girl he called . . . "the mother of my Emma." Who was the woman he had mentioned in connection with Patusan I can't say; but from his allusions I understand she had been an educated and a very good-looking Dutch-Malay girl, with a tragic or perhaps only a pitiful history.[5]

Stein replaces this woman's husband, Cornelius, who has lived with Jewel as her stepfather following the mother's death, with Jim, who then marries Jewel, depicting one of Conrad's few viable romances. Although Jewel had urged Jim to leave, "He said then he would not abandon her to Cornelius" (188). When Jim is menaced by Gentleman Brown and his crew, it is Cornelius who aids them, telling Brown: "Just you kill him" as he "almost danced with impatience and eagerness" (230). Jim does, of course, die, and Jewel returns to Stein's house and is seen there by Marlow: "When I rose to get back to the house I caught sight of Stein's drab coat through a gap in the foliage, and very soon at a turn of the path I came upon him walking with the girl. Her little hand rested on his forearm, and under the broad, flat rim of his Panama hat he bent over her, grey-haired, paternal, with compassionate and chivalrous deference" (213). Stein, having abandoned Jewel's mother (191) in the past, once she is absent, sends a suitor, Jim, to protect her from her stepfather Cornelius. Following Jim's death, the daughter returns to the house of her father, albeit unknowingly. Even if one does not accept Stein's actual paternity, he functions as a manipulative father in this triad.

Other novels that revolve around the theme include *The End of the Tether* (1902), *Nostromo* (1904), and *Under Western Eyes* (1910). All three novels end disastrously in one way or another. In the earlier one, the father summarizes his feelings for his daughter: "You can't understand how one feels. Bone of my bone, flesh of my flesh; the very image of my poor wife."[6] Two out of three of the stories in *'Twixt Land and Sea* (1912) involve fathers and daughters, with "The Secret Sharer," sandwiched between "A Smile of Fortune," and "Freya of the Seven Isles." "A Smile of Fortune" has many of the aspects of Hawthorne's "Rappaccini's Daughter," although it is slightly more explicit in its exposition of the incest theme.

In *Almayer's Folly* (1895), the relationship between Almayer and Nina, his half-caste daughter, is the result of the resolution of an earlier father/daughter relationship in which the surrogate father, Tom Lingard, renounced his possible claim and arranged to marry the "daughter" to Almayer instead. Nina's mother had been rescued twenty years before by Lingard, who then had exiled her to a convent, "acting under unreasoning impulses of the heart."[7] The relationship is made explicit: "She called Lingard father, gently and caressingly, at each of his short and noisy visits, under the clear impression that he was a great and dangerous power it was good to propitiate. Was he not now her master? And during those long four years she nourished a hope of finding favour in his eyes and ultimately becoming his wife, counsellor, and guide" (22). But her "white father" renounces his rights with an "abrupt demand" that Almayer marry her, enticing him with promises of a fortune. Two years after Almayer's reluctant but greedy acquiescence, a daughter, Nina, is born. She is a beautiful half-caste who becomes the object of Almayer's obsession and the source of all his anguish.

Lingard decides to send the six-year-old girl to Singapore for her education as the relationship between Almayer and his wife deteriorates. "She was jealous of the little girl's evident preference for the father, and Almayer felt he was not safe with that woman in the house." Almayer "meditated in silence on the best way of getting rid of her" (26). Almayer's desires to "remove" the mother fail, and she ultimately becomes an accomplice in Nina's escape.

Nina's exile has served the traditional function of enhancing the attractiveness for the father of the daughter who returns to be met with a love that has been reinforced by absence. When Nina returns at sixteen, she is "a woman, black-haired, olive-skinned, tall and beautiful, with great sad eyes . . ." (29). Her attractiveness and sexuality are well established before the appearance of the suitor, Dain Maroola. She has been ejected from a temporary Singapore home because she has attracted young men and thus competed with the white daughters of the Vinck household. Once established in her father's house, Nina becomes a focus for voyeuristic neighbors, and the object of design as a "favorite wife" for Reshid, an Arab.

At the time of Dain's appearance, Nina is nineteen, and manages to present herself to him in spite of her mother's contrivances to prevent it. Once the mother accepts the inevitability of the passionate love affair between Dain and Nina, she becomes their coconspirator in protecting their meetings from detection by Nina's father. During the period in which Dain and Nina are clandestinely meeting, Dain is frequently paying simultaneous business visits to her father. The repressed death wish of the father toward the suitor is revealed when Almayer smiles at the evidence that the unidentifiable body found near the river is really Dain's, although Nina and her mother both know that it is not.

The intensity of Almayer's feeling for his beautiful daughter is reflected in his wife's observation to Babalatchi as they plot Nina and Dain's escape: "To keep the daughter whom he loves he would strike into your heart and mine without hesitation. . . . when the girl is gone he will be like the devil unchained. Then you and I had better beware" (136). Almayer's almost insupportable existence has been sustained for a long period of time by his quixotic dream of building a new life for himself and his daughter with the wealth that he is sure is going to be his. And although Nina has always served Almayer well, when it is time to go, she has few regrets: "At the bottom of that passing desire to look again at her father's face there was no strong affection. She felt no scruples and no remorse at leaving suddenly that man whose sentiment towards herself she could not understand, she could not even see" (151).

When Almayer follows the pair up the river, Nina throws her own body between Dain and her father's gun. The resolution comes in Almayer's despairing renunciation of his daughter and in his cooperation in the final escape of the lovers. But it is not a renunciation that brings the promise of peace. Almayer's desolation is measured out in his return to his monkey, his only companion, his burning of the house, and his move into the empty "Almayer's Folly." His hallucinations of a child to whom he can be heard talking and his eventual surrender to opium, which is precipitated by the news of the birth of Nina's son, cap a series of events which culminate in his lonely death.

It is small wonder that Lenormand sought in his discussion with Conrad to make him admit to the strong theme of repressed incest that informs this first novel and it is important that Conrad could not do this, as Lenormand notes: "I had ventured into that zone where the fictive being, detached from his creator, enfolds himself in hypocritical veils and dupes him [the author] on the nature of his deep tendencies" (Lenormand, 43; quoted in Stallman, 7).

Conrad followed the publication of a second novel, *An Outcast of the Islands* (1896), with the writing of *The Sisters*, which he was discouraged from finishing by Garnett. Of special interest is the fact that Ford reported that "the theme was to be incest, not the consummation of the forbidden desire, but the rendering of the emotions 'of a shared passion that by its nature must be the most hopeless of all'" (Karl, 365–66). Karl offers conjectures regarding possible psychobiographical connections in Conrad's life: "[A]n incest pattern . . . would not be distant from his mind if he were thinking of marrying Aunt Marguerite, or even Emilie or Jessie, the latter two almost young enough to be his daughters" (366). This makes more puzzling Conrad's later reaction to Lenormand's observations on *Almayer's Folly*.

Joseph Conrad's *Chance* (1913) is one of the most explicit statements of the father/daughter theme in his canon, with striking plot similarities to *Pericles*. Perhaps as a result of Conrad's effort to produce a really "popular" work of fiction, *Chance* encompasses versions of all of the classic elements of the incest theme: the early death of the mother, the prolonged separation of father and daughter resulting in the father's intense reaction at the time of reunion, the daughter's arrangement of her marriage to a suitor to forestall the unspoken threat, the father's hatred for and efforts to eliminate the suitor culminating in the father's own destruction and the temporary transfer of the daughter to a "good" father/suitor who ultimately renounces her to a younger suitor.

The central figures are Flora de Barral, her father, and the suitor, Captain Anthony, a fellow seaman of the omnipresent narrator, Marlow. As in many other such narratives the chain of possessive fathers extends back into the past with the Captain's father, Carleon Anthony, the poet, and his daughter, Mrs. Fyne. The latter's courtship by Mr. Fyne had been clandestine "because of the lady's father. He was a savage sentimentalist who had his own decided views of his paternal prerogatives." Her brother had escaped by going to sea, but his sister had "remained in bondage to the poet for several years, till she too seized a chance of escape by throwing herself into the arms . . . of the pedestrian Fyne."[8]

In Marlow's first encounter with Flora he rescues her from a suicide attempt, a sequel to a number of earlier ones. During a short period when Marlow is absent, Captain Anthony, "a silent man" (46), visits the Fynes, and he too rescues Flora from a suicide attempt. The difference between the two rescuers lies in the Captain's eventual commitment to Flora. Prior to her father's release from jail, she flees to London to marry Anthony, ostensibly to provide for her father. But this only serves to disguise the more urgent reason for seeking protection in marriage, a reason reinforced by Flora's first encounter with this fixated father.

The relationship between Flora and her father had been altered by the death of the mother, and Conrad's awareness of his literary heritage is stated by Marlow: "I remembered what Mrs. Fyne had told me before of the view she had years ago of de Barral clinging to the child at the side of his wife's grave and later on of these two walking hand in hand the observed of all eyes by the sea. Figures from Dickens—pregnant with pathos" (162).

Flora's father had been imprisoned for swindling when she was sixteen and released seven years later, when she is twenty-three—the present time. During these seven years of exile, Flora's series of adventures are highly suggestive of the trials of Pericles' daughter, Marina. Her first experience of exploitation is with her governess and her "nephew" as they woo Flora in hopes that, through the "nephew's" marriage to the wealthy young girl, sufficient funds will be available for the governess and the nephew to carry on their affair. But when a financial crash deprives Flora of her money, Mrs. Fyne sends her husband to bring the abandoned girl to their hotel. The future attempts at sexual exploitation of Flora are foreshadowed in the description of Fyne's "rescue": "What might have been their thoughts at the spectacle of a middle-aged man abducting headlong into the upper regions of a respectable hotel a terrified young girl obviously under age, I don't know. . . . All he wanted was to reach his wife before the girl collapsed" (126).

But Flora's stay with the Fynes is brief, as she becomes involved in a series of triangles characterized by maneuvers to exploit her sexually or financially—or both. Even in her abortive "rescue" by the Fynes, one senses the possibility of exploitation by either Mrs. Fyne, who would enlist her as a "girl friend" (there are suggestions of lesbianism here), or by Mr. Fyne, who is living with a wife whose attentions are engaged elsewhere.

Marlow trusts that the past accumulation of disastrous encounters for Flora will influence Mrs. Fyne to give her a chance for happiness with her brother, Captain Anthony. But Mrs. Fyne is inexorable when it comes to marriage with her own brother. She tells Marlow, "[M]y feelings are mostly concerned with my brother. We were very fond of each other"

(184). But Flora gets no support from Mr. Fyne either. She functions as a nebulous figure in a family that is no family at all. She is the only one of the "girl-friends" that Fyne gets to know, but her tenuous existence within this family is indicated by her repeated suicide attempts while she is with them.

When Marlow tries in vain to reconcile Fyne to the marriage between Flora and his brother-in-law, Fyne sounds like a suitor himself: "'She loves no one except that preposterous advertising shark,' he pursued venomously" (244). Fyne is jealous of both her real father and of Anthony. Regarding her relationship with Anthony, he believes that "She said 'Yes' to him only for the sake of that fatuous, swindling father of hers" (246), but his assessment of Anthony's motivation is vehement: "'Generosity! I am disposed to give it another name. No. Not folly,' he shot out at me as though I had meant to interrupt him. 'Still another. Something worse. I need not tell you what it is,' he added with grim meaning" (251). The sexual implications disturb Fyne profoundly, and his arguments persuade Anthony to refrain from consummation of the marriage once Fyne has accused him of being "abominably selfish" (251). Fyne thus functions as an obstructive father in his efforts to dissuade his brother-in-law from the marriage; he only succeeds in delaying its consummation.

After de Barral's release from prison, the overtones of incest become pronounced and Fyne's sense of outrage over Flora's marriage pales beside that of her father's. The reunion between father and daughter is erotically suggestive: "Inside that rolling box . . . she felt . . . every fibre of her body, relaxed in tenderness, go stiff in the close look she took at his face. He was different. There was something. Yes, there was something between them, something hard and impalpable, the ghost of these high walls." After they have hugged each other, the cab rolls to the docks "with those two people as far apart as they could get from each other, in opposite corners" (355). The ensuing disclosure of her recent marriage produces a barrage of incest ramifications: "In strangled low tones he cried out, 'you—married? You, Flora! When? Married! What for? Who to? Married!' . . . He did really look as if he were choking" (359). When he finally is able to speak, he says, "You were just saying that in this wide world there we were, only you and I, to stick to each other," and "She was dimly aware of the *scathing intention* lurking in these soft low tones" (360, emphasis mine). When he tells her that she haunted him while he was in prison, she replies, "Then we have been haunting each other, . . . For indeed he had haunted her nearly out of the world, into a final and irremediable desertion" (360). Although Marlow has assumed that Anthony's proposal has given Flora a solution for caring for her father, it has also provided a resolution for a potentially incestuous situation.

Her father, realizing how recently the marriage has occurred, pleads, "Couldn't you wait at least till I came out?" and "she shook her head negatively" (361). He asks why she "couldn't let a father have his daughter all to himself even for a day after—after such a separation" (362), and her reply reinforces the suggestions that her marriage has had more than financial ramifications for her: "Papa! He came to me. I was thinking of you. I had no eyes for anybody. I could no longer bear to think of you. It was then that he came. Only then. At that time when—when I was going to give up" (363). But her father's response is violent: "I would like to break his neck" (363).

Marlow then summarizes the function of the suitor as means of resolution for the incestuous relationship: "[S]he mentioned that generosity of a stormy type, which had come to her from the sea, had caught her up on the brink of unmentionable failure, had whirled her away in its first ardent gust and could be trusted now, implicitly trusted, to carry them both, side by side, into absolute safety" (365).

The implications of induced impotence caused by Flora's disclosure to her father are summarized by Marlow: "The famous—or notorious—de Barral had lost his rigidity now. He was bent. Nothing more deplorably futile than a bent poker" (367). Flora's identification of her father and Captain Anthony is also suggested. The lengthy separation from her father has eliminated any bond: "Except for her childhood's impressions he was just—a man. Almost a stranger. How was one to deal with him?" But her newly realized alternative seems to have its own pitfalls, stated in terms any feminist would support: "And there was the other too. Also almost a stranger. The trade of being a woman was very difficult. Too difficult" (366).

Once the triad is isolated on board the *Ferndale*, Flora pleads with her father to give her "peace." The violence of his reaction to her marriage is only the beginning of de Barral's miserable sojourn "upon the floating stage of that tragi-comedy" (272) that culminates in his thwarted attempt to murder Anthony. This attempt is frustrated by young Powell and is followed by de Barral's suicide, which releases the delayed consummation of the marriage. The incestuous implications of Anthony as father figure has been a factor in the Fynes' reactions and in Anthony's own procrastination. As he slowly moves to consummate the marriage, he mutters to himself concerning de Barral's suicide: "No! No! I am not going to stumble now over that corpse" (435). Marlow attributes incestuous wishes to all fathers: "I have a certain notion that no usual normal father is pleased at parting with his daughter. No. Not even when he rationally appreciates 'Jane being taken off his hands' or perhaps is able to exult at an excellent match. At bottom, quite deep down, down in the dark (in some cases only by digging), there is to be found a certain repugnance" (371). Conrad thus states basic Freudian concepts in nonpsychoanalytic terminology.

Since Anthony is thirty-five years old and in the authoritative role of ship's captain, he can be read as a father-double, the "good" father as opposed to de Barral, the "bad" father. The young crewman, Powell, at first mistakes Flora's father for the Captain (285). The father/daughter relationship between the Captain and Flora is reinforced by Powell's impressions of her youthfulness: "To behold a girl where your average mediocre imagination had placed a comparatively old woman may easily become one of the strongest shocks" (289).

In an archetypal ritualization, the "bad" father, unable to fulfill his own incestuous desires because of his blood relationship, dies by drinking the poison he had intended to use to remove his daughter's husband; the "good" father is finally freed to consummate the marriage, described later by Flora in such idyllic terms: "I have had a fine adventure. . . . The finest in the world! Only think! I loved and I was loved, untroubled, at peace, without remorse, without fear. All the world, all life were transformed for me. . . . Yes, I have known kindness and safety. The most familiar things appeared lighted up with a new light, clothed with a loveliness I had never suspected" (444).

In spite of a wealth of critical comments to the contrary (Moser, Guerard, Roussel, etc.), Anthony's delay in consummating the marriage represents not his failure, but a desire for a mutuality that is free of the exploitation of Flora's gratitude and subservient position. The delay thus undercuts the role of autonomy in the father/daughter relationship, since Anthony heroically represses his own desires until Flora is able to come to him of her own free will.[9] Powell, potentially a young suitor, had saved Anthony's life, and this father-surrogate does not retain the daughter for very long. Four years later, when the ship is involved in a collision, Anthony saves Flora's life, but when Powell urges him to leave the ship, he replies: "'It isn't my turn. Up with you.' These were the last words he ever spoke on earth, I suppose" (439). As the crew of the rescuing *Westland* mistake Powell for the captain, the *Ferndale* goes "down like a stone" (440). Anthony's renunciation to make room for the young suitor foreshadows similar action in *The Rover*. The other surrogate "good" father, Marlow the narrator, urges the union of Flora and Powell at the end of the novel.

In *Chance*, Conrad has blended some of the Shakespearean elements of the incest theme with innovations of his own. As in *Pericles*, the father and daughter are separated early on and Flora then survives (but just barely) a series of disastrous triangular misadventures. As the time for her father's release approaches, she attempts suicide and is rescued twice by father surrogates. De Barral attempts to "save" his daughter by murdering her husband who in turn is saved by the young suitor. A counterpart to Lysimachus, Captain Anthony, the "good" father, retains the daughter for four idyllic years before renouncing her to the young suitor whose eventual possession of her is left unresolved at the end of the novel. Conrad thus allows a "good" father to retain the daughter, but only for a short time before he relinquishes her—presumably to the young suitor.

Just as *Chance* relates to *Pericles*, so does Conrad's final completed novel, *The Rover* (1923), relate to *The Tempest*.[10] In this novel, the "daughter" Arlette is protected by a mother surrogate, Catherine, from both father-surrogates, Peyrol and Citizen Scevola. Against the background of the French Revolution, Citizen Scevola has destroyed both of Arlette's parents in the course of their trip to Toulon to retrieve their daughter from a convent, taking over their tartane (a Mediterranean vessel having one mast and a large sail). The triangle is established with the arrival of Eugene Réal, a young seaman on a military mission. In spite of the fact that Scevola and Arlette are referred to as "master" and "mistress" of the Escampobar farm, Scevola's possession of the girl has been prevented by Catherine, who shares sleeping quarters with Arlette.[11]

The other father figure, Peyrol, has lived on the farm for eight years when the three rivals encounter each other for the first time. Scevola strolls in front of the other two carrying "a manure fork on his shoulder," and it is later with this same fork that he will attempt to murder the young seaman. Although the sailor has arrived to spy on military shipping, Peyrol makes it clear that he views him as a possible threat in terms of Arlette: "Lieutenant, . . . if I had not seen from the first what was in your heart I would have contrived to get rid of you a long time ago in some way or other" (44). Réal reports that he has seen the shadow of the girl prowling at night and comments: "I know a shadow when I see it, and when I saw it, it did not frighten me, not a quarter as much as the mere tale of it seems to have frightened you. However, that sans-culotte friend of yours must be a hard sleeper" (44).

Thus early in the novel the stage is set with the tempted good father, Peyrol, the young girl who roams at night and fills Peyrol "with an uneasiness which he did not attempt to conceal," Scevola, one of the "purveyors of the guillotine," and the young suitor, Réal (44). Like Arlette, Réal has lost his parents in the French Revolution, and as with other isolated Conradian heroes: "He had no place in the world to go to, and no one either" (71). Although Guerard called *The Rover* "a story for boys," Bradbrook's assessment of the novel as "lurid" is much more accurate. The tartane has served as the bloody scene of the massacre of the victims of Scevola's savagery.

> [Peyrol] wrenched off the enormous padlock himself with a bar of iron and let the light of day into the little cabin which did indeed bear the traces of the massacre in the stains of blood on its woodwork. . . . He could without very strong emotion figure to himself the little place choked with corpses. He sat down and looked about at the stains and splashes which had been untouched by sunlight for years. . . . He, at any rate, had never been a butcher. (87)

The tartane constitutes the link between all of Arlette's "fathers," since her actual father had owned it and both she and the ship had been plundered by Scevola. The abandoned ship is then turned over to Peyrol by Scevola, and it will later be the scene of the latter's attempt on Réal's life. It is the ship on which Peyrol plans to send the young suitor to his death, but it becomes instead the bier of the two surrogate fathers, as the "good" father relinquishes the daughter and takes both himself and the "bad" father to their deaths. The plot varies from that of *The Tempest,* since the father leaves the daughter and suitor on the island and takes himself away on the vessel. Conrad's reference supports this analogy after Peyrol has cleaned the boat and anchored it in a "little basin": "She was safe from the tempests there as a house ashore" (99) and it holds the promise of "his escape from a desert island" (88).

The first signs of Peyrol's sexual interest in Arlette are accompanied by signs of his ambivalence toward Eugene Réal as potential suitor: "The way she had taken to dressing her hair in a plait with a broad black velvet ribbon and an Arlesian cap was very becoming. She was wearing now her mother's clothes. . . . It was quite time that this confounded lieutenant went back to Toulon. This was the third day. His shore leave must be up. Peyrol's attitude towards naval officers had been always guarded and suspicious" (103).

When Peyrol seats himself beside Réal, the situation is made clear: "Yet he did not absolutely hate Lieutenant Réal. Only the fellow's coming to the farm was generally a curse and his presence at that particular moment a confounded nuisance and to a certain extent even a danger. . . . he continued to look immovable—or at least difficult to get rid of" (104). After a long discussion between the two men concerning Peyrol's past and the movements of the English ship, Réal says, "You are a strange man, Peyrol . . . I believe you wish me dead" (109), and Peyrol's response is, "No, only out of this." Peyrol and Réal spar with each other over which one is to undertake the military mission that has been ordered from Paris. As Peyrol succeeds in sending Réal for the necessary papers, Réal says, "I see you want me out of the way for some reason or other" (120).

Shortly after Arlette's realization of her love for Réal, the reciprocity of which is confirmed by his "passionately" kissing her hand, the sexual intentions of Scevola are made clear, even to Arlette. He had been confined to a small, narrow room, "his lair" (161), by Catherine ever since he had first brought Arlette to her. Catherine explains to Peyrol how she had kept Scevola from Arlette, protesting that she was too young, and that "he would walk up and down for hours talking of her and I would sit there listening to him with the key of the room the child was locked in, in my pocket" (167). But she also reports that "he was sure to have Arlette for his own" (167), which made Catherine shiver. Catherine indicates that she felt great relief when the grey-haired Peyrol appeared, indicating that he has "roused the child wonderfully" and although Catherine remains unaware of the true nature of Peyrol's feelings, it is made clear to the reader that there is not the safety in his grey hair that Catherine thinks. She urges Peyrol to warn the young lieutenant against the possibility of murder by Scevola whose "awful fancies have come back," and who "is not sleeping at night" (171).

Arlette, overhearing Catherine and Peyrol talking, wants to know what they are plotting and the scene has strong sexual overtones both for "Papa Peyrol" and for Arlette:

> She dazzled him. Vitality streamed out of her eyes, her lips, her whole person, enveloped her like a halo and . . . yes, truly, the faintest possible flush had appeared on her cheeks, played on them faintly rosy like the light of a distant flame on the snow. She raised her arms up in the air and let her hands fall from on high on Peyrol's shoulders, captured his desperately dodging eyes with her black and compelling glance, put out all her instinctive seduc-

tion—while he felt a growing fierceness in the grip of her fingers. (175)

During the absence of the Lieutenant for whom Arlette is waiting eagerly, both fathers show evidence of a lovesickness. Peyrol, remembering how Arlette had looked at Réal, "felt positively sick at the recollection" (179), and Scevola, realizing that Arlette had been locked in Réal's room when he had tried the handle earlier, felt "such a sickening shock that he thought he would die of it" (182). Although Peyrol protests that only Scevola could be suspected of treachery, Peyrol too makes his own subtle plans for doing away with the young suitor. What is said of Scevola is true also of Peyrol: he fears he is to be robbed "of his right to Arlette" (183). The threat implicit in the young suitor electrifies the other characters into activity.

While the girl is periodically locked into rooms for her protection, Scevola, seeking Réal with the pitchfork, is locked into the cabin on the tartane by Symons from the English ship. Peyrol, meeting Réal on board the tartane, is tempted to treat him to the same fate that Scevola has in mind for him. He finds the stable fork, and after looking up and seeing Arlette's face in the window of Réal's room, Peyrol asks himself, fork in hand: "Shall I pick him up on that pair of prongs, carry him down and fling him into the sea?" (206). He desists, however, and Réal returns to the house.

Réal has fought fiercely against his fatal attraction to Arlette, for a variety of reasons. The damage she has incurred in her war experiences makes her seem to him a "body without mind" (214), but when he finds her in his room on his return, his resistance ends: "He flung his arms round her waist and hugged her close to his breast" (216). She immediately warns him against both Scevola and Peyrol, saying of the former that he "is thirsting for your blood" and of the latter that "he has changed. I can trust him no longer" (216). The function of Peyrol as surrogate father for Arlette is summarized in terms of what Réal does not understand:

He could not know that Peyrol, unforeseen, unexpected, inexplicable, had given by his mere appearance at Escampobar a moral and even a physical jolt to all her being, that he was to her an immense figure, like a messenger from the unknown entering the solitude of Escampobar; something immensely strong, with inexhaustible power, *unaffected by familiarity* and remaining invincible. (219, emphasis mine)

The concept of "unaffected by familiarity" echoes the idea that the threat of incest is reduced and dissipated when the members of the family live together over a long period of time. The ambivalence in Arlette's recollection of Peyrol's first appearance reinforces this reading: "I can't help being fond of him, but I begin to fear him now. When he first came here and I saw him he was just the same—only his hair was not so white— big, quiet. It seemed to me that something moved in my head. He was gentle, you know. I had to smile at him. It was as if I had recognized him. I said to myself: 'That's he, the man himself'" (219).

Prematurely separated from her own father, the recognition that Arlette feels is oedipal; she sees him as a father, although she is not aware that this is what her recognition entails. When Catherine, outside Réal's room, insists that Arlette come out, the girl says to him: "I am the daughter here, she must do what I tell her" (223). Catherine, an ambiguous mother-fig-ure, also tries to keep Arlette and her suitor apart. Réal suffers intensely after Arlette leaves: "He felt like a man chained to the wall and dying of thirst, from whom a cold drink is snatched away," and "Natures schooled into insensibility when once overcome by a mastering passion are like vanquished giants ready for despair" (224). He now fears separation and death, and Catherine comes to remind him that he must leave on his mission the next day. She tries to discourage his attachment for Arlette by telling him that "there is death in the folds of her skirt and blood about her feet"—but this fails to deter Réal who protests that "if she had all the madness of the world and the sin of all the murders of the Revolution on her shoulders, I would still hug her to my breast" (225).

The dramatic intensity of the novel increases notably from this point on. Peyrol locks Scevola up on the tartane, still intending to send Réal off at least to long-term imprisonment. When Peyrol returns to the house, Catherine relates the events of the previous evening, finishing with the statement that the lieutenant is "an honest man" (229). When Peyrol in-forms her that Réal is going away "she dreaded the moment when that fatal Arlette would wake up and the dreadful complications of life which her slumbers had suspended would have to be picked up again" (229). She indicates to Peyrol that the abbé had wanted to put Arlette in a convent and when Réal comes down for his coffee, Peyrol says he is going to shave, again echoing *Pericles* in which Pericles vows to leave his hair uncut until Marina marries (3.3.27–30). But again, Conrad reverses Shakespeare. Pericles intends to celebrate the renunciation to the suitor while Peyrol intends to celebrate the elimination of the suitor: "This is a great day—the day we are going to see the lieutenant off" (231).

Before leaving for the tartane, Peyrol looks in on Arlette asleep: "Her black hair lay loose on the pillow; and Peyrol's gaze became arrested by the long eyelashes on her pale cheek. Suddenly he fancied she moved, and he withdrew his head sharply, pulling the door to. He listened for a moment as if tempted to open it again, but judging it too risky, continued on his way downstairs" (234). The relative positions of Peyrol and Catherine in this oedipal situation are explicit as Peyrol leaves to go to the boat, and he replies to Catherine's statement that she is "tired of life." "I will tell you what it is; you ought to have been married . . . if one of my old-time chums came along and saw me like this, here with you . . . He would say to himself perhaps, 'Hullo! here's a comfortable married couple'" (235).

As one aspect of the reversal of Shakespeare's *Tempest*, in *The Rover* the storm occurs at the end of the drama rather than at the outset; the movement that accompanies the storm is from the island to the ship, rather than the reverse; and the storm is not produced by Peyrol/Prospero, but by "Jupiter's caprices" (237). Peyrol has not yet made his crucial decision and "he felt that his conduct was at the mercy of an internal conflict" (237). Scevola is now "tied up to a stanchion by three turns of the mainsheet" and Peyrol says to Réal, "Le moment approche. . . . The great moment— eh?" Addressing the lieutenant, this surrogate father who has confined his "bad" double says, "You may depend on me for sending you off when the moment comes. For what is it to you? You have no friends, you have not even a petite amie" (238). To Réal, he says of Scevola, "he has a sacré mauvais caractère" (239). The *Tempest* analog is augmented by Scevola's being "somewhat soothed by the assurance that he would not die by drowning" (265), mirroring Gonzalo's similar anxiety (1.1.64–67).

The lieutenant upsets Peyrol by informing him that he has left 2,500 francs as the price of the tartane. Peyrol's change of heart is precipitated by Arlette's shriek as she awakens from a dream in which Eugene is being killed by a mob and she rushes from the house down to the boat. The dream is accompanied by thunder and lightning and Peyrol is "swinging his cudgel regularly" (246), suggesting Arlette's fear of Peyrol in phallic terms.

> Arlette flew down the slope. The first sign of her coming was a faint thin scream which really the rover alone heard and understood.
> . . . The next moment he saw, poised on a detached boulder and thinly veiled by the first perpendicular shower, Arlette, who, catching sight of the tartane with the men on board of her, let out a prolonged shriek of mingled triumph and despair: "Peyrol! Help! Pey—rol!" (247)

Arlette came on board with such an impetus that Peyrol had to step forward and save her from a fall which would have stunned her (248). Before Arlette faints after striking Peyrol in the face with her fists, her pleas are explicit: "Misérable! Don't you dare! . . . Peyrol, my friend, my dear old friend. Give him back to me" (248). And again tempest imagery occurs: "A heavy squall enveloped the group of people on board the tartane. Peyrol laid Arlette gently on the deck. . . . The rain swept over the tartane with an angry swishing roar to which was added the sound of water rushing violently down the folds and seams of the precipitous shore vanishing gradually from his sight, as if this had been the beginning of a destroying and universal deluge—the end of all things" (248).

This combines tempest and biblical flood imagery; the Flood was a punishment for the mating of the gods with the daughters of men. Peyrol and Réal carry the limp Arlette off the boat and the lieutenant "looked as if he had just saved her from drowning" (249). The conscious change in Peyrol's plans signals the resolution of his incestuous desire and occurs when he looks at the girl on the deck and says, "She has fainted from rage at her old Peyrol" (249).

While Réal is delivering the girl to Catherine, Peyrol and Michel prepare to sail and Citizen Scevola demands, "Unbind me. Put me ashore." But no attention is paid the "blood-drinking patriot, who had been for so many years the reputed possessor not only of Escampobar, but of the Escampobar heiress that, living on appearances, he had almost come to believe in that ownership himself" (251). He is finally untied "for a little excursion at sea" (252), and from the shore Réal watches the tartane and the English ship maneuver, feeling betrayed. Arlette joins him under the tree telling him "that if she had not found him she would have thrown herself over the cliff" (258, 259). The motivation for Peyrol's renunciation is made clear: "It was as though the rover of the wide seas had left them to themselves on a sudden impulse of scorn, of magnanimity, of a passion weary of itself. However come by, Réal was ready to clasp for ever to his breast that woman touched by the red hand of the Revolution; for she, whose little feet had run ankle-deep through the terrors of death, had brought to him the sense of triumphant life" (260).

The final running maneuvers of the tartane and the *Amelia* receive critical accolades even from those critics who have little use for this novel otherwise. The captain of the large ship refers to Peyrol as a man "determined on making his escape" and the double resonance of the phrase can be viewed in terms of the incest motif. This meaning is confirmed: "If those words by some miracle could have been carried to the ears of Peyrol, they would have brought to his lips a smile of malicious and triumphant exultation. Ever since he had laid his hand on the tiller of the tartane every faculty of his resourcefulness and seamanship had been bent on deceiving the English captain" (263). He plans, indeed, to be caught, but in so doing lies his escape.

Peyrol's relationship to Prospero becomes increasingly evident as he assumes control of the situation in the craft which "had been spirited away" (254). Promising Scevola that he will "not die by drowning," he says of Captain Vincent, "I know that man's mind" (264). Explaining to Michel that the *Amelia* will begin firing on them in less than half an hour, Peyrol spells out his control; he is his own Ariel:

"Because her captain has got to obey what is in my mind. . . . He will do it as sure as if I were at his ear telling him what to do. He will do it because he is a first-rate seaman, but I, Michel, I am just a little bit cleverer than he." He glanced over his shoulder at the *Amelia* rushing after the tartane with swelling sails, and raised his voice suddenly. "He will do it because no more than half a mile ahead of us is the spot where Peyrol will die!" (266)

After he has been shot, "A feeling of peace sank into him, not unmingled with pride. Everything he had planned had come to pass. He had meant to play that man a trick, and now the trick had been played. Played by him better than by any other old man on whom age had stolen, unnoticed, till the veil of peace was torn down by *the touch of a sentiment unexpected like an intruder and cruel like an enemy*" (267, 268, emphasis mine).

Shakespeare's old man had required supernatural devices with which to accomplish the resolution of his father/daughter relationship; Peyrol has done the same thing with the means to hand, and served political and military purposes to boot. As he dies, looking in vain for the other two men who are either dead or dying, he recalls Arlette's scream, "Peyrol, don't you dare!" with its double implication of not daring to do away with her suitor, and not daring to keep her for his own.

When the vanquished ship is boarded, it contains a registry with no name, and the clothing of "E. Réal" (270); the nature of Peyrol's success is suggested by the names of the two English ships that appear, the *Superb* and the *Victory*. Captain Vincent never understands why Peyrol had courted death and tells Nelson: "Considering that they all could have saved their lives simply by striking their sails on deck, I can not refuse them my admiration and especially to the white-haired man" (274). But

later, when contemplating the affair he realizes that "they have been asking for it. There could be only one end to that affair" (277).

The symbolism of being "locked in" is continued to the end as the
bodies of the three men are locked in the cuddy, while the key is on the
Amelia. The tartane, owned by a series of "fathers" in this novel, becomes
in the end the coffin for two of them. The novel concludes with another
reference which confirms its relationship to Shakespeare's final play: "The
blue level of the Mediterranean, the charmer and the deceiver of auda-
cious men, kept the secret of its fascination—hugged to its calm breast the
victims of all the wars, calamities and tempests of its history, under the
marvellous purity of the sunset sky" (286).

Both Shakespeare's *Tempest* and Conrad's *Rover* are couched in political plots. Rank comments on the relationship between the political narrative and the incest theme: "That the political drama is a continuous facade for the incest drama is characteristically reflected in a motive
relevant in the development of the dramatic plot" (63). In both works,
order is restored, both politically and familially: Prospero has averted di-
saster and will return to Milan for his daughter's nuptials. Réal eventually
serves as "Mayor of the Commune in that very same little village which
had looked on Escampobar as the abode of iniquity, the sojourn of blood-
drinkers and of wicked women" (283). The implications of incest as anar-
chy are apparent.

Conrad then, in an early, a middle, and a final work, parallels both
Shakespeare and Dickens. In *Almayer's Folly,* the father's renunciation is
imposed, not by a Duke Theseus, but by the armed daughter. The father
does not accept, and his "folly" ultimately destroys him. In *Chance,* the
"bad" father, after his failure to destroy the "good" father, destroys himself.
The "good" father retains the daughter for a short period of happiness,
whereupon he relinquishes her to the young suitor. In the final novel, the
"good" father, tempted to destroy the suitor, ultimately renounces and
destroys both himself and the "bad" father, freeing the daughter for the
young suitor. A tempest figures in the two later novels. In *Chance,* Conrad's evident ambivalence regarding fatherly retention is apparent in his
interim transfer of the daughter to a father/suitor prior to a final relinquishment to a young suitor. This ambivalence was later reflected in his
unfinished novel, *Suspense* (1925), which he was working on when he
died.

A final word should be said about the significant relationship between
sexuality and death in the works of Conrad—an aspect of his work that
more closely corresponds to Shakespeare's canon than it does to either the

work of Dickens or of James. Both Almayer and Peyrol find death the only viable alternative to their frustrated sexuality, and Flora continually flirts with suicide as the daughter's only way out. Of Conrad himself, Meyer reports:

> In the course of his proposal of marriage to Jessie George, which was as dismaying as it was abrupt, she later reported Conrad conveyed a similar forecast of his early destruction by informing her that he had not long to live—an assertion for which there was not the least evidence. Following her acceptance, she noted on his face an expression of "acute suffering." Suddenly he left her, hailed a passing cab, and urging the driver on to greater speed, fled from her presence. During the next three days she did not hear from him, and when he finally saw her again he insisted that the marriage take place in less than six weeks' time and that they go abroad to live. Just before the wedding he demanded that she burn all his letters in his presence.[12]

There are several elements commonly found in the fiction in this description. The sense of urgency overlayered with a sense of shame suggests incest-related anxieties, which Conrad repeatedly elucidated in his novels.

'Tis as human a little story
as paper could well carry.
James Joyce, *Finnegans Wake*

6

The Triangle in
James Joyce

The singular appropriateness of the Joyce corpus as the conclusion to an overview of the father/daughter theme in a selected body of literature needs little elaboration. Of all twentieth-century writers, James Joyce (1882–1941) stands out as the most significant heir, both to Shakespeare and to the Victorian novelists. In his determination to be all things to all readers, and to encompass the totality of human history and human experience in a very few works, Joyce managed to distill and resynthesize most of the literature that had preceded him. Homer Brown accurately notes: "The biography of Joyce's particular forms is part of the biography of the novel in general."[1] Joyce had an early encounter with the father/daughter incest theme in literature when he translated Hauptmann's *Vor Sonnenaufgang* into *Before Sunrise* in 1901 at the age of twenty while spending time in Mullingar with his father, who was then taking the census.[2] Rank had noted of the play: "[O]ne scene depicts the father's crude lust for his daughter" (331).

Evidence of Joyce's preoccupation with the incest theme and with fathers and daughters in particular is less evident in his early works than is true of any of the other writers. By the same token, there has probably been more critical speculation regarding the relationship between the Joyce family dynamics and the content of both *Ulysses* and *Finnegans Wake* than has been true of the other writers. Joyce's background as a child was closest to that of Dickens in the gradual economic deterioration of the family's stability into a state approaching destitution. In both situations, it was not unreasonable to blame the father. Joyce's mother, dead at forty-four, had been pregnant seventeen times by an irresponsible and unsympathetic husband. Joyce's lifelong mate, Nora, had already managed her own escape from a household in which an irate uncle had beaten her when she was nineteen for "walking out" with a Protestant.[3] Unlike the artists who preceded him, Joyce's early work displays few examples of father/suitor conflict over the daughter. To our knowledge, Joyce did not experience this sort of conflict as a young man and Nora's ready acquiescence in fleeing Ireland occurred in the absence of any obstructive father. Joyce seems to have consciously circumvented the omnipresent "fathers" in his refusal to bow to convention and marry the young woman: "But why should I have brought Nora to a priest or a lawyer to make her swear away her life to me?"[4] However, in later bouts of jealousy over Nora's supposed past affairs, Joyce generated the emotional intensity usually associated with the conflict between the father and the suitor.

In Joyce and Nora's family, their daughter Lucia was the most ill-fated since she suffered from schizophrenia and was institutionalized for the latter part of her life. Needless to say, this was a great trauma for her family, especially her father. Lucia seems to have had considerable effect on the development of the characters of Milly (*Ulysses*) and Issy (*Finnegans Wake*), and was herself an adolescent as *Ulysses* was being written. Maddox points out that both *Ulysses* and the *Finnegans Wake* notebooks "contain references to the kind of eye defect, a 'turnedin eye,' about which Lucia and her parents were increasingly worried as she reached adolescence."[5]

In *Dubliners* (1914), the father/daughter/suitor configuration is central to "Eveline" with the compression of its presentation being particularly reminiscent of early Dickens. The stark simplicity of Joyce's story succinctly encompasses the missing mother, the domineering father, the ambivalent but submissive daughter and the seductive suitor, concluding with the daughter's compulsive return to the father—an agonized withdrawal that suggests a closing-off of all future possibilities. Margaret

Church supports this view: "Psychologically and mythically, the age of the sons is the age of the Oedipus and Electra complex. Eveline is as incapable of leaving her father as Mr. Duffy . . . is of abandoning the interpretation he holds of Mrs. Sinico as a mother figure."[6]

"The Dead" has been less commonly viewed as an example of the father/daughter/suitor triangle, but it can be read from that point of view. Gabriel exerts the same kind of authority over his wife Gretta as he does over his children; they all rebel futilely together, indicated by her complaint to his aunts: "He's really an awful bother, what with green shades for Tom's eyes at night and making him do the dumb-bells, and forcing Eva to eat the stirabout. The poor child! And she simply hates the sight of it. . . . O, but you'll never guess what he makes me wear now!"[7] Although Gretta can laugh, she identifies herself with the children and obviously does not have the power to intervene, even on her own behalf. Later, when his wife excitedly pleads to visit Galway again, Gabriel "coldly" replies, "You can go if you like" (191). This disdain for her wishes bears no relevance in Gabriel's mind to his later frustrated physical desire "to overmaster her" (217). His chagrin is profound when he learns of her fixation on the past and on the boy she remembers as having died for her. Although Gabriel had married Gretta in rebellion against his mother, "he had never felt like that himself towards any woman but he knew that such a feeling must be love" (223).

Viewed in father/daughter/suitor terms, "The Dead" becomes an inversion of the theme, since it is the young suitor who is dead and on whom Gretta's attachment is forever fixed. Although Brown perceptively observes that "Gabriel acknowledges that discovery of her separateness which marks the end of his attempt to control or manipulate her" (98), he fails to note that this same renunciation in effect renders him impotent. Both Gretta and Gabriel are prevented from the enjoyment of immediate experience by the ghost of Michael Furey, frozen forever in the idealized stasis of the lovers on the Grecian urn. Sexuality based on fatherly autonomy is undermined. In *Dubliners*, "Eveline" and "The Dead" balance each other out. Eveline's father wins and Gabriel loses, but the inevitable result in both instances is that paralysis characteristic of the world of these stories; there is no joy either way.

In both the early *Stephen Hero* and *A Portrait of the Artist as a Young Man*, the rival for the suitor, Stephen Dedalus, is not his own father or the girl's father, but the omnipresent Church Fathers. In *Stephen Hero*, his hostility is much more explicit than in the later version: "Stephen watching this young priest and Emma together usually worked himself into a state of unsettled rage"[8] and toward the end of the available manuscript, he openly propositions her in terms that cause Lynch to tell him, "To the ordinary intelligence it looks as if you had taken leave of your senses for the time being" (200). Stephen's implied adversary is the "young priest" under whose sway it is highly unlikely that Emma would ever consent to his rather crude advances. But this suggests a distancing of the father's authority, and the immediate conflict is between the suitor and the young woman.

In *A Portrait of the Artist as a Young Man* (1916), although most of Stephen's encounters are with prostitutes followed by his confession to the priests, the nature of the rivalry in his nebulous involvement with Emma has not changed from the earlier version: "His anger against her found vent in coarse railing at her paramour, whose name and voice and features offended his baffled pride: a priested peasant. . . . To him she would unveil her soul's shy nakedness, . . . rather than to him, a priest of eternal imagination."[9] Also in *Ulysses*, following the death of Stephen's mother, it is the daughter Dilly who remains to cope with the father's instability and irresponsibility. Dilly might well become an Eveline; there are no suitors in evidence to rescue her from her drab existence. But it is in *Ulysses* (1921) that the incest theme becomes significant.

In this more complex novel, the father/daughter relationship becomes intensely personalized between Bloom and the absent Milly and the incest theme recurs in fragmented references throughout the novel. Toward the end of *Ulysses*, Bloom reflects on "the insecurity of hiding any secret document behind, beneath or between the pages of a book" (*U*, 17.1413–14). Insecurely hidden in the pages of this book, unsuccessfully buried in an excess of verbiage, lies the oedipal theme in the guise of the Odysseus theme, the former raising the problems of sin, guilt, and incest which lie at the heart of the novel. Evidence of Joyce's preoccupation with the Oedipus myth can be found in the Zurich Notebook (1918), in which he summarizes the myth in perhaps its most succinct form: "Tiresias revealed all. after never fucked her."[10] The blind stripling can be viewed as a Tiresias figure, his tap-tapping echoing the incest-motif in the Sophocles play. Many aspects of the incest theme are stated obliquely and must be "pieced together from hints":

There are sins or (let us call them as the world calls them) evil memories which are hidden away by man in the darkest places of the heart but they abide there and wait. He may suffer their memory to grow dim, let them be as though they had not been and all but persuade himself that they were not or at least were otherwise. Yet a chance word will call them forth suddenly and they will rise up to confront him in the most various circumstances. (*U*, 14.1344–50)

Two opposing critical positions on *Ulysses* with regard to themes of sin and guilt stand for the myriad oppositions that have emerged in critical commentary about this novel since it first appeared. Lionel Trilling maintained that "the conception of sin has but a tangential relevance to the book. The element of sexuality which plays so large a part in the story does not raise considerations of sin and evil; it is dealt with in the way of poetic naturalism."[11] Mark Shechner recognizes Bloom's sense of guilt, but hedges on its cause: "For 'Circe' is, at bottom, a *mea culpa*, an admission of a great burden of sin that is struggling for expression. Yet, the precise nature of the sin remains hidden."[12] The discrepancy in these assessments points up the fact that the theme of sin that I believe permeates the novel and has its roots deep within "the darkest places" of Bloom's heart is so overlayered in his consciousness that his skillful repression of his "evil memories" escaped critical recognition for many years. In a novel viewed by many as a tribute to man's ability to endure, the twin motifs of incest and suicide continue to resurface throughout.[13] Such a reading brings to mind Ibsen's influence on Joyce in this recurrent preoccupation with sexual frustration, the power of the dead over the living, man's relentless need to cope with his guilt, and possibly also, *kindermord*. Freud's reference to the incest theme in *Rosmersholm* as "subterranean" and requiring piecing "together from hints" (*SE*, 14:327) also applies to *Ulysses*.

The nature of incest is elaborated upon by Stephen in the library discussion, following Mr. Best's comment, "But *Hamlet* is so personal, isn't it? . . . I mean, a kind of private paper, don't you know, of his private life" (*U*, 9.362–63). Bloom moves through this chapter as a ghost, a shadow, and Stephen's words on incest are particularly applicable to him:

Saint Thomas, Stephen, smiling said, . . . writing of incest from a standpoint different from that of the new Viennese school Mr Magee spoke of, likens it in his wise and curious way to an avarice of the emotions. He means that the love so given to one near in blood, is covetously withheld from some stranger who, it may be, hungers for it. Jews, whom christians tax with avarice, are of all races the most given to intermarriage. (*U*, 9.778–84)

This passage closes with an oblique reference to the daughter as Stephen concludes: "No sir smile neighbour shall covet his ox or his wife or his manservant or his maidservant or his jackass" and Mulligan adds, "Or his jennyass" (*U*, 9.790–92). Later, Bloom expresses the wish "to amend many social conditions," some of which are the product of "avarice" (*U*, 17.990–91).

The conventional precipitating factor contributing to father/daughter incest, the "missing" mother, is obliquely present in *Ulysses*. June 16, 1904, is the date of Molly's assignation with Blazes Boylan, but the marital relationship of the Blooms was altered following the birth of Rudy and his death eleven days later, an alteration summed up by Molly: "we were never the same since" (*U*, 18.1450). During the "10 years, 5 months and 18 days" since the event, they have practiced *coitus interruptus*, a fairly common method of contraception at that time: "there remained a period . . . during which carnal intercourse had been incomplete, without ejaculation of semen within the natural female organ" (*U*, 17.2282–84). The reason for this is probably the fact that Rudy was a defective child, as indicated by Molly's "what was the good in going into mourning for what was neither one thing nor the other" (*U*, 18.1307–8). This is supported by Bloom's musings on the midwife's instinct that the infant was better off dead (*U*, 4.419), and his recollections in the cemetery: "Dwarf's body, weak as putty, . . . Baby. Meant nothing. Mistake of nature. If it's healthy it's from the mother. If not from the man. Better luck next time" (*U*, 6.326–30).

That the Blooms' relationship has been shadowed by the fear of producing another defective child seems probable, but a new factor has disturbed their relationship for the past nine months and one day, since there has been a "limitation of activity mental and corporal, inasmuch as complete mental intercourse between himself and the listener had not taken place since the *consummation of puberty*" by Milly on September 15, 1903, exactly nine months and one day ago—a human gestation period (*U*, 17.2284–86, emphasis mine).

That Joyce has here telescoped the consummation of puberty with a sexual consummation can be deduced by the theme of exile that is simultaneously indicated, because since that time, Bloom's "complete corporal liberty of action had been circumscribed. . . . By various reiterated feminine interrogation concerning the masculine destination whither, the place where, the time at which, the duration for which, the object with which in the case of temporary absences, projected or effected" (*U*, 17.2291–97). The novel is subsequently sprinkled with references to

Bloom's "projected" trips to see Milly in Mullingar; he is the *"god pursu-ing the maiden hid"* (*U*, 9.616–17). His liberty has been curtailed "in con-sequence of a preestablished natural comprehension in incomprehen-sion between the *consummated females"* (*U*, 17.2289–92, emphasis mine).

Why has Milly been sent to Mullingar at the age of fourteen? Is she another "Cordelia. *Cordoglio*. Lir's loneliest daughter?" (*U*, 9.314). Throughout *Ulysses*, as Stephen says of the Shakespeare corpus: "The note of banishment, banishment from the heart, banishment from home, sounds uninterruptedly" (*U*, 9.999–1000). The first reference to a "ban-ished" Milly also introduces the recurrent theme of "reduplication of per-sonality" (*U*, 15.2523) with its implications of Milly as a replication of Molly. Buck Mulligan reports that his friend Bannon in Westmeath has found "a sweet young thing. . . . Photo girl he calls her." The response is: "Snapshot, eh? Brief exposure" (*U*, 1.684–86). Milly, working for a photog-rapher in Mullingar, is a duplication for Bloom of Molly. The recurrent "metempsychosis" and "parallax" reinforce the duplication/identification theme throughout the novel. Again, a Shakespearean allusion acquires resonance: *"My dearest wife*, Pericles says, *was like this maid*. Will any man love the daughter if he has not loved the mother?" (*U*, 9.423–24). The question is thus raised as to the precise nature of the "brief exposure," with a possible hint in: "Riddle me, riddle me, randy ro. / My father gave me seeds to sow" (*U*, 2.88–89).

Bloom's preoccupation with his daughter is delineated twice early in the novel: during his breakfast and in the cemetery. Before he sets out on the day's peregrinations, he receives a letter from Milly (a fact he reports "carefully"), while Molly gets a card, a discrepancy later noted by Molly. As Bloom takes his tea, a metaphor for sexuality both in *Ulysses* and in *Finnegans Wake*, he reads her letter, conveyed to the reader in fragments: "Thanks: new tam: Mr. Coghlan: lough Owel picnic: young student: Blazes Boylan's seaside girls" (*U*, 4.281–83), the last being a Proustian merged identity refrain. The first reading is followed by Bloom's imagin-ing the verse:

O, Milly Bloom, you are my darling.
You are my lookingglass from night to morning.
I'd rather have you without a farthing
Than Katey Keogh with her ass and garden. (*U*, 4.287–90)

The looking glass is immediately given sexual connotations as Bloom re-calls the discovery by a young Milly of the mirror in the voyeuristic old professor Goodwin's hat: "Sex breaking out even then. Pert little piece she was" (*U*, 4.293–95).

After delivering Molly's tea, Bloom eats and drinks his tea in the kitchen, rereading the letter three times. Mark Shechner points out that "for Bloom, eating is an act of love and love a matter of eating" (75). Bloom muses about Milly's report of the picnic with the young student, and in the carriage-ride to the funeral, "picnic" is equated with sexual intercourse as Mr. Power says, "Someone seems to have been making a picnic party here lately," to which Mr. Dedalus replies resignedly, "After all, it's the most natural thing in the world" (*U*, 6.98, 108).

Bloom's thoughts following the first rereading of Milly's letter give us some of the clues to the situation:

> Coming out of her shell. Row with her in the XL Café about the bracelet. Wouldn't eat her cakes or speak or look. Saucebox. He sopped other dies of bread in the gravy and ate piece after piece of kidney. . . . Young student. . . . O, well: she knows how to mind herself. But if not? No, nothing has happened. Of course it might. Wait in any case till it does. A wild piece of goods. Her slim legs running up the staircase. Destiny. Ripening now. Vain: very. He smiled with troubled affection at the kitchen window. (*U*, 4.422–31)

In *Ulysses*, the theme of exile that is so frequently an exile by water in other works is compressed into the trip which Milly and her father take on the *Erin's King* around the Kish light. Robert Adams comes close to this reading when he observes: "Unlike Odysseus, Bloom is not much of an ocean voyager; the one occasion when he gets on a boat ought to be rich in import. . . . given the paucity of domestic incident chez Bloom, the participation of Milly seems particularly promising."[14] Although Adams accurately observes that *Erin's King* refers both to a real boat and to Parnell, the allusion probably also entails Parnell as a symbol of exile following a disastrous love affair. Imagery, which in more obscure passages I read as suggestive of Milly, (blue scarf, wind, hair), is established in the first *Erin's King* reference:

> On the *Erin's King* that day round the Kish. Damned old tub pitching about. Not a bit funky. Her pale blue scarf loose in the wind with her hair.
> *All dimpled cheeks and curls.*
> *Your head it simply swirls.*

Seaside girls. Torn envelope. . . . Swurls, he says.
Piers with lamps, summer evening, band.
Those girls, those girls.
Those lovely seaside girls.
Milly too. Young kisses, the first. Far away now past.
Mrs Marion. (*U*, 4.434–44)

Bloom's sexual fantasies are then interwoven with thoughts of Milly in language that foreshadows his later experience with Gerty on the beach:

A soft qualm regret flowed down his backbone, increasing. Will happen, yes. Prevent. Useless: can't move. Girl's sweet light lips. Will happen too. He felt the flowing qualm spread over him. Useless to move now. Lips kissed, kissing kissed. Full gluey woman's lips.
Better where she is down there: away. Occupy her. Wanted a dog to pass the time. Might take a trip down there. August bank holiday. Might work a press pass. Or through M'Coy. (*U*, 4.447–54)

Joyce characteristically gets double or triple meaning from a number of words in the passage. Bloom undoubtedly does have "qualms" about his erotic feelings; Milly's encounter with the young student "will happen," he cannot "prevent" it because he is not free to "move"—but all of these words also describe his erotic sensations of the moment.

The trip on the *Erin's King* is elaborated upon twice more, the second occurrence suggesting that it was on this trip that Bloom told Milly that she would have to go to Mullingar: "not forgetting the Irish lights, Kish and others, liable to capsize at any moment, rounding which he once with his daughter had experienced some remarkably choppy, not to say stormy, weather" (*U*, 16.649–52).

Clues to the Bloom/Milly relationship which accompany the letter-reading are augmented by his musings on the way to the funeral, following his thoughts about his lost son and how wonderful it would have been to "see him grow up. Hear his voice in the house. . . . My son. Me in his eyes" (*U*, 6.75–76).

Molly. Milly. Same thing watered down. Her tomboy oaths. O jumping Jupiter! Ye gods and little fishes! Still, she's a dear girl. Soon to be a woman. Mullingar. Dearest Papli. Young student. Yes, yes: a woman too. Life, Life. (*U*, 6.87–90)

All the components of the incest theme are compressed here: the daughter as replica of the mother, attachment to the father (dearest Papli), exile (Mullingar), and suitor (young student). Shortly before this, as Mr. Dedalus comments on "the wise child that knows her own father. Mr. Bloom smiled joylessly on Ringsend road" (*U*, 6.53–54), suggesting a double entendre in the biblical "know." Thoughts of Milly continue in counterpoint to thoughts of death as they drive along the canal:

> Athlone, Mullingar, Moyvalley, I could make a walking tour to see Milly by the canal. Or cycle down. Hire some old crock, safety. . . . Developing waterways. . . . Cheaper transit. By easy stages. Houseboats. Camping out. Also hearses. To heaven by water. Perhaps I will without writing. Come as a surprise. (*U*, 6.444–50)

The novel contains many such combinations of water imagery and sexuality, reinforced by puns such as "come." As the carriage passes the burial section for murderers, Bloom thinks, "Murder will out," then muses: "She mightn't like me to come that way without letting her know. Must be careful about women. Catch them once with their pants down. Never forgive you after. Fifteen" (*U*, 6.482–85).

Fifteen has double significance as a birthday and as an indication of Milly's "consummation of puberty." In addition to being Milly's newly turned age, it was her mother's age in her first sexual encounter with Mulvey. In her soliloquy, Molly boasts: "I knew more about men and life when I was 15 than they'll all know at 50" (*U*, 18.886–87).

The importance of the date for Bloom is reflected as he reads Milly's letter: "Fifteen yesterday. Curious, fifteenth of the month too. Her first birthday away from home. Separation" (*U*, 4.415–16). But June 16, 1904, has additional birthday ramifications; it is the birthday of Mrs. Purefoy's son. However, since it is nine months and one day since Milly's "consummation of puberty" (*U*, 17.2287), it is also possibly, in Alice's words, "an unbirthday," the day on which Bloom's and Milly's son might have been born, but is not. This suggests another reason for Bloom's preoccupation with the outcome of Mrs. Purefoy's prolonged labor.

This delivery culminates in the passage on sins and evil memories "hidden away by man in the darkest places of the heart." These "will rise up to confront him in . . . a vision or a dream" ("Oxen of the Sun"), "while timbrel and harp soothe his senses" ("Sirens"), "amid the cool silver tranquility of the evening" ("Nausicaa"), "or at the feast, at midnight, when he is now filled with wine" ("Circe"; *U* 14.1344–52). The first of this series is explicitly noted by Mulligan at its termination: "His soul is far away. It is as painful perhaps to be awakened from a vision as to be born" (*U*, 14.1165).

Bloom, in this vision, becomes a "knighterrant," "errant" meaning both "wandering" and "erring" (in a world where *Erin's King?*). In a passage reversing the "wise child that knows his own father" allusion to Telemachus, to the Shakespearean "wise father that knows his own child,"[15] the original transgression can be "pieced together from hints":

> But hey, presto, the mirror is breathed on and the young knight-errant recedes, shrivels, dwindles to a tiny speck within the mist. Now he is himself paternal and these about him might be his sons. Who can say? *The wise father knows his own child.* He thinks of a drizzling night in Hatch street . . . the first. Together (she is a poor waif, a child of shame, yours and mine and of all for a bare shilling and her luckpenny), . . . Bridie! Bridie Kelly! *He will never forget the name, ever remember the night: first night, the bridenight.* They are entwined in nethermost darkness, the willer with the willed, and in an instant (*fiat!*) light shall flood the world. Did heart leap to heart? Nay, fair reader. In a breath 'twas done but— hold! Back! It must not be! In terror the poor girl flees away through the murk. She is the bride of darkness, a daughter of night. She dare not bear the sunnygolden babe of day. No, Leopold. Name and memory solace thee not. That youthful illusion of thy strength was taken from thee—and in vain. No son of thy loins is by thee. There is none now to be for Leopold, what Leopold was for Rudolph. (*U*, 14.1060–77, emphasis mine)

Bloom's designation as "knighterrant" transforms the girl into a "daughter of (k)night," and Bloom is the wise father who "knows his own child." Hatch street, a Dublin street facing the Kish light, also fits with other chicken/egg allusions which culminate in "Silly-Milly burying the little dead bird in the kitchen matchbox, a daisychain and bits of broken chainies on the grave" (*U*, 6.952–53).

The impossibility of Bloom's having a son by his daughter is suggested in "murderers of the sun," which may refer either to contraception or to abortion; I favor the former. "Hold! Back! It must not be!" suggests coitus interruptus. Following the reiteration of Milly motifs: "the everlasting bride," "the bride, ever virgin," "Millicent the young, the dear, the radiant," "sandals of bright gold," "a veil of . . . gossamer" (*U*, 14.1101–4), Bloom reawakens to the life around him identified as "that vigilant wanderer, soiled by the dust of travel and combat and *stained by the mire of an indelible dishonour*" (*U*, 14.1217–19, emphasis mine), again, highly suggestive of incest.

"Sirens," in which "timbrel and harp soothe" Bloom's senses, is intricately laced with significant phrases from *Martha* and *La Sonnambula*. While *Martha* suggests the blurred identities of Martha Clifford and Milly, Bellini's *La Sonnambula* tells of the young sleepwalker allowed to escape from the room of the older man who is probably her father; it also contains the key aria, from which Bloom hears fragments:

> "All is lost now,
> By hope and joy am I forsaken
> Never more can love awaken
> Past enchantment, no, nevermore."[16]

As Simon sings "to a dusty seascape there: *A Last Farewell*. . . . A lovely girl, her veil awave upon the wind upon the headland" (*U*, 11.590–92), the imagery again suggests Milly on the deck of the excursion boat. Bloom's thoughts blend the sleepwalking in the opera with the departure of Milly the sleepwalker, reinforcing a reading of the *Erin's King* trip as the onset of her exile:

> Yes, I remember. Lovely air. In sleep she went to him. Innocence in the moon. Brave. Don't know their danger. Still hold her back. Call name. Touch water. Jingle jaunty. Too late. She longed to go. That's why. Woman. As easy stop the sea. Yes: all is lost.
>   A beautiful air, said Bloom, lost Leopold. I know it well.
>
> * * *
>
> He knows it well too. Or he feels. *Still harping on his daughter.* Wise child that knows her father, Dedalus said. Me?
>   Bloom askance over liverless saw. Face of the all is lost. (*U*, 11.638–46)

Joyce had handwritten a change in the italicized sentence above, crossing out "my" and substituting "his."[17] The final reference to Milly in this chapter, against the background of the reiterated tap-tap of the blind stripling, blends the aging Bloom's disappointment over leaving no heir with Milly's possible union with a young suitor: "I too. Last of my race. Milly young student. Well, my fault perhaps. No son. Rudy. Too late now. Or if not? If not? If still? / He bore no hate. / Hate. Love. Those are names. Rudy. Soon I am old" (*U*, 11.1066–69). Shortly, another possible reference to Bloom's "darkest sin" occurs: "Who fears to speak of nineteen four?" (*U*, 11.1072–73).

The most succinct allusion to the Bloom/Milly relationship occurs "amid the cool silver tranquility of the evening" on the beach following

Bloom's encounter with Gerty when "far on Kish bank the anchored lightship twinkled, winked at Mr Bloom" (*U*, 13.1180–81). Bloom has "sinned against the light" (*U*, 14.1575–76), and "all is lost" (*U*, 11.641).

"Circe" includes in its abundance of material the memories aroused at the feast at midnight. Joyce's additions to the typescript (in double brackets) illustrate his expansion on the theme of Bloom's negative qualities as a father. The first hint comes from the Bawd: "Ten shillings a maidenhead. Fresh thing was never touched. Fifteen. [[There's no-one in it only her old father that's dead drunk]]" (*U*, 15.359–60).[18]

Bloom recalls a past time when Milly was called "Marionette" (*U*, 15.540), and Beaufoy states explicitly: "Why, look at the man's private life! Leading a [[quadruple]] existence! Street angel and house devil. [[Not fit to be mentioned in mixed society!]]" (*U*, 15.853–54).[19] The "quadruple" designation was changed from "double" and indicates Bloom's involvement with Molly, Milly, Martha, and Gerty. The latter's function as a daughter-double is quite explicit in Bloom's musings after his sexual encounter on the beach: "Three years old she was in front of Molly's dressingtable just before we left Lombard street west. *Me have a nice pace.* Mullingar. Who knows? Ways of the world. Young student. Straight on her pins anyway not like the other. Still she was game" (*U*, 13.925–29).[20] The importance of the doubling characteristic in Bloom's relationships with women is reiterated.

Bloom protests that "*there might have been lapses of an erring father*" (*U*, 15.905–6), but J. J. O'Molloy, speaking in his defense, says that "The trumped up misdemeanour was due to a momentary aberration of heredity, brought on by hallucination, such familiarities as the alleged guilty occurrence being quite permitted in my client's native place, the land of the Pharaoh" (*U*, 15.944–47), incest having been a prerogative of Egyptian royalty.

Another reiterated suggestion made here is that Milly has sleepwalked, echoed in Bellini references, and that Bloom has been a sort of hapless victim: "I would deal in especial with atavism. There have been cases of shipwreck and somnambulism in my client's family. If the accused could speak he could a tale unfold—one of the strangest that have ever been narrated between the covers of a book" (*U*, 15.949–53). But in his further defense of Bloom against the accusations of Mary Driscoll, the household maid, O'Molloy comments: "I say it and I say it emphatically . . . accused was not accessory before the act and the prosecutrix has not been tampered with. The young person [[She was treated by defendant as if she were his very own daughter]]" (*U*, 15.972–73).[21]

Later, in Molly's soliloquy, we learn that Mary's accusations had been correct and that Molly had discharged her (*U*, 18.60–70). Both Gerty (*U*, 13.432) and Dr. Mulligan (*U*, 15.1783) refer to Bloom as "more sinned against than sinning," the guilt/incest reference from *King Lear*. Bloom, replying to the Fan's statement that he is married, replies, "Yes. Partly, *I have mislaid*" (*U*, 15.2757, emphasis mine). Bloom has a vision in which he thinks he is seeing Molly the first night at Mat Dillon's, but Bello:

> (*Laughs mockingly.*) That's your daughter, you owl, with a Mullingar student.
> (*Milly Bloom, fairhaired, greenvested, slimsandalled, her blue scarf in the seawind, simply swirling, breaks from the arms of her lover and calls, her young eyes wonderwide.*)
>   MILLY
> My! It's Papli! But, O Papli how old you've grown! (*U*, 15.3165–71).

A short time later, referring again to Shakespeare, Bello tells Bloom that he has made his "secondbest bed and others must lie in it" (*U*, 15.3198–99). Boylan is already lying in his first bed, and passages from "Oxen of the Sun" indicate that others will be lying in Milly's (secondbest) bed also.

Key material pertinent to the Bloom/Milly relationship occurs in "Ithaca," with sleepwalking again alluded to: "What proposal did Bloom, diambulist, father of Milly, somnambulist, make to Stephen, noctambulist?" (*U*, 17.929–30). There is evidence that although Milly's sleepwalking has precipitated the first encounter, this was not the only incident. Following the song about a "jew's daughter" (*U*, 17.813–28), with its castration imagery, the words of Stephen, a "judge of imposters" (*U*, 15.4490–91), are offered in condensed form: "One of all, the least of all, is the victim predestined. *Once by inadvertence, twice by design* he challenges his destiny. It comes when he is abandoned and challenges him reluctant and, as an apparition of hope and youth, holds him unresisting. It leads him to a strange habitation, to a secret infidel apartment, and there, implacable, immolates him, consenting" (*U*, 17.833–37, emphasis mine). The references then become more explicit, suggesting the shame and secrecy attached to incest:

> Why was the host (victim predestined) sad?
> He wished that a tale of a deed should be told of a deed not by him should by him not be told.
>
>   * * *
>
> Why was the host (secret infidel) silent?

He weighed the possible evidences for and against ritual murder: . . . the sporadic reappearance of atavistic delinquency, the
mitigating circumstances of fanaticism, hypnotic suggestion and
somnambulism.

From which (if any) of these mental or physical disorders was
he not totally immune?

From hypnotic suggestion. . . . From somnambulism . . .
(U, 17.838–54)

Bloom too is a sleepwalker.

There is more than ample evidence of the sexuality of Milly, the somnambulist. She is a "bold bad girl from the town of Mullingar" (U,
14.1494–95), "a skittish heifer," "big of her age and beef to the heel" (U,
14.502), and "just getting out of bounds" (U, 18.1027). When Bloom compares the departures of Milly and his cat, they are held to be similar "because actuated by a secret purpose the quest of a new male (Mullingar
student) or of a healing herb (valerian)" (U, 17.890–91), valerian being a
tranquilizer. If Milly's quest is for a "new male," there must have been an
"old male." The incest motif is reinforced by the summary of similarities
between Milly and the cat: "In passivity, in economy, in the instinct of
tradition, in unexpectedness" (U, 17.894). But the differences between
Milly and the cat are even more important: "Differently, because of different possible returns to the inhabitants or to the habitation" (U, 17.891–92).
Cats always return home; daughters are not as predictable.

When Bloom encounters another suitor for Milly, there is no textual
evidence that he is aware of it. During his time with the medical students,
Crothers, looking at a picture in a locket, tells Bloom of his meeting with
a young girl who was wearing "her new coquette cap (a gift for her feast-
day as she told me prettily)" (U, 14.758–59), and he toasts Bloom with
"mille compliments" (U, 14.746–47). He then makes a possible reference
to Bloom's three encounters, "Thrice happy will be he whom so amiable
a creature will bless with her favours" (U, 14.763–64). Bloom is evidently
not shown the picture, and there is no clue as to whether he understands
that the student is talking about Milly, who had written to thank her father
for the "new tam"; Bloom had been aware of one suitor, but possibly not
of several.

A "piecing together of hints" scattered throughout the novel seems to
indicate that Milly is in exile in Mullingar due to three transgressions that
have occurred with her father, "once by inadvertence, twice by design."
Joyce's use of "inadvertence" echoes Landor's Imaginary Conversation

between Beatrice Cenci and Pope Clement VIII, who condemned her to death following her father's murder. Clement denies Beatrice's plea for mercy, saying, "An inadvertence peradventure yea / Never a parricide."[22] Clement dismisses the father's actions as inadvertence, but not the daughter's revenge.

Aware of Molly's four o'clock assignation with Boylan, Bloom sporadically considers possible ways of getting to Mullingar to see Milly, countered by the recurrent image of a "young student," the possible solution for both Bloom and Milly. But at one point, thoughts of Milly and of suicide are linked: "Looking down he saw flapping strongly, wheeling between the gaunt quaywalls, gulls. Rough weather outside. If I threw myself down?" And shortly after: "He threw down among them a crumpled paper ball. . . . Also the day I threw that stale cake out of the Erin's King" (U, 8.51–60).

The stale cake, as symbolic as the wedding cake in *Great Expectations*, reflects the futile, abortive quality of Bloom's relationship with his daughter who "wouldn't eat her cakes or speak or look" (U, 4.423). The food of love is stale and only fit to be thrown to the gulls:

> She kissed me. Never again. My youth. Only once it comes. Or hers. Take the train there tomorrow. No. Returning not the same. . . . The new I want. Nothing new under the sun. . . . Are you not happy in your? Naughty darling. Curious she an only child, I an only child. So it returns. Think you're escaping and run into yourself. Longest way round is the shortest way home. (U, 13.1102–11)

Most of this musing seems to be about Milly, but Martha's letter has reminded Bloom that for several reasons he is not happy in his home.

The essential components of the incest theme, both in psychoanalytic literature and in the literary tradition, are in evidence in *Ulysses*: (1) the missing mother, (2) the father's attachment to the daughter, (3) banishment or exile (frequently involving a trip by water), and (4) the suitor as means of resolution. The mother in *Ulysses* is, of course, only qualitatively missing—as the mother of a possible son and as an unfaithful wife; she has been an important factor for Milly, however, until her departure. A careful textual reading suggests an interpretation of Bloom's bringing Stephen into his home and on his hopes that he will stay that differs from that of most critics who have emphasized the possibility of a relationship between Stephen and Molly, reinforced by Molly's fantasies. But Bloom is focused on Stephen as a potential suitor for Milly, deeming him "the best of that lot" (U, 15.640). Bloom's intended transfer of his daughter to this suitor was symbolized in his relinquishment of the cup Milly had given him on his twenty-seventh birthday: "Relinquishing his symposiarchal right to the moustache cup of imitation Crown Derby presented to him by his only daughter, Millicent (Milly), he substituted a cup identical with that of his guest" (*U*, 17.361–63). The transfer from father to suitor would have many benefits:

> What various advantages would or might have resulted from a prolongation of such an extemporisation?
> For the guest: security of domicile and seclusion of study. For the host: rejuvenation of intelligence, vicarious satisfaction. For the hostess: disintegration of obsession, acquisition of correct Italian pronunciation.
> Why might these several provisional contingencies between a guest and a hostess not necessarily preclude or be precluded by a *permanent eventuality of reconciliatory union between a schoolfellow and a jew's daughter*?
> Because the way to daughter led through mother, the way to mother through daughter. (*U*, 17.935–44, emphasis mine)

Bloom's "vicarious satisfaction" would come through Stephen's union with Milly, which would also eliminate Molly's "obsession" regarding Milly and her father. Bloom is thus envisioning the kind of quadrilateral reconciliation that concludes both *The Winter's Tale* and *Pericles*—the pairing of the nubile daughter with a suitor, and the concomitant reconciliation of the father with the mother. But the best laid plans of this modern day Odysseus go astray, since Stephen refuses to cooperate, and Bloom's "proposal of asylum" is "promptly, inexplicably, with amicability, gratefully . . . declined" (*U*, 17.955). Thus Bloom's plans for "vicarious satisfaction" in a Stephen/Milly relationship, and the "disintegration" of Molly's "obsession" are both brought to an abortive conclusion. The "spirit of reconciliation" that Stephen sees as the essence of Shakespeare's later plays is absent from *Ulysses*.

Lionel Trilling's observations on sin and evil in *Ulysses* are not without validity, but a validity that must be modified by a recognition that sin and guilt function in the novel in much the same way that they function in the consciousness of Leopold Bloom, an Everyman/Noman, who must find ways to live with his guilt. Notwithstanding Mark Shechner's contention that "despite the ubiquity of confession in *Ulysses* and Joyce's other books, that crime remains as mysterious as Earwicker's crime in Phoenix Park" (150), there is sufficient textual support in the novel, not only for fantasies of father/daughter incest, but for the actual occurrence as well. Over-whelmed by guilt, Bloom might well succumb to the temptation to jump into the Liffey. Stephen's "Agenbite of inwit: remorse of conscience" (*U*, 9.809–10) haunts Bloom also, and makes him an even more poignant character for us. Having "crossed bridge of Yessex" (*U*, 11.229), as in *Hamlet*, "il se promène, lisant au livre de lui-même" (*U*, 9.114).

In spite of the challenges that *Finnegans Wake* presents, the incest theme has been widely acknowledged by critics from the beginning.[23] The novel serves as an extended metaphor for the motif, since the riddle is the form in which incest is frequently presented. The novel's unique blurring of boundaries and merging of identities is ideally suited to the incest theme. Of the passages referring to incest, some echo Milly passages from *Ulysses*, some allude to Ibsen's *The Master Builder*, and some allude to the works of other authors, the ones focused on here being among them.

In a novel in which duplication of personality is the order of the day and it is difficult to say "Who is Who When Everybody is Somebody Else,"[24] the doubling aspect of mother and daughter is frequently reiterated: "Two dreamyums in one dromium? Yes and no error. And both as like as a duel of lentils? Peacisely" (*FW*, 89.3–4). Father/daughter incest is stated explicitly more than once:

> And, speaking anent Tiberias and other incestuish salacities among gerontophils, a word of warning about the tenderloined passion hinted at. . . . but we grisly old Sykos who have done our unsmiling bit on 'alices, when they were yung and easily freudened, in the penumbra of the procuring room and what oracular comepression we have had apply to them! could (did we care to sell our fee-bought silence *in camera*) tell our very moistnostrilled one that *father* in such virgated contexts is not always that undemonstrative relative (often held up to our contumacy) who settles our hashbill for us . . . and, finally, what a neurasthene nympholet, endocrine-pineal typus, of inverted parentage with a prepossessing drauma in her past and a priapic urge for congress with agnates before cognates fundamentally is feeling for under her lubricitous meiosis when she refers with liking to some feeler she fancie's face. And Mm. We could. Yet what need to say? '*Tis as human a little story as paper could well carry.* (*FW*, 115.11–36, emphasis mine)

In the context of Earwicker's family, "agnates before cognates" would be "father before brothers" for sister Issy, who is probably that same "deepseep daughter which was bourne up pridely out of medsdreams unclouthed when I was pillowing in my brime" (FW, 366.13–14). But this father also speaks out forthrightly against suitors: "*And no damn loutll come courting thee or by the mother of the Holy Ghost there'll be murder!*" (FW, 399.1,2). Words of warning are also scattered in this text regarding "courting in blankets, enfamillias" (FW, 395.15), since we are told: "Especially beware please of being at a party to any demoralizing home life. That saps a chap. Keep cool faith in the firm, have warm hoep in the house and begin frem athome to be chary of charity" (FW, 433.36; 434.1–3). Joyce is leery of the proverbial "charity that begins at home."

The tension between the father's repressed desire and his anger over the daughter's suitors is reinforced when he says: "I'd be tempted rigidly to become a passionate father" (FW, 457.6–7), the injunction to the daughter being graphic: "The pleasures of love lasts but a fleeting but the pledges of life outlusts a lieftime. I'll have it in for you. I'll teach you bed minners, tip for tap, to be playing your oddaughter tangotricks with micky dazzlers if I find corsehairs on your river-frock and the squirmside of your burberry luptially covered with chiffchaff and shavings. . . . Cutting chapel, were you? and had dates with slickers in particular hotels, had we? Lonely went to play your mother, isod? You was wiffriends? Hay dot's a doll yarn!" (FW, 444.24–35). But incest in *Finnegans Wake* is sometimes a total family affair, since "she is dadad's lottiest daughterpearl and brooder's cissiest auntybride" (FW, 561.15–16), incorporating the reference to Lot and his daughters.

Many of the incest passages are strong echoes of Milly-passages in *Ulysses:* "in her ensemble of maidenna blue, with an overdress of net, tickled with goldies, Isolamisola" (FW, 384.30–31). The *Ulysses* allusions to sleepwalking are also repeated in *Finnegans Wake* as assurances are given to the young girl that she had not been disturbed by her father: "You were dreamend, dear. The pawdrag? The fawthrig? Shoe! Hear are no phanthares in the room at all, avikkeen. No bad bold faathern, dear one. Opop opop capallo, muy malinchily malchick!" (FW, 565.18–21). One of the most lyrical passages combines Milly echoes with "Bridie Kelly" allusions:

> Madame Isa Veuve La Belle, so sad but lucksome in her boyblue's long black with orange blossoming weeper's veil, for she was the only girl they loved, as she is the queenly pearl you prize, because of the way *the night that first we met* she is bound to be, methinks, and not in vain, the darling of my heart, sleeping in her april cot, within her singachamber, with her greengageflavoured candy-

whistle duetted to the crazyquilt, Isobel, she is so pretty, truth to
tell, wildwood's eyes and primarose hair, quietly, all the woods so
wild, in mauves of moss and daphnedews, how all so still she lay,
neath of the whitethorn, child of tree, like some losthappy leaf, like
blowing flower stilled, as fain would she anon, for soon again 'twill
be, win me, woo me, wed me, ah weary me! deeply, now evencalm
lay sleeping. (*FW*, 556.9–22, emphasis mine)

In *Ulysses*, we read: "He will never forget the name, ever remember the
night, first night, the bridenight" (*U*, 14.1068–69). The view of incest in
Finnegans Wake is a much more benign and lighthearted one than is true
in the earlier novel.

Possibly the most important incest references revolve around Issy, the
niece of Earwicker, and the riddle of the Prankquean. The pattern of
threes, suggested in *Ulysses* by "once by inadvertence, twice by design," is
taken up in a riddle:

[A]nd everybilly lived alove with everybiddy else, . . . And, be
dermot, who come to the keep of his inn only the niece-of-his-
in-law, the prankquean. . . . And spoke she to the dour in her petty
perusienne: Mark the Wans, why do I am alook alike a poss of
porterpease? And that was how the skirtmisshes began. (*FW*,
21.9–19)
And she made her witter before the wicked, saying: Mark the Twy,
why do I am alook alike two poss of porterpease? (*FW*, 22.4–6)
And the prankquean picked a blank and lit out and the valleys
lay twinkling. And she made her wittest in front of the arkway of
trihump, asking: Mark the Tris, why do I am alook alike three poss
of porter pease? But that was how the skirtmishes endupped. (*FW*,
22:26–30)

Although there is little critical agreement on the full import of these passages, I would venture to tie them to the three occurrences of incest in
Ulysses, a case of "trihump." I would also read the three "Mark" references
as relevant not only to Tristan, but to Mark Twain. It is the trihumping,
the three actual occurrences of incest that are being "marked" here as
Twain marked the depths of the river from the boat. The "skirtmishes" —
a skirmish with a skirt—begin and end within three specifically delineated times: Wan, Twy, and Tris.[25]

The daughter/nieces in *Finnegans Wake* continue to blend with Milly:
"with the gust of a spring alice the fossickers and swaggelers with him on
the hoof from down under piked forth desert roses in *that mullingar scrub*"

(*FW*, 321.31–33, emphasis mine). Also incorporated in *Finnegans Wake* are the hints of disguise, so prominent in *Ulysses:* "Fairhair, frail one. Listen, meme sweety! . . . My veil will save it undyeing from his ethernal fire! It's meemly us two, meme idoll. Of course it was downright verry wickred of him, reely meeting me disguised, Bortolo mio, peerfectly appealling" (*FW*, 527.21–26). McHugh identifies Bortolo as the "old man" in *The Barber of Seville*,[26] but in keeping with the theme of father/daughter incest in Joyce's final work, he is the older guardian with marriage designs on his beautiful young ward, ultimately thwarted by the suitor.[27]

The blurring of mother-niece-daughter is repeated a number of times: "when I would touch to her dot and feel most greenily of her unripe ones as it should prove most anniece and far too bahad, nieceless to say, to my reputation on Babbyl Malket for daughters-in-trade being lightly clad" (*FW*, 532.22–26). But the elements of guilt and trial so prominent in "Circe" are given a humorous cast by the language of *Finnegans Wake:* "whereas by reverendum they found him guilty of their and those imputations of fornicolopulation with two of his albowcrural correlations on whom he was said to have enjoyed by anticipation when schooling them in amown, mid grass, she sat, when man was, amazingly frank, for their first conjugation" (*FW*, 557.15–20).

Joyce owned many literary works involving the incest theme, most of them mentioned by Rank, including George Bernard Shaw's *Misalliance*, Oscar Wilde's *Salome*, Percy Bysshe Shelley's *The Cenci*, and *Vor Sonnenaufgang* (Before Sunrise) and *Hanneles Himmelfahrt* (Hannele, A Dream Poem) by Hauptmann. Not surprisingly, Joyce owned most of Ibsen's plays, including two copies of *Bygmester Solness*, one a German translation. Especially relevant to my focus here is the fact that his own library resources included most of Shakespeare's plays, several Dickens novels including *Bleak House*, a number of Conrad's works including *Chance*, and three Henry James works, but evidently not *The Golden Bowl*. As I noted in chapter 1, the *Wake* includes many oblique references to the works of these writers.

One of the most pervasive literary analogs for *Finnegans Wake* in terms of the father/daughter theme is Ibsen's *The Master Builder*. As Glasheen points out, the family configurations are similar, with both the Solness and the Earwicker (Porter) families having twin boys. However, in the Ibsen play, the twins have died in infancy. There are two daughter-surrogates in Ibsen, one of whom is Kaja, Solness's niece. The second daughter-figure is Hilde Wangel with whom Solness has had an ambiguous relationship ten years prior to the time of the play. The end of the play can be read as sexual metaphor, since Mrs. Solness, seeing that her husband has climbed the tower, cries out, "I must make him come down."[28] But he has climbed at the instigation of the young girl and then falls to his death, perversely cheered on by young Hilde.

In the *Wake*, the sexual implications of the master builder's fear of heights are clear: "Begetting a wife which begame his niece by pouring her youngthings into skintighs. That was when he had dizzy spells" (*FW*, 373.26–27). Joyce acknowledges the self-destructive aspect of Solness's confrontation with sexual experience in the person of the daughter-surrogate, Hilde Wangel: "And people thinks you missed the scaffold. Of fell design. I'll close me eyes. So not to see. . . . All men has done something" (*FW*, 621.28–32).

Again, Joyce comments on what happens in the Ibsen drama: "Amid the soleness. Tilltop, bigmaster! Scale the summit! You're not so giddy any more. All your graundplotting and the little it brought!" (*FW*, 624.10–13). In spite of his "graundplotting" with Hilde, and his dreams of a renewal through her, the play ends in defeat. Joyce's awareness of the sexual metaphor in the final climb to the tower is also indicated: "Such was a bitte too thikke for the Muster of the hoose so as he called down on the Grand Precurser who coiled him a crawler of the dupest dye and thundered at him to flatch down off that erection and be aslimed of himself for the bellance of hissch leif" (*FW*, 506.4–8).

The works of artists dealt with here in earlier chapters are often referred to in *Finnegans Wake*, *King Lear* being one of the most common: "Now listen, Mr. Leer!" (*FW*, 65.4); "old Luke with his kingly leer"(*FW*, 398.22–23); and "But on what do you again leer? I am not leering, I pink your pardons. I am highly sheshe sherious" (*FW*, 570.24–25). Correspondences with *Henry VIII* will be examined in the final chapter.

Although *Bleak House* is mentioned elsewhere in the *Wake*, to me the most pertinent allusion to this novel does not include the title, but does correspond to my reading of Jarndyce:

> Let us wherefore, tearing ages, presently preposterose a snatchvote of thanksalot to the huskiest coaxing, experimenter that ever gave his best hand into *chancerisk*, wishing him with his famblings no end of slow poison and a mighty broad venue for themselves between the devil's punchbowl and the deep angleseaboard, that they may gratefully turn a deaf ear clooshed upon the desperanto of *willynully*, their *shareholders from Taaffe to Auliffe*, that will curse them below par and *mar with their descendants, shame, humbug*

and profit, to greenmould upon mildew over *jaundice* as long as ever there's wagtail surtaxed to a testcase on enver a man. (*FW*, 582.2–12, emphasis mine)

"Shame, humbug and profit" have a true Dickensian ring, and the passage combines the risks in chancery with the many legal and financial implications, concluding with jaundice/Jarndyce.

Although Bernard Benstock and others have discussed the many "Maggie" references in *Finnegans Wake* (34), he fails to include Henry James's Maggie Verver as a possibility for "The Mime of Mick, Nick and the Maggies" (*FW*, 219.19). Mick and Nick would be Adam Verver and the Prince, and the two Maggies, Maggie and Charlotte. The intricate syntax in *The Golden Bowl* prefigures Joyce's own innovations in the latter part of *Ulysses* and to some extent in the final novel. Certainly my reading of *The Golden Bowl* would have appealed to Joyce, with the Porter family analogous to the pair in Portland Place:

> Tell me something. The Porters, so to speak, after their shadow-stealers in the newsbaggers, are very nice people, are they not? Very, all fourlike tellt. And on this wise, Mr Porter . . . is an excellent forefather and Mrs Porter (leading lady, a poopahead, gaffney-saffron nightdress, iszoppy chapelure) is a most kindhearted messmother. A so united family pateramater is not more existing on papel or off of it. As keymaster fits the lock it weds so this bally builder to his streamline secret. *They care for nothing except everything that is allporterous. Porto da Brozzo!* Isn't that terribly nice of them? You can ken that they come of a rarely old family by their costumance. . . . *I think I begin to divine so much.* (*FW*, 560.22–35, emphasis mine)

The end of the passage here suggests Joyce's own thoughts as he had read about the Ververs. *Porto da Brozzo*, with its reference to an Italian village (McHugh, 560.31–32) suggests the Prince's origins and he does come "of a rarely old family." The key/lock image (with James as the keymaster), recalls the description of the Prince's marriage, reinforced by the "papel" reference. But the text yields a number of other allusions which suggest the "funny" foursome of James's novel, one with specific reference to Grandfather Verver and his having both his daughter and her double, his wife—two Maggies:

> [O]ld grum has his gel number two (bravevow, our Grum!) and he would like to canoodle her too some part of the time for he is

downright fond of his number one but O he's fair mashed on
peaches number two so that if he could only canoodle the two,
chivee chivoo, all three would feel genuinely happy, it's as simple
as A.B.C., the two mixers, we mean, with their cherrybum chappy
(for he is simply shamming dippy) if they all were afloat in a
dreamlifeboat, hugging two by two in his zoo-doo-you-doo, a toff-
toff for thee, missy-missy for me. (*FW*, 65.23–31)

This passage also picks up on boat imagery in *The Golden Bowl* as it
describes the idyllic possibilities of the Ververs' isolated life together: "[I]t
was wonderfully like their having got together in some boat and paddled
off from the shore where husbands and wives, luxuriant complications,
made the air too tropical" (468). A further *Golden Bowl* allusion incorpo-
rates the foursome and a reference to James himself:

The quobus quartet were there too, if I mistake not, . . . in an
amenessy meeting, metandmorefussed to decide whereagainwhen to
meet themselves, flopsome and jerksome, . . . and *mastersinging* always
with that consecutive fifth of theirs, eh? Like four wise elephants
inandouting under a twelve-podestalled table? (*FW*, 513.29–36)

There has been a sort of amnesty meeting before the couples part and they
do not know "whereagainwhen to meet themselves." The consecutive
fifth would seem to be the Principino, and the "twelve-podestalled table"
suggests James's intricate time-sequence, delineated month by month.
    There is also textual evidence for relating the much-discussed letter
uncovered by the hen as one sent from Adam Verver to Maggie. Belinda
"a more than quinquegintarian," suggests Fanny Assingham, who loves to
dig things up. It was sent from "Boston (Mass.) of the last of the first to
Dear . . . Maggy." Adam Verver was the first and we have already learned
he will be the last Adam Verver. The "hate turned mild" refers to the
dissipation of Charlotte's initial anger as she is separated from the Prince
and returned to exile in America. The "funferall of poor Father Michael"
perhaps refers to Father Mitchell who presided over a luncheon at Fawns
prior to the breakup of the quartet.
    The farthest one might carry this lies with the closing of the letter: "&
Muggy well how are you Maggy and hopes soon to hear well & must now
close it *with fondest to the twoinns*." Has Maggie borne twins who have
two different fathers: the Prince and Adam? This actually occurs on rare
occasions when two impregnations are close in time. Perhaps this was
Joyce's own little humorous postscript chiding James for his obfuscation

in this novel: "(the *overcautelousness of the masterbilker* here, as usual, signing the page away)" (*FW*, 111.5–24). The Master has bilked the reader. But another passage, applied by some to the *Wake* itself also describes the reader's experience of James's novel: "sentenced to be nuzzled over a full trillion times for ever and a night till his noddle sink or swim by that ideal reader suffering from an ideal insomnia: all those red raddled obeli cayennepeppercast over the text, calling unnecessary attention to errors, omissions, repetitions and misalignments" (*FW*, 120.14–16).

Although Joyce's Trieste library contained six of Conrad's books, he is rarely cited as one of Joyce's sources.[29] In the *Wake*, several references seem quite specific. Nina's confrontation of her father with the gun is suggested: "she been goin shoother off almaynoother onawares" (*FW*, 371.26). Captain Walley of "The End of the Tether" appears as "Jonah Walley" (*FW*, 536.32–33), and Flora's first suitor as "Charley Chance" (*FW*, 65.16), also a reference to Marlow. The reference to Powell's escape from the doomed ship combines the key incident in *Lord Jim* with one regarding *Chance*: "And a good jump, Powell! Clean over all their heads. We could kiss him for that one, couddled we, Huggins?" (*FW*, 376.21–23).

Finnegans Wake is of signal importance in relation to the father/daughter incest theme for two reasons which bring into focus the essential difference between Joyce and all of his predecessors except for Shakespeare's *Henry VIII* in final resolution. The difference lies in the shift in emphasis from the father and daughter into the consciousness of the mother, first employed in Molly's soliloquy at the conclusion of *Ulysses*. But Molly differs from Anna Livia, Molly being closer to the myriad mothers of Dickens especially, who have rejected their husbands for one reason or another, throwing them unwittingly upon the daughter for companionship.

Molly ponders the Bloom/Milly relationship as she identifies Milly with her own earlier self, and Molly is well aware of the possibilities of being usurped by her daughter but is not ready to relinquish: "I noticed he was always talking to her lately at the table explaining things in the paper and she pretending to understand sly of course that comes from his side of the house . . . and helping her into her coat. . . . I suppose he thinks Im finished out and laid on the shelf well Im not no nor anything like it" (*U*, 18.1017–23). Unlike her later counterpart, Anna Livia, Molly intends to stave off Milly's usurpation: "wanting to put her hair up at 15 my powder too only ruin her skin on her shes time enough for that all her life after of course shes restless knowing shes pretty with her lips so red a pity they wont stay that way

I was too but theres no use going to the fair with the thing answering me like a fishwoman" (*U*, 18.1063–67).

Molly is glad that Milly has been sent away because of Boylan, who can thus be seen as a displacement in the oedipal configuration: "I couldnt turn round with her in the place lately unless I bolted the door first gave me the fidgets coming in without knocking first" (*U*, 18.1009–11). The lack of communication between the Blooms is pointed up by the discrepancy between views of Leopold's attempt to persuade Stephen to remain in the Bloom household, since Molly views him as a possible lover for herself, while Bloom is planning on a "union between a schoolfellow and a jew's daughter" (*U*, 17.941–42). Both possibilities are negated by Stephen's refusal of asylum.

If, as Homer Brown has maintained, the Joyce corpus is the biography of the novel itself, then Joyce's treatment of the father/daughter theme is a condensation and compression of the "revolution" of the theme into a very few works. In "Eveline," the father retains the daughter; in "The Dead," the father-surrogate has never really possessed the daughter, who is still fixated on an earlier suitor; in *Ulysses*, the father first possesses the daughter and then tries to relinquish her to his choice of one of a group of possible suitors. In *Finnegans Wake*, with its cyclical form, Anna Livia leaves her father for the suitor, but returns to her father at the end of the novel, after renouncing Earwicker to the daughter. The *Wake* not only attempts to encompass all of human history; it also encompasses all possibilities in family relationships, based on a cyclic pattern in which "everybilly lived alove with everybiddy else" (*FW*, 21.9).

Abnegation is Adaptation.
James Joyce, *Finnegans Wake*

7

Incest and Death

It is very tempting to impose an order on the oeuvres of the artists here being considered and simply conclude that each one of them, as the culmination of his various treatments of the father/daughter theme, toward the end of his career wrote a "Tempest," distinguished by the autonomous renunciation of the daughter by the father to a suitor. But honesty prevents such pat conclusions. Shakespeare contributed to the writing of a final work, *Henry VIII* (1613), which serves as the historical paradigm for the cyclical abandonment of the mother in favor of a daughter—frequently involving for this particular king, the physical destruction of the mother. In *Finnegans Wake* (1939), Joyce too completed a final work in which the mother relinquished the father to the daughter, as she returned to her own father.

Dickens, James, and Conrad, on the other hand, all left unfinished novels that offer ample evidence that the theme was still very much with them. All of these examples would seem to extend Ella Freeman Sharpe's contention regarding Shakespeare to the other writers: *"The Tempest shows this poet's way of attaining a solution of, or respite from, inner conflict. It is a psychical solution achieved by many personalities of the manic-depressive type to which what we call 'genius' often belongs. A 'solution' of conflict is reached again during longer or shorter intervals with infinite degrees of stress, for it is a 'revolutionary' solution, not 'resolution' of conflict through further psychical evolution"* (215). Although the "manic-depressive" judgment remains problematic, a cursory examination of the father/daughter theme in the unfinished, post-"Tempest" works of these authors will serve to support Sharpe's thesis of "revolution" rather than of resolution. Rank augments this view in his comments on fragments:

> In fact, they [fragments] prove even more useful than outlines, since they clearly demonstrate which problems led to the cessation of the artistic process of sublimation. . . . In this case erotic fantasy life emerges so strongly that the repressive tendency necessary to hold it within bounds actually brings the whole stream of creativity to a standstill. (56)

Henry James's preoccupation in his 1907 essay on *The Tempest* is with Shakespeare's ostensible decision to cease writing:

> [O]ur poor point, for which *The Tempest* once more gives occasion, strikes me as still, as always, in its desperate way, worth the making. How did the faculty so radiant there contrive, in such perfection, the arrest of its divine flight? By what inscrutable process was the extinguisher applied and, when once applied, kept in its place to the end? *What became of the checked torrent*, as a latent, bewildered presence and energy, in the life across which the dam was constructed?[1] (emphasis mine)

James's intense reaction to Shakespeare's determination to cease writing is further amplified by his conclusion that "our hero may have died — since he did so soon — of his unnatural effort" (310). Why James chose to ignore *Henry VIII*, I have not determined. Although there has always been some critical controversy over how much of that play can be attributed to Shakespeare himself, there has been little doubt that he at least shared in the writing — most probably with Fletcher. It was produced at various times in London during Henry James's period in England, first in 1855 (when it had the longest run of any play up to that time), in 1859, and again in 1892. The play itself, as either contemporaneous with or just subsequent to *The Tempest* seems tailor-made to fit Sharpe's theories. By utilizing historical material, Shakespeare could deal with the recurrently threatening theme while at the same time putting it at a distance since the materials for the drama already lay to hand in Holinshed's *Chronicles* (1587) and other sources. His collaboration with another playwright would also have served that purpose.

The inclusion in *Henry VIII* of the renunciation by the mother, Katherine, can also be seen as a forerunner of that element in James Joyce's *Finnegans Wake*. The Prologue to the play begins: "I come no more to make you laugh,"[2] itself a signal of the cyclical movement in the plays, and the artist's own awareness of it. Anne Bullen is a daughter-surrogate, both by virtue of being "Sir Thomas Bullen's daughter," and Katherine's lady-in-waiting, "one of her Highness' women." Henry's immediate attraction to her is made clear: "By heaven, she is a dainty one. Sweetheart, / I were unmannerly to take you out, / And not to kiss you" (1.4.92–96).

The surrounding court is not deceived by Henry's scruples regarding the twenty-year marriage to Katherine, who had been married to his brother for five months before her husband had died:

LORD CHAMBERLAIN: It seems the marriage with his brother's wife
Has crept too near his conscience.
DUKE OF SUFFOLK: [aside] No, his conscience
Has crept too near another lady. (2.2.16–19)

Certainly one aspect of the theme that may have proved compellingly attractive for Shakespeare was the fact that not only was the mother not "missing," she was such a "good" mother that even Anne Bullen bemoans her dismissal: "after this process, / To give her the avaunt, it is a pity / Would move a monster!" (2.3.9–11). But Henry never argues the exemplary qualities of his wife, only arguing in his own defense: "for her male issue / Or died where they were made or shortly after / This world had air'd them. Hence I took a thought / This was a judgment on me, that my kingdom / (Well worthy the best heir o' th' world) should not / Be gladded in't by me" (2.4.189–94). Henry argues that his marriage to his brother's widow constituted incest and that was the reason for the judgment which resulted in no male children. Katherine herself declares that she no longer serves as the King's sexual partner: "Alas, 'has banish'd me his bed already, / His love, too long ago. I am old my lords, / And all the fellowship I hold now with him / Is only my obedience" (3.1.119–22). The displacement from mother to daughter is summed up by Wolsey: "The late queen's gentlewoman? a knight's daughter, / To be her mistress' mistress? The queen's queen?" (3.2.94–95).

Shakespeare altered historical fact in arranging that Katherine had died before the birth of Anne's child—ironically enough another girl, Elizabeth. To complete the cycle, Katherine commends her own daughter to Henry's care before she dies: "In which I have commended to his goodness / The model of our chaste loves, his young daughter / . . . and a little / To love her for her mother's sake, that lov'd him, / Heaven knows how dearly" (4.2.131–38).

Shakespeare's Epilogue to this play is deeply ironic:

> I fear,
> All the expected good w'are like to hear
> For this play at this time, is only in
> The merciful construction of good women,
> For such a one we show'd 'em: if they smile,
> And say 'twill do, I know within a while
> All the best men are ours; for 'tis ill hap
> If they hold, when their ladies bid 'em clap. (7–14)

A definite strain of antifeminism can be detected in these final lines, and their correspondence to the substance of the play itself offers fertile ground for speculation. Henry's desire for a son is undercut by the fact that he never indicates his displeasure over the birth of another daughter. When he decided to abandon Anne Boleyn, he accused her of incest with her brother.

Of the three novelists who left unfinished works, Charles Dickens's *The Mystery of Edwin Drood* has proved most tantalizing to critics and readers alike. Conclusions to the novel are published from time to time, and at least two films have been made.[3] The treatment of the father/daughter/ suitor triad is partially disguised in this novel through the extensive use of surrogates. But dead fathers exert the power that establishes the triangular situations. The fathers of Rosa and Edwin are dead but have stipulated that the two should marry. The father of Helena and her brother Neville is also dead and John Jasper has been appointed guardian for the two men. Although Jasper and Edwin function as father and suitor, they are really uncle and nephew and both focus their attentions on the orphaned Rosa, Edwin largely because that is the will of the fathers.

Again, the obfuscations in the relationship of surrogate father (Jasper) to the suitors (Edwin and Neville) has enabled Dickens to deal with an explosively threatening theme. As in other literary works embodying the incest theme, the elimination of the undesired member of the triangle involves death in *Drood,* the unsolved murder that is at the heart of the novel. Dickens, moving from his harmoniously resolved "Tempest," augmented by his explicitly renunciatory "George Silverman's Explanation," began a novel which was to deal with the father/daughter/suitor configuration in its most violent expression.

Although John Jasper is only twenty-six to Edwin's twenty, "he looks older than he is, as dark men often do."[4] Opium, to which this father figure is addicted, is notorious for accelerating the aging of its users. His role as Rosa's "music-master" establishes him in an authoritarian position, which he also holds with regard to his nephew. Rosa's anxiety toward Jasper's unwanted attentions reflects the menace he represents:

> He has made a slave of me with his looks. He has forced me to understand him, without his saying a word; and he has forced me to keep silence, without his uttering a threat. When I play, he never moves his eyes from my hands. When I sing, he never moves his eyes from my lips. When he corrects me, and strikes a note, or a chord, or plays a passage, he himself is in the sounds, whispering that he pursues me as a lover, and commanding me to keep his secret. I avoid his eyes, but he forces me to see them without looking at them. (70)

But when Rosa is asked by Helena Landless what this threat means, she replies: "I don't know. I have never even dared to think or wonder what it is" (71).

Jasper's plans for Edwin's murder and Neville's implication as perpetrator are premeditated and deliberate as he plies the two young men with spiked drinks to abet their hostility, and deliberately plants suspicion regarding Neville's role as murderer in the minds of the Crisparkles. Following the disappearance of Edwin, Jasper's confrontation with Rosa in the garden is suggestive of incipient rape, concluding with threats of blackmail geared toward the implication of Neville in the murder. Jasper's protestations of love are violent: "I love you, love you, love you! If you were to cast me off now—but you will not—you would never be rid of me. No one should come between us. I would pursue you to the death" (217). After fainting inside the house, Rosa flees for protection to her "good" father, Grewgious, who had been hopelessly in love with her mother years before; as she enters his room, he tells her: "My child, my child! I thought you were your mother!" (222).

But the father/daughter theme continues to be the salient one in the projected conclusion for the novel. Rosa, at one point described as "a dove in a high roost in a cage of lions," is protected by Grewgious "in the stoutness of his knight errantry" (229). Rosa is introduced to Mr. Tarter who "had been a sailor, roving everywhere for years and years" (234), and had many years before saved Crisparkle, his senior schoolmate (now thirty-five and unmarried), from drowning. As Tarter shows an interest in Rosa, the imagery becomes subtly phallic: "This a little confused Rosebud, and may account for her never afterwards quite knowing how she ascended (with his help) to his garden in the air, and seemed to get into a marvellous country that came into sudden bloom like the country on the summit of the magic beanstalk. May it flourish forever!" (235). The emergence of Mr. Tarter as a suitor is a compromise solution since he is not the young suitor Neville had been, and his age and life-experience place him as a modified father figure.

Although Dickens died before completing chapter 23, there is enough evidence in Forster's biography to strongly suggest the importance this novel had for him as a post-Tempest return to a work in which an obsessive father did not intend to renounce the daughter:

> The story, I learnt immediately afterward, was to be that of the murder of a nephew by his uncle; the originality of which was to consist in the review of the murderer's career by himself at the close, *when its temptations were to be dwelt upon as if, not he the culprit, but some other man, were the tempted.* The last chapters were to be written in the condemned cell, to which his wickedness, all elaborately elicited from him *as if told of another,* had brought him. . . . all discovery of the murderer was to be baffled till towards the close. . . . Rosa was to marry Tarter, and Crisparkle the sister of Landless, who was himself, I think, to have perished in assisting Tarter finally to unmask and seize the murderer.[5] (emphasis mine)

This revelation to Forster yields two highly significant implications which go to the very heart of the artistic function itself—the distancing of threatening material which is lodged within the play or the novel and told as if "some other man were the tempted." In this unfinished work by Dickens, although the two young suitors had been attracted to the two young heroines (Edwin/Helena; Neville/Rosa), both these young suitors are destroyed, and the girls are married to men placed by age somewhere between young suitors and true father figures.

But even more important from the psychoanalytic viewpoint is the possible identification of the artist, Dickens, with the artist, Jasper, at the end of the novel as it was projected to Forster. Are we not reading a "review" of the murderer/artist's "career by himself at the close" in which his "wickedness" is "all elaborately elicited from him as if told of another?" Isn't this the artist's delineation of the artistic process? As Shakespeare returned to that "other man," Henry VIII, and dramatized his initial elimination of the mother, followed by his marriage to the daughter, so too did Dickens/ Jasper murder the two young suitors and confer the daughters on surrogate fathers, concluding with Jasper's disclaimer that it had been "told of another." The author of one of the 1980 completions carries this further, relating the fiction to Dickens's liaison with Ellen Ternan: "Jasper represents Dickens himself. At times the affair with a girl so much younger must have appalled Dickens, who had conventional moral views" (Kanfer, 100–101).

Dickens died at a point in the narrative at which it seems that certain characters are beginning to close in on the guilty father figure, Jasper. He died several days after spending time with his two older daughters, Mary and Katey, the former having refused a loved suitor because of her father's disapproval, and the latter having married a man she did not love in order to remove herself from her father's house. After Katey and her new husband had departed following the wedding, Dickens was found sobbing into her wedding dress, reproaching himself for having driven her to marry a man she didn't love (Johnson, 961). He had spent all night talking with Katey a few days before his death, and although it was not his custom, he had worked all day on *Drood* the day before he died (Johnson, 1153).

Neither Henry James nor Joseph Conrad yields such dramatic material either biographically or in the content of their final works as did Charles Dickens. Also, identifying James's last unfinished novel is more problematic than for either of the other novelists, bringing to mind the ambiguous categorization of what constituted his first novel. He had begun *The Sense of the Past* in 1890 and abandoned it in 1900 with the judgment that it was "unworkable" (Lewis, 516). He began *The Ivory Tower* just before a 1910 illness to comply with a request from his publisher "to balance *The Golden Bowl*" (Edel, *Master,* 477). Later, his rationale for not finishing it and returning instead to *The Sense of the Past* was that the experience of World War I made the theme of *The Ivory Tower* seem irrelevant. Edel defined the theme as one "of Americans who inherit great wealth only to have it stolen by other Americans" (Edel, *Master,* 501). James worked on *The Sense of the Past* up until the time he died in 1916, and the fragment published in 1917 included extensive notes outlining the plot through to the end. James had written these when he first began work on the novel.[6] Reminiscent of James's first two novels, the two incomplete novels show indications of contrasting modes of closure, thus meriting being read one against the other.

The Ivory Tower does not tantalize and engage the reader's speculation in the same way that *The Mystery of Edwin Drood* does; nevertheless, there is ample evidence that James was not abandoning the father/daughter theme. The novel deals with two suitors, Graham Fielder and Horton (Haughty) Vint and two daughters, Cissy and Rosanna. Those inclined to Freudian interpretations of names would be struck by the fact that Graham was originally to be called "Rising," and Horton, "Crimper."[7]

The novel opens with all mothers missing and the deaths of two fathers imminent. One is Mr. Betterman, Gray's uncle; the second is Rosanna Gaw's father, who has lived for a long time with his attachment for his inordinately heavy daughter as his only human connection: "Here was a parent who clearly appealed to nobody in the world but his child, and a child who condescended to nobody in the world but her parent" (16).

The ivory tower serves as the repository for an unopened letter written to Gray by Rosanna's father just prior to his death, his "very last lines" (144). Gray's decision to hide the unread letter gives its subjects a sense of release: "With this question at rest it seemed at once, and as with an effect out of proportion to the cause, that a great space before them had been cleared: they looked at each other over it as if they had become more intimate, and as if now, in the free air, the enormities already named loomed up again" (150). The mystery of the contents of the letter remains unanswered since James did not indicate in his notes for the novel what the letter contained; he failed in fact to mention the ivory tower at all.

The usual Jamesian complexities are involved in the relationships of the foursome, Gray, Rosanna, Cissy, and Horton, all of whom have histories of past connections with each other. Cissy had been strongly attached to the older Mr. Northover, a former suitor of Gray's mother. She explains her father-fixation to Horton, which she feels will forever prevent her forming a viable relationship with one of the younger suitors, even though Northover has died.

> Don't you know I fell so in love with Mr. Northover . . . that I've kept true to him forever, and haven't been really in love with you in the least, and shall never be with Gray himself, however much I may want to, or you perhaps may even try to make me?—any more than I shall ever be with anyone else. (164)

Haughty Horton, frustrated by Cissy's fixation on a ghost of "sexagenarian charms" (166), feels helpless in his "comparison with the memory of a rococo Briton he had no arms to combat" (167). Gray's musing about his former stepfather's infatuation for the young Cissy defines the father-surrogate as having maintained a safe distance:

> It wasn't, either, as if this blest associate had been by constitution an elderly flirt, or some such sorry type, addicted to vain philanderings with young persons he might have fathered: he liked young persons, small blame to him, but they had never, under Gray's observation, made a fool of him, and he was only as much of one about the young lady in question, Cecilia Foy . . . as served to keep all later inquiry and pleasantry at the proper satiric pitch. (261)

In the notes for this novel, James referred to Cissy both as "My Girl" (271), and as "my Heroine" (274), an interesting contrast to his references to Maggie Verver as "our young woman" (486). With all fathers removed by death, the young suitors and the daughters remain, with Cissy's fixation, the inherited money, and the unread letter as unresolved elements. Dead fathers dominate the action, reinforcing the importance of the oedipal configurations in *The Ivory Tower*. If James planned to retain the daughters under fatherly control, it would be the ghostly control that the dead often exert over the living.

But *The Ivory Tower*, with its Newport setting and its emphasis on material considerations, was supplanted by James with his attempt to finish *The Sense of the Past*. The completed fragment breaks both with his own narrative traditions and with those of his peers. Critics have agreed on the complexities of the project: "Its subject had always been difficult" (Edel, *Master*, 539) and "[H]ow could he ever have exhausted a theme so essentially complicated as that of *The Sense of the Past*?" (Squire, Prefatory Note, in *Sense*, v). How indeed?

Reading the notes has aspects of reading a case history or listening to a stream-of-consciousness narrative with infinite ambiguities. Although a thorough psychoanalytic reading is not feasible here, the finished fragment has several characteristics not present in the main body of James's work: (1) a compression of the action akin to that occurring in dreams, (2) an openness and immediacy in relations between the sexes, and (3) a frankness approaching crassness about the function of money in motivating the characters.

James had declared in the notes that he would employ "enormous foreshortening, great compression and presentation of picture." He had planned a six-month span for the entire action of the novel and envisioned the work as incorporating elements of what he dubbed "the 'Screw'."[8] The central configuration of characters is highly reminiscent of *The American*. Ralph Pendrel, a wealthy American travels to England where he encounters a family in which the father is dead and a mother and brother are in control of two daughters. The oedipal configurations are filled out by the American ambassador consulted by Ralph shortly after his arrival in England; by the brother, Perry, who has explicitly replaced his dead father in relation to his sisters; and by Sir Cantopher, an Englishman of wealth and standing who has unsuccessfully courted both daughters and is referred to as the "H.W. [Horace Walpole] man" in the notes.[9] Ralph and the older daughter are in their thirties in contrast to the younger daughter, Nan, "a Cinderella" (312). The contrast between "elder" and "younger" sister is often reiterated and Molly is identified with her mother on more than one occasion.

Ralph Pendrel had been rejected as suitor for the American, Aurora, and traveled to England to take possession of a house he has inherited from an English relative impressed with a historical book he has published. Shortly after entering his newly acquired house on a second visit, he meets and immediately becomes engaged to Molly, the elder sister in a family evidently desperately in need of his wealth. As in James's other unfinished work, dead fathers hover: Molly's father has left the family destitute and Ralph's father had written to Molly to sanction the relationship between her and his son.

The references to the family's prospective dependence on Ralph's wealth are blatant. When he asks the brother, Perry, "Do you mean you want money?" Perry replies, "Indeed I do, by God!" (269). Ralph then indicates that an unlimited amount is available and as he takes some out of his pocket, Nan enters and her brother tells her that she can be the first to take some.

The plot is made more intricate by an elaborate time-scheme in which Ralph is living in 1910 and the English family in 1820, by the existence of a double for Ralph from the earlier period, and by certain occult occurrences. The intricacies of such a plot can well serve to mask basic psychological dynamics. The compression is evident in the fact that Ralph's first encounter with the family, his physical approach to Molly along with his declaration of love and their engagement, his conversations with the family and Sir Cantopher followed by his subsequent encounter with Nan all occur during a single morning. There is minimal background description or action.

The third-person narrative adheres solely to Ralph's point of view and consists mainly of conversations and Ralph's assessment of the other characters' reactions. Ralph's encounter with Nan takes place at the end of the completed fragment and initiates their instant ability to communicate in ways that have been unavailable to him with the others. But the narrative depicting their falling in love and Nan's renunciation of him so that he can return into his own time-period are only spelled out in the notes. The projected dénouement also entails the arrival of Aurora from America to reclaim him.

But the puzzle remains ultimately insoluble. There is sufficient evidence between the existing text and the notes to suggest that James was going to depart from what seemed to be undefeated fatherly control in *The Ivory Tower* and revert to the renunciation by the daughter of a suitor who is really a father-surrogate in a relationship similar to that between Adam Verver and Charlotte in *The Golden Bowl*. Molly breaks her engagement and Nan views Ralph as one who will side with her against her family's efforts to get her to accept Cantopher, "a person she can't get over her dislike of" (303). Much of the late action was to be precipitated by "*the particular thing taking, or having taken place*" (315, emphasis James's). But ultimately, the notes explain that Nan's understanding of Ralph's predicament will force her to "bring the whole situation to the point of its dénouement" (325); James explains: "I have grabbed for my solution in the line of her *making* the sacrifice" (335, emphasis James's). Since James's death intervened, one can only invoke, with regard to this novel, Freud's poignant words written in the midst of his lengthy analysis of his daughter Anna: "With all these insoluble conflicts, it is a good thing that life at some time comes to an end" (Gay, 441).

Joseph Conrad's final, unfinished novel did not diverge as radically from earlier work as did that of James. As had been true of *The Rover, Suspense: A Novel of Napoleonic Times* (1925) is set in the historical past of the French Revolution, but at the time of Napoleon's exile on Elba. Jean-Aubry reports that its untimely breaking-off was anticipated by its creator:

> I am going to set to work to deal with Napoleon's influence on the western Mediterranean: two volumes with notes, appendices and statistical tables. And this is to be a novel. I have an idea I shall never finish it. This notion is not unwelcome to me. There will always be idiots to say: he aimed so high that it killed him. A fine epitaph.[10]

As with the other unfinished novels, the father/daughter theme is apparent at several levels. The central daughter is Adèle d'Armand whose paternal parentage is questionable from the outset. Sir Charles Latham, father of the hero, Cosmo, had been deeply in love with Adèle's mother, and had avoided passing through Paris following the birth of the child. Eventually, due to the exigencies of the political situation, Adèle and her parents live for a period under Sir Charles's roof:

> From the depths of the Italian chimneypiece the firelight of blazing English logs would fall on Adèle d'Armand sitting quietly on a low stool near her mother's couch. Her fair hair, white complexion, and dark blue eyes contrasted strongly with the deeper color scheme of Henrietta Latham, whose locks were rich chestnut brown and whose eyes had a dark lustre full of intelligence rather than sentiment. Now and then the French child would turn her head to look at Sir Charles, for whom in her silent existence she had developed a filial affection.[11]

After the d'Armands' return to France and the subsequent announcement of Adèle's impending marriage to an older man, Count Helion Montevesso, Sir Charles becomes deeply upset: "It had not been difficult for him to learn to love that fascinating French child as though she had been another daughter of his own. For a moment he experienced an anguish so acute that it made him move slightly in his chair" (36).

The center of action in the novel then shifts to Sir Charles's son, Cosmo, and his impending meeting with Adèle in Italy. He is quite comfortable in this reunion until he watches "her lips move to form the words which quite frightened him. 'Did Sir Charles give you a message for me?'" Although the reply is negative, he tells her that when his father had heard of her marriage, he "could think of nothing for days but you" (88). Adèle at this point is twenty-six and has been married ten years to Count Helion, a man "more than twice her age" (113).

Another daughter-figure, Clelia, ostensibly Helion's niece, is also introduced—a primitive, erotic figure: "Her green flounced skirt was spread on each side of the seat. The bodice of her dress, which was black, was cut low, her bare arms were youthfully red and immature" (115), and the Count's antipathy for Cosmo is established early on. As he watches his departure, "all at once, his eyes started to roll about wildly as if looking for some object he could snatch up and throw down the stairs at Cosmo's head" (156). Conrad was not above a Dickensian name choice in "Helion."

While Cosmo promptly falls in love with Adèle, in spite of the fact that, as Guerard points out, he may in fact be her brother,[12] the young Clelia, in a scene with her "uncle," filled with erotic overtones, tells Helion that she wants Cosmo: "I want that young signor that came today to make eyes at my aunt." Helion's reply is "Impossible" (169), but Dr. Martel is not fooled: "It was not because of that little savage that that gloomy self-tormenting ass of a drill sergeant to an Indian prince wanted young Latham removed from Genoa. Oh, dear no. That wasn't it at all. It was much more serious" (186–87). He concludes that Cosmo's stay in Genoa would be better terminated. But we still do not have enough information at this point to judge whether Martel is correct in his appraisal. Perhaps Helion really wants both Adèle and Cosmo out of the way so that he can pursue the "little savage."

Helion as a father-substitute is spelled out graphically, since Adèle had married him in a spirit of "self-sacrifice," telling Cosmo that "the only genuine passion in my heart was filial love" (132). The platonic nature of their marriage is suggested by her childlessness (of which the Emperor once spoke to her), and her view of her marriage, which had made her feel as though she "had taken the veil" (135). Adèle reminds Cosmo of a portrait he had seen in the past, a woman "with her left breast pierced by a dagger" (195).

Although Dr. Martel reports Cosmo's subsequent disappearance to Adèle, the novel switches to Cosmo and his adventures in a boat in which an old man dies with a prophetic passage suggesting Conrad's misgivings regarding his own final place in the artistic galaxy:

> "We have thrown a bit of canvas over him. Yes, that is the old man whose last bit of work was to steer a boat, and strange to think perhaps it had been done for Italy."
> "Where is his star now?" said Cosmo after looking down in silence for a time.
> "Signore, it should be out," said Attilio with studied intonation. "But who will miss it out of the sky?" (274)

Again, with Conrad, we find the main components of the oedipal configuration in an unfinished work. Helion, the father-surrogate in possession of the daughter, seeks to do away with the threatening suitor, Cosmo. But Adèle has two other possible fathers: her legal one who lives in the palace with them, and Sir Charles who is also the suitor's father. If Cosmo's vision of the portrait is a foreshadowing, we can surmise the destruction of Adèle by Helion who would still retain another daughter, the savage Clelia, who has her designs on Cosmo, repeating the other triangular configuration. But, lacking the conclusion, we can only speculate. As a parallel to the chronology of James's unfinished works, the chronology of Conrad's handling of the theme is also an example of the dangers of oversimplification in attempting to establish a cyclic movement for any artist. Guerard says that "*Suspense* was conceived as early as 1907" (287), and Jean-Aubry gives us the details of the complex time sequence: "The whole summer long he grappled desperately with this book. The bad old days of *The Rescue* seemed to have come back. Shut up for hours at a time in his 'torture chamber,' he managed only a few pages of this book every day—and he was not pleased with those."[13] He switched at this point to a collection of short stories, one of which he elongated into *The Rover*. The message seems clear here: He was able to go ahead with the renunciatory "Tempest"-theme while leaving the other novel unfinished, only to return to grapple with it later, believing that he might never finish it and proving to be right.

The provocative question is then raised of the relationship between the theme of the unfinished works, the psychological difficulties they presented for the artists, and their intervening deaths. It was James's opinion that Shakespeare's decision to cease writing with *The Tempest* contributed to his death, and Prospero's speech at the end suggests this. A glance at the chronology of the other authors' final works will perhaps prove equally suggestive. Dickens's *Our Mutual Friend* (1865) was followed by "George Silverman's Explanation" (1868), and the incomplete *Mystery of Edwin Drood* in 1870, the year of his death. Henry James, having completed *The Golden Bowl* in 1904, abandoned *The Ivory Tower* in 1910, and returned to *The Sense of the Past* in 1914, when many changes were made in the original 1900 plans. He died in 1916, still determined to finish the novel. Joseph Conrad told Richard Curle of "six different lines of treatment which might be followed in *Suspense*" the day before his death in 1924.[14] All three novelists gave every indication of an ongoing determination to finish the current work; they were working against the clock and were aware of it.

James Joyce, alone of the novelists, did not leave us an unfinished work, although he did, at one point, arrange for a fellow-artist, James Stephens, to complete *Finnegans Wake* if he died before finishing it. However, when asked in 1940 whether he had plans for a new book, he said, "Yes, I think I'll write something very simple and very short" (Ellmann, *James Joyce*, 731). "Eveline" had been very simple and very short, and Clive Hart some time ago elucidated the interesting parallels between its conclusion and the conclusion of *Finnegans Wake*.[15] However, Hart fails to make the crucial distinction: Eveline is never able to transfer her affections to the young suitor and returns to her father's house in a state of fixated paralysis. Anna

Livia has lived a full life with Earwicker before her renunciation and return to Father/Sea. But there is also the possibility here that Anna's first
lover had been her own father and that the movement comes full circle.
Anna's final passages entail a blurring of the identities of her husband and
her father. Although she begins talking to her husband, there is a shift to
her father and, like Issy in the present, she has usurped her own mother in
the past.

Shakespeare and Joyce, in their final, completed works, *Henry VIII* and
Finnegans Wake, shift into the consciousness of the mother/wife, as she
renounces the father to the daughter. In the play, the shift is politically
masked, since Henry's new wife will now be "queen's queen" (3.2.94,95).
But Katherine seems to will her own death—she does not accept a subservient position for long:

> Remember me
> In all humility unto his highness:
> Say his long trouble now is passing
> Out of this world. Tell him in death I bless'd him,
> For so I will; mine eyes grow dim. Farewell
> My lord. (4.2.160–65)

In *Finnegans Wake*, in a poignant, lyrical passage, Anna Livia simultaneously renounces the father to the daughter and returns symbolically to
her own father, the sea:

> How you said how you'd give me the keys of me heart. And we'd
> be married till delth to uspart. And though dev do espart. O mine!
> Only, no, *now it's me who's got to give. As duv herself div*. Inn this
> linn. And can it be it's now fforvell? Illas! I wisht I had better
> glances to peer to you through this baylight's growing. But you're
> changing, acoolsha, you're changing from me, I can feel. Or is it
> me is? . . . Yes, you're changing, sonhusband, and you're turning,
> I can feel you, for a daughterwife from the hills again. Imlamaya.
> And she is coming. Swimming in my hindmoist. Diveltaking on
> me tail. Just a whisk brisk sly spry spink spank sprint of a thing
> theresomere, saultering. . . . I pity your oldself I was used to. Now
> a younger's there. Try not to part! Be happy, dear ones! . . . *And let
> her rain now if she likes*. Gently or strongly as she likes. Anyway
> let her rain for my time is come. I done me best when I was let.
> Thinking always if I go all goes. A hundred cares, a tithe of troubles

and is there one who understands me? (*FW*, 626.30–36; 627.1–15, emphasis mine)

Anna Livia's words, "I wisht I had better glances to peer to you through this baylight's growing" (*FW*, 626.33–35) echo Katherine's "mine eyes grow dim." And a pun on Katherine's "reign" becomes Anna's "let her rain" as she renounces to her daughter.

Are we listening to Anna Livia's final words as she too wills her death and walks into the sea to drown? As she relinquishes her husband to the daughter, the cycle is completed as she returns to her own father: "And it's old and old it's sad and old it's sad and weary I go back to you, my cold father, my cold mad father, my cold mad feary father . . . and I rush, my only, into your arms" (*FW*, 627.36; 628.1–4). Since the cyclic movement of this novel has been widely explicated, it should come as no surprise that Anna Livia perhaps once was the usurper of her own mother. As in *Ulysses*, three occurrences are mentioned: "And one time you'd rush upon me, darkly roaring, like a great black shadow with a sheeny stare to perce me rawly. And I'd frozen up and pray for thawe. *Three times in all*. I was the pet of everyone then. A princeable girl. And you were the pantymammy's Vulking Corsergoth" (*FW*, 626.23–28, emphasis mine). Earwicker himself was a duplicate of Anna Livia's father: "he was like to me fad" (*FW*, 626.10).

In a body of literature dealing with fathers and daughters who interact for the most part in the absence of mothers, *Henry VIII* and *Finnegans Wake* are strange but striking bedfellows. They also are representative of the evolution of the incest theme in literature as it relates to a cultural shift that seems to have taken place between Shakespeare and Joyce in man's concept of individuation. The incest taboo is, above all, an acknowledgment of individual differences, of the unique nature of each person. The movement in Joyce's work, which Homer Brown noted as paralleling the history of the novel itself (6), moves away from the individuation of *Dubliners*, *Portrait of the Artist*, and *Ulysses*, until in *Finnegans Wake*, there is a blurring of identities and obliteration of individual differences, with incest as a pervasive theme: "everybilly lived alove with everybiddy else" (*FW*, 21.9). Nietzsche, who saw individuation as the root of mankind's problems, linked its removal to the obliteration of incest-boundaries:

If we examine Oedipus, the solver of riddles and the liberator of his mother . . . we may conclude that wherever soothsaying and magical powers have broken the spell of present and future, the rigid law of individuation, the magic circle of nature, extreme unnaturalness—in this case incest—is the necessary antecedent.[16]

Although one might question whether Oedipus was the "liberator of his mother," incest serves well as the focal point both for the principle of individuation and for its denial. The choice of an incestuous love-object is at once an affirmation of the most restricted choice and a rejection of all limitations on such a choice.

An overview of the unceasing preoccupation of a variety of artists with relationships between fathers and daughters should tell us more about ourselves. This assumes an acceptance of the view of the artist as put forward by Freud and later elucidated by Lionel Trilling:

> Nothing is so characteristic of the artist as his power of shaping his work, of subjugating his raw material, however aberrant it be from what we call normality, to the consistency of nature. It would be impossible to deny that whatever disease or mutilation the artist may suffer is an element of his production which has its effect on every part of it, but disease and mutilation are available to us all— life provides them with prodigal generosity. What marks the artist is his power to shape the material of pain we all have.[17]

Working from the premise that the individual tends to repeat the oedipal pattern established in his original relationship to his parents, sometimes resulting in an "undoing" of that pattern, autonomous renunciation functions as a fantasy of total control—what is given up can never again be taken away. "Abnegation is adaptation" (FW, 306). But the fact that with the possible exception of Henry James, the final works of the artists seem to involve a possible return to possession of the original love-object suggests that the attempt to resolve a desire for union with a lost object can never be completely and finally accomplished. Leopold Bloom, contemplating his loss of Molly to Boylan, and his probable loss of control over Milly, attempts to resign himself:

> If he had smiled why would he have smiled?
> To reflect that each one who enters imagines himself to be the first to enter whereas he is always the last term of a preceding series even if the first term of a succeeding one, each imagining himself to be first, last, only and alone, whereas he is neither first nor last nor only nor alone in a series originating in and repeated to infinity. (U, 17.2126–31)

Bloom, who is only "an artist in his spare time" (*U*, 16.1448–49), has no control over this cycle; only Joyce the artist can control it through the artistic process. The microcosmic world of the one-to-one relationship serves as Joyce's paradigm of world history; the Viconian cycle functions at all levels of human experience: The "longest way round is the shortest way home" (*U*, 13.1110–11).

There are many factors to be considered in the analysis of the five authors here under consideration based on the family dynamics of each. Did their particular relationships with their parents have a direct effect on their compulsion to repeat many times over the triangular conflict in evidence in their works? How did the fact that a given artist did or did not have daughters of his own affect the cycle of resolution of the incest threat in the various works? Certain critics or analysts have focused on rivalries between brothers or between fathers and sons. However, in considering these specific artists, the most reliable psychobiographical inquiry must rely on the original oedipal triangle with the parents. All five artists did not have brothers, sisters, or daughters, but they all had mothers and fathers.

Rank's assessment of the function of the artists' fathers differs somewhat from the essays in Norman Holland's *Shakespeare's Personality*. Rank maintained: "In nearly all important writers, we have observed a noticeably uniform childhood development. . . . [which] results from the oppressive presence of a strict, stern father, whom the son opposes, and a gentle, tender, loving mother" (570). Holland points, however, to Shakespeare's early relationship with a failed father.[18] But this factor applies to Dickens, Conrad, and Joyce as well. Again, as in other instances, Henry James seems to stand apart, and due to a number of variables, his relationships throughout his life with the members of his family were the most stable.

About Shakespeare's relationship with his mother we know very little except that she was still alive throughout most of his productive life. Most critics view Anne Hathaway as a mother-figure for Shakespeare. Charles Dickens's relationship with his mother was deeply affected by her attitude when he was banished from home and sent to the blacking factory. Recalling that she had later urged his return to the factory, he indicated that he would never forgive her.

Although Leon Edel lamented the dearth of direct commentary by James regarding his mother, there is sufficient evidence to suggest a strong attachment on both sides. Mary James seems to have fit into the traditional concept of the devoted, self-effacing Victorian mother—"she listened to her husband with 'complete availability'." Edel reports that James wrote in his notebook just after her death, "she was the keystone of the arch" (Edel, *Untried*, 41). The family seems to have been a singularly open one in terms of permitting a wide latitude of expression, including a great deal of sibling antagonism which included making fun of their father: "We were delightedly derisive with her even about pride in our father." But there are hints of oedipal rivalry with the father in James's making it a point to embrace his mother "in his presence" (Edel, *Untried*, 50). Edel finally concludes that the mother's very real strength of character and his father's concomitant dependence on her led the son to see women as basically threatening. But one family friend, commenting at the time of her death on the shock to her children, said that it was true of "Harry especially who had a passionately childlike devotion to her" (Lewis, 336).

Joseph Conrad's unfortunate family situation abortively deprived him of his mother before he had much chance to come to terms with that relationship. Since it was his father's political activities that had propelled the family into Siberian exile when he was still a child, the father could thus have been viewed as being a direct cause of her early death. It is easy to believe that this was seen by him as a hostile act on the part of his father for the rest of his life. His father's obsessive mourning, to which his son was daily exposed, probably did little to mitigate that reality. Conrad's jealousy of his firstborn infant suggests a sense of himself as competing for a mother's attention. On a railroad trip with his wife and the infant Borys, he threw the child's clothes out of the train window. Later, when Borys finally informed his mother of his marriage that he had been keeping a secret, she refrained from telling his father for a period of time but considered herself the best person to "drop the bombshell" (Karl, 885). Conrad had only sons but following the birth of Borys, he wrote to Mrs. E. L. Sanderson "I don't mind owning I wished for a daughter. I can't help thinking she would have resembled me more and would have been perhaps easier to understand."[19]

James Joyce's relationship with his mother has probably received more critical attention than that of many other artists. Much of the information is gleaned from his letters, from material left by his brother Stanislaus, and from the reactions of Stephen Dedalus within the fiction. Joyce's letters home to his mother after his first arrival in Paris indicate great dependency and lack of understanding of how traumatic they must have been for the receiver, who was told of his inevitable health problems, of the trials of poverty, and of imminent starvation. Joyce returned from Paris to participate in the long vigil of his mother's last illness, some of the details of which were later documented in *Ulysses*. The behavior of his profligate father during the ordeal did nothing to soften the trauma of the experience. However, even a deathbed request could not induce Stephen/Joyce to feign religious compliance for his mother's peace of mind. The mother of Stephan Dedalus haunts him throughout the pages of *Ulysses*, and about Leopold Bloom's mother we are told almost nothing.

The question of the artists' daughters also raises important issues. Since Conrad and James were the only two out of the five writers without daughters, it is important to note any differences in their treatment of the resolution of the incest-threat. I have selected two general factors as meriting analysis: the variations in the portrayals of *actual* as opposed to *surrogate* fathers, and the relationship between the occurrence of *death* as a component of the narrative and the mode of resolution of the incest-threat.

In an Early Work:

Author		Fathers; "D"=Death
Shakespeare	*Midsummer Night's Dream:*	Actual
Dickens	*Pickwick Papers:*	Actual/surrogate
James	*Watch and Ward:*	Actual/surrogate/D
	Roderick Hudson:	Surrogates/D
Conrad	*Almayer's Folly:*	Actual/D
Joyce	"Eveline":	Actual

In a Middle Work:

Shakespeare	*King Lear:*	Actual/D
Dickens	*Bleak House:*	Surrogate/D
James	*Portrait of a Lady:*	Actual/surrogate
Conrad	*Chance:*	Actual/surrogate/D
Joyce	*Portrait Artist/as Young Man:*	Surrogates

In a Late Work:

Shakespeare	*The Tempest:*	Actual
Dickens	*Our Mutual Friend:*	Actual/surrogate
James	*The Golden Bowl:*	Actual/surrogate
Conrad	*The Rover:*	Surrogates/D
Joyce	*Ulysses:*	Actual

In a Final Work:

Shakespeare	*King Henry VIII:*	Surrogate/D
Dickens	*The Mystery of Edwin Drood:*	Surrogate/D?
James	*The Ivory Tower:*	Actual/surrogate/D
	The Sense of the Past:	Surrogate

| Conrad | *Suspense:* | Actual/surrogate/D |
| Joyce | *Finnegans Wake:* | Actual/D |

Conclusions Regarding Father/Daughter Relationships

In the early work (total 6 works):
Actual/5; Surrogates/3; Death/3.
In the middle work (total 5 works):
Actual/3; Surrogates/4; Death/3.
In the late work/"Tempest Schema" (total 5 works):
Actual/4; Surrogates/3; Death/1.
In the final work (total 6 works):
Actual/3; Surrogates/5; Death/5.

In surveying these summaries, it becomes apparent that a number of the works contained both actual and surrogate fathers and these were counted in both categories. *The Golden Bowl*, for example, focuses on an actual father and daughter, but the father marries a surrogate daughter. The balance between portrayal of actual as against surrogate relationships seems so even that its importance is canceled out. What is more significant is to look at that balance in the works of individual artists. Shakespeare, partly due to his place in time, usually treated actual fathers and daughters until he wrote *Henry VIII* with its given historical relationships. Henry James, on the other hand, used surrogates frequently, but portrayed two of his most intense father/daughter relationships in *The Portrait of a Lady* and in *The Golden Bowl* between actual fathers and daughters.

The death of one of the parents often sets the stage for the ensuing action of the play or the novel. However, in the tally above, I have only included those deaths that occurred in the course of the narrative. The most interesting evidence regarding death as a factor in the resolution of the incest threat appears in the late "Tempest" works of renunciation and in the final, unfinished works which point to retention. In the former, out of five works, death only occurs in *The Rover* and it is a renunciatory death rather than a destructive death as in *King Lear*. It is also the death of one surrogate who had earlier destroyed the actual father.

It is, of course, impossible to draw conclusions about the final works, since we don't know the endings. But even without this certainty, death occurs in three out of six works and seems probable in *Suspense*. Although deaths preceded the action in both of the James novels, my method precludes including those. The significance lies in the absence of death in narratives of renunciation and the presence of death in narratives of retention.

Not surprisingly, evidence of patriarchal control remains evident in many of the works. Both Emma in *Bleak House* and Bella Wilfer in *Our Mutual Friend* are manipulated by a patriarchal figure into a happy solution with a suitor. In Shakespeare's and Joyce's final works, Katherine and Anna Livia both relinquish to younger women—surely the ultimate male fantasy. Rank elaborates on this: "The mother's death when her daughter reaches marriageable age not only is an expression of the father's wish to exchange his spouse for his daughter but . . . also corresponds to the jealous wish of the daughter, who wishes to take her mother's place with the father (identification)" (309). But the fact that the creators of these daughters are male artists suggests that this too is a male fantasy, even though it also corresponds to accepted psychoanalytic theory. In both literary works, the mothers and daughters have been controlled by patriarchal husbands in a male dominated society.

The manipulation by the autonomous daughter of the father's relinquishment remains an unusual element in the modern plot as found in novels by the two daughterless artists, Henry James and Joseph Conrad, in *Almayer's Folly*, *What Maisie Know*, and *The Golden Bowl*. Although the evidence is uncertain, *The Sense of the Past* also seemed destined to move in that direction. However, the daughter's intervention to control her own fate is by no means a modern development. In the Greek fable of Hippodamia, the suitors are required to defeat her father in a chariot race, and after thirteen youths have died, Hippodamia "cunningly brings about her father's death by loosening the spokes of his chariot wheels" (Rank, 313).

With the exception of *Almayer's Folly*, in all of the novels depicting autonomous daughters, the woman makes the sacrifice while the hero still retains a viable alternative in another woman. Maisie, Maggie Verver, and Nan all forsake their love-objects, but Claude retains Mrs. Beale, Adam Verver still has Charlotte, and Ralph Pendrel flees to America with Aurora. Although Maggie does retain the Prince, James had told us enough of the basis of the marriage to make it seem not much of an option for either Maggie or the Prince. It would seem that the daughter's assumption of autonomy is still in the service of a patriarchal structure.

Death has long been a recurrent motif accompanying the incest theme, either as punishment for infractions or as a means of resolving the incest threat by elimination of one of the parties. Infrequently, suicide serves as an option for the heroine's means of escape from the tyranny of the father or from an unwanted suitor. Shakespeare's Juliet briefly entertains the idea, but James, who lived through the traumas of having a number of his women friends commit suicide, doesn't depict this in the works considered here. Only Conrad, who himself had made a suicide attempt when young, pictures his heroines as either attempting (*Chance*) or threatening (*The Rover*) suicide as a solution to the problem.

But death also intervened in the artistic process for three of the artists who, having completed "Tempest" novels, died in the midst of writing another work treating the father/daughter theme. In their cyclical returns to novels in which retention of the daughter by the father seems probable, it becomes tempting to speculate on the anxieties faced by the artist in this venture as possibly hastening his demise.

Although both Shakespeare and Joyce managed to survive their cyclical return to fatherly retention, Shakespeare died three years after completing *Henry VIII* and Joyce two years after *Finnegans Wake*. But these works had entailed a certain built-in protection for their creators. Shakespeare selected a well-known historical account and worked with a coauthor, mitigating some of the anxiety. Joyce resorted to an intricate and complex "new" language that was to prove inaccessible to many readers. But even Joyce's revolutionary use of language did not entirely make his efforts easy. Morris Beja reports that he kept skipping around while working on *Finnegans Wake* in an effort to avoid the sections of Book 2 involving Issy.[20] Rank commented unwittingly on Joyce's ultimate production:

Thus what we perceive from the author's subjective point of view as a necessary condition of production is seen from the spectator's point of view as one of the technical artistic devices that, by distracting the viewer's interest from content to form, make personal complexes and fantasies of the author suitable for presentation and enjoyment by the viewer.

Schiller had called this "the destruction of content through form" (55).

Toward the end of his study Rank contended that artistic repression in treatment of the incest theme in literature would gradually decrease as humanity became freer and better informed: "[I]n modern literature the incest theme . . . appears with surprising frequency in its fully conscious manifestations" (548). It is true that there has been a decrease in repression of the theme in a number of modern novels. While certain earlier literature in English treated father/daughter incest overtly (Shakespeare's *Pericles* and Shelley's *The Cenci*), since that time the theme has usually occurred in the more subtle guise of the triangular configuration which results from conflict between the father and suitor over possession of the daughter. As mentioned earlier, many modern American novelists have dealt with the theme in more overt ways.[21] Recent works by Jane Smiley (*A Thousand Acres* [1991]), Margaret Atwood (*The Robber Bride* [1993]), and

Marilyn French (*Our Father* [1994]) culminated in one reviewer's dubbing the incest theme "the Cool Whip of serious fiction."[22]

The many modern literary examples invite a reexamination of Rank's predictions regarding the evolvement of the incest motif in modern literature supported by Rudnytsky's observation that "The 'tragic conflicts and solutions of Sophoclean Athens' continue to resonate even in our postmodern era" (xxxi). Very few examples in the foregoing pages have dealt with actual incest and many have dealt in terms of surrogates, distancing the theme for both the author and the reader. Since Rank compiled his data, literature has almost entirely replaced emphasis on conflict between fathers and sons with conflicts between fathers and suitors. Joyce's *Finnegans Wake*, widely recognized as the paradigm of modern fiction, in its pervasive preoccupation with the incest theme rendered in singularly obscure language, goes beyond anything Rank could have imagined, establishing a signal exception to Rank's prediction that the theme would become more overtly handled in modern literature. The contrast with other modern works which have dealt with the theme overtly invites reconsideration of Rank's most provocative speculation:

> It is works with undisguised sexual content that are renewed with each generation and disappear most quickly from the literary scene. By contrast . . . it is those works derived through the highly valued process of repression and sublimation (cf. *Hamlet*) that remain young and effective for centuries, precisely because they correspond more and more closely to the effects of progressing repression, in which their writers were far ahead of their contemporaries. (549)

One writer far ahead of his contemporaries gave the world *Finnegans Wake* (1939), in which language reveals and fails to reveal in a unique way that has never been duplicated. Unlike *Hamlet*, this novel will remain a special case due to its inherent limitations for a broad readership. Only time will tell if such a work will prove more enduring than the many other modern works which have treated the incest theme in a less obscure manner.

Notes

Preface

1. Frye, "The Archetypes of Literature," 91.
2. J. Hillis Miller, "Georges Poulet's Criticism of Identification," 196.

Introduction

1. Freud, "On the History of the Psycho-Analytic Movement," *Standard Edition*, 14:37 (hereinafter referred to in text as *SE*).
2. Rudnytsky, introductory essay, in Rank, *The Incest Theme in Literature and Legend*, xx, xxi.
3. Rank, *The Incest Theme in Literature and Legend*, 301. Translation from Rank, *Das Inzest-Motiv in Dichtung und Sage*, 369.

> Der Inzest zwischen Sohn und Mutter, sowie die ihn ersetzenden Phantasien, gelten dem Bewusstseon, zunächst wohl aus physiologischen Empfindungen, als schwereres Vergehen wie eine Verbindung von Vater und Tochter. Denn die innerliche körperliche Blutsverwandtschaft, die den Sohn mit der Mutter verbindet, ist ja im Verhältnis von Vater und Tochter nicht in dem Masse gegeben.

4. Rank included *Frau Inger of Oestraad, Ghosts, John Gabriel Borkman, Little Eyolf, The Master Builder, Peer Gynt, When We Dead Awaken, The Wild Duck*, and *Woman from the Sea*, 542–48; 395–96; 559.

5. Boose, "The Father and the Bride in Shakespeare," 325.
6. Rank, *Das Inzest-Motiv in Dichtung und Sage*, 1912, 381n.1. In the 1992 translation, footnotes were omitted unless referred to in the text. I am indebted to Jean Kimball for pointing this note out and for a translation: "The relation of the father who seeks to protect his daughter from the suitors so that he might keep her as beloved for himself also underlies one of the last works of Shakespeare, *The Tempest*."
7. Freud, "Totem and Taboo," *SE*, 13:17.
8. Freud, "A Special Type of Choice of Object Made by Men," *SE*, 11:165.
9. Levy-Bruhl, 1931, 247, quoted in Maisch, *Incest*, 41, 42.
10. Maisch, *Incest*, 34–36.
11. Morgan, *The Doctrine of Marriage, Adultery and Divorce* (Oxford: W. Baxter, 1826). Quoted in Samuel Kirson Weinberg, *Incest Behavior*, 7.
12. H. d'Arbois de Jubainville, *La Familie celtique: Etude de droit comparé* (Paris: Librarie Emile Bouillon, 1905), 197. Quoted in Weinberg, 35.
13. Masters, *Patterns of Incest*, 18.
14. Bruni, "Joyce Stripped Naked in the Piazza," *James Joyce Quarterly* 14, no. 2 (1977):149. Quoted in a lecture on Joyce given by his close friend Alessandro Francini Bruni in Trieste in 1922.
15. Renvoize, *Incest: A Family Pattern*, 32.
16. *The Holy Bible*, ed. Rev. C. I. Scofield, Genesis 4.8.
17. Sade, *Eugénie de Franval*, 394.
18. Mead, *Sex and Temperament*, 68.
19. Joyce, *Ulysses: A Critical and Synoptic Edition*, 9.780–83 (hereinafter referred to in text as *U*).
20. Bentham, *The Theory of Legislation*, 220.
21. Boose, "The Father's House and the Daughter in It," 71.
22. Herman, *Father-Daughter Incest*, 108.
23. Taylor, *Sex in History*, 242.
24. Grimble, "From Birth to Death in the Gilbert Islands," *Journal of the Royal Anthropological Institute of Great Britain and Ireland* 51 (1921): 26. Quoted in Weinberg, 8.
25. Vanderbilt, "Incest: A Chilling Report," 69.
26. Bloch, *New Research on the Marquis de Sade and His Times*, 701. Quoted in Rank, *Incest Theme*, 355.
27. Ward, *Father-Daughter Rape*, 159.
28. *New York Times*, March 4, 1993.
29. Meiselman, *Incest: A Psychological Study of Causes and Effects with Treatment Recommendations*, 159.
30. Girard, *Deceit, Desire and the Novel: Self and Other in Literary Structure*, 186, 187n.1.
31. Freud, "The Taboo of Virginity," *SE*, 11:193.
32. Jones, *Papers on Psycho-Analysis*, 656.

Chapter 1

1. Freud, "Some Character-Types Met with in Psycho-Analytic Work," *SE*, 14:327.
2. Sophocles, *Oedipus at Colonus*, 1:291.
3. Dundes, "'To Love My Father All'." In *Cinderella: A Folklore Casebook*, 234.
4. In Chaucer's *Troilus and Criseyde* (c. 1385), it is the heroine's father, Calchas, who maneuvers his daughter out of Troilus's bed and into the arms of the enemy, although the reasons are ostensibly political and military. Pandar can be read as a "good" father-surrogate in his manipulations of the lovers. At least two of the *Canterbury Tales* (c. 1386), "The Man of Law's Tale," and "The Physician's Tale," involve fathers, daughters, and suitors. The transformation that takes place in "The Wife's Tale" can be viewed as a projection of the common male fantasy in which the unattractive older woman is changed into the beautiful young daughter-figure through love. Chaucer, of course, was using earlier sources and the theme could be traced back through a number of earlier works.
5. Chaucer, Prologue to "The Man of Law's Tale," in *The Canterbury Tales*, 139.
6. In Maxim Gorky's "The Hermit," the twelve-year-old daughter gets her father released by the court, claiming that it was "her fault." Guy de Maupassant's *Monsieur Jocaste* (1883) features "conscious incest between father and daughter" (Rank, 331), and although conscious incest is not a component, father/daughter relationships are central to Balzac's *Père Goriot* and *Eugénie Grandet* (1835/1833). In addition to Henrik Ibsen's *Rosmersholm* (1886), explicated by both Rank and Freud, *The Master Builder* (1892) so central to *Finnegans Wake*, with its "masterbilker" (111.21), has the theme at its core, displaced onto an uncle and a niece. Tolstoy's *War and Peace* (1869) has its unnatural father/daughter attachment in Marya Bolkonsky and her father who live at "Bleak Hills," a name possibly derived from the Dickens novel replete with triangular configurations. Max Frisch's *Homo Faber* (1964) returns to the recurring convention of a father unwittingly sleeping with a woman whom he later discovers to be his daughter.
7. Gilbert, "Life's Empty Pack," 273.
8. Although *Northanger Abbey* (1803) is ostensibly a spoof of the Gothic novel (a genre itself significant for treatment of the theme), there are strong hints of incestuous tendencies in General Tilney. Dickens's contemporary, Thackeray, gives us Becky Sharpe (1847), who rejects Sir Pitt with the suggestion that she be his daughter rather than his wife.
9. Cory and Masters, *Violation of Taboo: Incest in the Great Literature of the Past and Present*, 133–39.
10. Freud, "Fragment of an Analysis of a Case of Hysteria," *SE*, 7:20.
11. Erik H. Erickson, "Reality and Actuality: An Address," 52.
12. George Yost, *Pieracci and Shelley: An Italian Ur-Cenci*.
13. Beyle [De Stendhal], "The Cenci," 180–82.

14. Ricci, *Beatrice Cenci*, 168, 206.

15. Browning, "Cenciaja," 1009.

16. Pepper, *Guido Reni*, 1984. Stephen Pepper declines to attribute *Lot and His Daughters* to Reni, saying that it is probably by Cantarini. Nevertheless, the official catalog for the touring Reni exhibition at the Los Angeles County Museum in 1994 not only included a color reproduction of the painting in the catalog, but used it on a brochure for the show. The dust jacket for the 1992 translation of the Rank tome on the incest theme also displays it. Pepper designates the Beatrice portrait, now in the Hermitage, as *Sibyl* by Elisabetta Sirani. Copies hang in the Uffizi and in a gallery in Rome. He believes that it was a copy of such turbaned sibyls as were being done by Reni and his studio (303, 304).

17. Mary Shelley, *Mary Shelley's Journal*, 210.

18. Percy Bysshe Shelley, *The Cenci*, ed. George E. Woodberry, ix.

19. Percy Bysshe Shelley, *The Cenci*, ed. Roland A. Duerksen, 10.

20. Huntington Library MS. 1335, "Relazione della morte famiglia Cenci, sequita in Roma li de Maggio, 1599." Copied in Rome, February 26, 27, 1813, from Muratori, *Annals of Italy*, vol. 10. I wish to express my thanks to the authorities of the Huntington Library for permission to consult this manuscript. Matthew Josephson, *Stendhal: or the Pursuit of Happiness*, 164, put forth the opinion about Stendhal providing the Shelleys with their copy.

21. Mary Shelley, *Mathilda*, ed. Elizabeth Nitchie, x.

22. Shakespeare, *The Tempest*, 3.2.59–60.

23. Steffan, "Seven Accounts of the Cenci and Shelley's Drama," 605.

24. Dickens, *American Notes and Pictures from Italy*, 391.

25. Melville, *Pierre*, 489.

26. Curran, *Shelley's Cenci*, 11.

27. Evan Carton, "A Daughter of the Puritans," 220.

28. Erlich, *Family Themes and Hawthorne's Fiction*, 33.

29. Hawthorne, *The Marble Faun*, 54.

30. Edel, *Henry James: The Conquest of London: 1870–1881*, 90.

31. James, "The Real Thing." The artist in the story, needing models to pose for an illustrated novel about the aristocracy, tries and then rejects two impoverished members of that class and chooses instead two down-at-heel members of the working class, having concluded that "the real thing" does not serve the ends of artistic creativity.

32. Joyce, *Giacomo Joyce*, 11.

33. Ellmann, introduction to *Giacomo Joyce*, xxi–xxvi.

34. Richard Ellmann, *James Joyce*. New York: Oxford University Press, 1982. Review from *Evening Telegraph*, December 21, 1909, 303.

35. Tresize, Review of *Beatrice Cenci*, by Goldschmidt (opera [CD]). *Opera Now*, August/September 1995.

36. For confirmation, see Catherine Clement, *Opera of the Undoing of Women*.

37. Browning, "Cenciaja," 1009. In a July 27, 1876, letter to Buxton Forman, Browning quoted Beatrice's words from the trial taken from the "old yellow book" which he had used for "The Ring and the Book": "That which I ought to confess, that will I confess; that to which I ought to assent, to that I assent; and that which I ought to deny, that I will deny."

38. Kahane, introduction to Bernheimer and Kahane, In Dora's Case: Freud-Hysteria-Feminism, 31.

39. Freud to Fliess, May 31, 1897, in The Complete Letters of Sigmund Freud to Wilhelm Fliess, 1887–1904, ed. Masson, 252.

40. Freud, "Civilization and Its Discontents," SE, 21:104.

41. Rieff, ed., Dora: An Analysis of a Case of Hysteria, 9.

42. Marcus, "Freud and Dora: Story, History, Case History," in Bernheimer and Kahane, In Dora's Case: Freud-Hysteria-Feminism, 81.

43. Freud to Fliess, October 14, 1900; January 25, 1901, in Freud/Fliess Letters, 427, 433.

44. Cohen, The Daughter's Dilemma, 164.

45. Willbern, "Filia Oedipi: Father and Daughter in Freudian Theory," 89.

46. Freud, "The Paths to the Formation of Symptoms," Lecture 23, SE, 16:370.

47. Gay, Freud: A Life for Our Time, 95.

48. Renvoize, Incest: A Family Pattern, 24.

49. Froula, "The Daughter's Seduction: Sexual Violence and Literary History," 119.

50. Freud to Fliess, May 31, 1897, in Freud/Fliess Letters, ed. Masson, 249.

51. Lieberman, Acts of Will: The Life and Work of Otto Rank, 4.

52. Fitch, Anaïs: The Erotic Life of Anaïs Nin, 4, 164.

53. Nin, Incest: From a Journal of Love, 210.

54. Conrad, A Personal Record, 71.

55. James, The Notebooks of Henry James, 35.

56. Edel, Henry James: The Untried Years—1843–1870, 277.

57. "The Limitations of Dickens," in The Portable Henry James; "The Tempest," in Selected Literary Criticism, ed. Shapira.

58. Cheng, Shakespeare and Joyce: A Study of Finnegans Wake; Fogel, Covert Relations: Joyce, Woolf, and James; Ford, "James Joyce and the Conrad Connection: The Anxiety of Influence"; Schutte, Joyce and Shakespeare: A Study in the Meaning of Ulysses.

59. Atherton, The Books at the Wake.

60. Ford, "James Joyce and the Conrad Connection: The Anxiety of Influence."

61. Boose, "The Father's House and the Daughter in It: The Structures of Western Culture's Daughter-Father Relationship," 60.

62. "Translator's Note: 'Dampening' by the unconscious of one concept to another, less offensive one is referred to at times [by Rank] as Abschwächung and at times as Abmilderung." Richter, trans., in Rank, Incest Theme, xxxix–xl.

63. Joyce, Finnegans Wake, 110.15 (hereinafter referred to in text as FW).

64. Freud, "Beyond the Pleasure Principle," *SE*, 18:22–23.

Chapter 2

1. Schoenbaum, *William Shakespeare: A Compact Documentary Life*, 76.
2. Chambers, *Sources for a Biography of Shakespeare*, 62.
3. Kay, *Shakespeare: His Life, Work and Era*, 395.
4. Kimball, "James Joyce and Otto Rank: The Incest Motif in *Ulysses*."
5. William Shakespeare, *Romeo and Juliet*, 3.5.119–20.
6. Shakespeare, *A Midsummer Night's Dream*, 1.1.96–98.
7. Quoted in Norman Holland, *Psychoanalysis and Shakespeare*, 255–56.
8. Shakespeare, *Othello*, 1.3.193–95.
9. Pauncz, "The Lear Complex in World Literature," 52.
10. Shakespeare, *King Lear*, 1.1.288–89.
11. I am indebted for this observation to Norman Holland, *Psychoanalysis and Shakespeare*, 112.
12. Introduction to Shakespeare, *Pericles*, xv.
13. Introduction to Shakespeare, *Pericles*, xv.
14. Thorne, "*Pericles* and the Incest-Fertility Opposition," 44.
15. Mueller, "Hermione's Wrinkles, or, Ovid Transformed: An Essay on *The Winter's Tale*," 226.
16. Shakespeare, *The Winter's Tale*, 5.3.121.
17. Shakespeare, *The Tempest*, 1.2.13.
18. Sharpe, "From *King Lear* to *The Tempest*," 237.
19. Paris, "*The Tempest*: Shakespeare's Ideal Solution," in *Shakespeare's Personality*, ed. Norman Holland, 210.

Chapter 3

1. Johnson, *Charles Dickens: His Tragedy and Triumph*, 1:32.
2. Hardwick, "Born under Aquarius," 90.
3. Tomalin, *The Invisible Woman: The Story of Nelly Ternan and Charles Dickens*.
4. Adrian, "Dickens and Inverted Parenthood," 11.
5. Zabel, Introduction to *Charles Dickens' Best Stories*, 13.
6. In "The Mistaken Milliner. A Tale of Ambition," the narrator explains: "Now, 'coming out,' either in acting, or singing, or society, or facetiousness, or anything else, is all very well, and remarkably pleasant to the individual principally concerned, if he or she can but manage to come out with a burst, and being out to keep out, and not go in again; but it does unfortunately happen that both consummations are extremely difficult to accomplish, and that the difficulties of getting out at all in the first instance, and if you surmount them, of keeping out in the second, are pretty much on a par, and no slight ones either—and so Miss Amelia Martin shortly discovered" (254).
7. Charles Dickens, *Sketches by Boz*, 244–49.

8. *Nicholas Nickleby* (1839) treats the theme in the oblique terms of uncles and doubles and resolution lies in the punishment of the father figures: suicide for Ralph and murder for Gride, and in the marriages of the daughter-figures to appropriate suitors. In *The Old Curiosity Shop* (1841), the sinister, sexual aspects of Quilp and the innocence of Nell, who finally escapes into death, have been extensively commented upon. Of *Barnaby Rudge* (1841) one critic has observed of Gabriel: "He obviously wants Dolly for himself; he is well-intentioned, but, for all that, a tyrant" (Kincaid, *Dickens and the Rhetoric of Laughter*, 123). Many other novels present classic variations on the theme: *Hard Times* (1854), *Little Dorrit* (1857), and *Great Expectations* (1861).

9. Butt and Tillotson, *Dickens at Work*, 92.

10. Ian Miller, "The Dickens Dramas: Mr. Dombey," in *Dickens Centennial Essays*, ed. Nisbet and Nevius, 161.

11. Dickens, *The Posthumous Papers of the Pickwick Club*, v.

12. Dickens, preface to the 1st ed., in Wall, *Charles Dickens: A Critical Anthology*, 44.

13. Manning, *Dickens as Satirist*, 41.

14. Erikson, "Human Strength and the Cycle of Generations," in *Insight and Responsibility*, 133–34.

15. Charles Dickens, *David Copperfield*, 57.

16. Dickens, *Bleak House*, 51.

17. Gissing, "Characterization," in Wall, *Charles Dickens: A Critical Anthology*, 233.

18. Shaw, foreword to Charles Dickens, *Great Expectations*. Reprinted in Wall, *Charles Dickens: A Critical Anthology*, 293.

19. House, "The Changing Scene," 344.

20. Van Ghent, "The Dickens World: A View from Todgers's," 32–33.

21. Dickens, *Our Mutual Friend*, 128.

22. Kincaid, *Dickens and the Rhetoric of Laughter*, 245.

23. Dickens, "George Silverman's Explanation."

24. Marcus, "Dickens: From Pickwick to Dombey," 40.

25. Fleissner, *Dickens and Shakespeare: A Study in Histrionic Contrasts*, 289.

Chapter 4

1. Edel, *Henry James: The Master—1901–1916*, 212.

2. Edel carefully documents the progression of all of these various relationships in his five-volume biography.

3. James, *Watch and Ward*, introduction by Edel, 5; *Roderick Hudson*, v.

4. Fish, "Form and Revision: The Example of *Watch and Ward*."

5. James, *Watch and Ward* (Macmillan, 1923), 31. Notes in text to this edition.

6. Edel, introduction to *Watch and Ward*, 7.

7. James, *The Portrait of a Lady*, 39.

8. James, *The Golden Bowl*, 94.

9. Portigliotti, *The Borgias: Alexander VI, Caesar, Lucrezia*, 249. See also Rank, *Incest Theme*, 384–85; Mallett, *The Borgias*, 89; Maisch, *Incest*, 29,30; and Masters, *Patterns of Incest*, 31ff.

10. James, *Italian Hours*, 308.

11. Zwinger, *Fathers, Daughters, and the Novel: The Sentimental Romance of Heterosexuality*, 87.

12. "*A la guerre comme à la guerre*" can be translated as either "il faut accepter les inconvénients, les privations qu'imposent les circonstances (V. *Résignation*), ou encore: la guerre justifie les moyens" (Le Robert, 3:387. Used in Balzac, *La rabouilleuse*, Oeuvr., 3:1002).

Translation: "It is necessary to accept the problems, the privations which circumstances impose (see Resignation), or: "'War justifies the means'" (trans. Barbara Ford).

13. Howells, *Life in Letters of W. D. Howells*, 116–18, 394–99. Quoted in Edel, *Henry James: The Untried Years: 1843–1870*, 274.

14. James, Preface to *The Turn of the Screw*, xxiv.

15. Although J. A. Ward, *The Search for Form: Studies in the Structure of James's Fiction*, indicates that some critics see Maggie's creation of her marriage as "a predatory aggression, and ingenious shrewdness, and a calculating empiricism" (213), in general, critical appraisal is weighted heavily toward Maggie's innocence and toward the Ververs as victims of the adultery of the *sposi*. Oscar Cargill praises the "precious moral sense" (391) of the Ververs, while Joseph J. Firebaugh sees them as lacking "passion, either physical or emotional" (402). Halperin's afterword views Maggie as "essentially innocent, weak, and self-indulgent" (555), while Jean Kimball maintains that "One could hardly fling the accusation of incest at these charmingly naïve people" (449). Frederick Crews sees Maggie as a redeemer (105), while Carl Maves notes her "combination of innocence and insensitivity" (131). Charles Samuels says the Ververs "had enjoyed a kind of paradisical affection" (210) but Ferner Nuhn is perhaps the most ecstatic: "Maggie Verver is the female knight errant who wins the day, who redresses wrong . . . restores the palace to its former life and beauty" (127), but goes on to say that if we see something unnatural in the Verver relationship, James himself would have been "horrified" (138). Although Laurence Holland refers to familial affection which "becomes instituted incest" (356), he does not elaborate. F. R. Leavis possibly comes closest to my position, indicating that the Prince and Charlotte "represent what, against the general moral background of the book, can only strike us as a decent passion; in a stale, sickly and oppressive atmosphere they represent life" (160). Leon Edel, in spite of his psychoanalytic orientation, also takes a benign view of what happens, evidently ignoring the obvious pain on the part of all parties as the novel ends: "Charlotte ends with the wealth and power and freedom of her marriage to an American tycoon" (215).

Three recent critics who have provided interesting and provocative readings of this novel offer interpretations of Maggie's role that differ crucially from my own. None of them shares my positive view of what I see as her assumption of autonomy at the end of the novel. Paula Marantz Cohen in *The Daughter's Dilemma: Family Process and the Nineteenth-Century Domestic Novel* concludes: "Maggie Verver recaptures her husband at the expense of her father, and in such a way as to make her triumph seem bizarre and morally dubious" (179). Lynda Zwinger, in *Fathers, Daughters, and the Novel: The Sentimental Romance of Heterosexuality*, views Maggie as still subjected to the strictures of a paternalistic society, stating: "[W]e're not talking about literal incest between father and daughter" (93). A third critic, Mary Ann Caws in "What Can a Woman Do for the Late Henry James?" agrees that the separation of the couples has "somehow been brought about by Maggie" but refers to Maggie's "symbolic incestuous relation to her father" (1).

16. Freud, "On the Universal Tendency to Debasement in the Sphere of Love," *SE*, 11:187.

Chapter 5

1. Lenormand, "Note sur un séjour de Conrad en Corse," 668–69; quoted and translated in Stallman, ed., *Joseph Conrad: A Critical Symposium*, 6.

> Un jour que nous regardions passer la fille de son ami P., une enfant de dix-huit ans, dont les yeux égarés et le masque de sauvagesse me faisaient penser à la recluse de *A smile of fortune*, il me dit: "Toute ma vie, j'ai été extrêmement préoccupé par les rapports de père à fille." Nous parlâmes de *la Folie Almayer*. "C'est un livre que j'ai écrit à trente-six ans, sans aucun but. Je ne savais pas que je deviendrais un homme de lettres. J'ai fait cela d'un seul jet et comme malgré moi." Je lui demandai s'il n'avait jamais eu l'intention de suggérer que l'obscurcissement et la déchéance d'Almayer devaient être attribués à une passion inconsciente de l'exilé pour sa fille, tendresse incestueuse abritée derrière un amour paternel. Il protesta contre l'existence d'un pareil sentiment chez son héros. Quand je lui signalai les passages qui m'avaient conduit à cette interprétation, — les rêves de futile grandeur qu'Almayer caresse pour Nina, les alternatives de colère et d'exaltation qu'il traverse en présence de l'enfant, l'impulsion meurtrière qui le précipite contre l'homme qu'elle aime, la scène qui suit, toute sillonnée d'éclairs de jalousie, — Conrad se tut, visiblement gêné, puis détourna la conversation.

2. Jessie Conrad, *Conrad and His Circle*, 24. Quoted in Meyer, *Joseph Conrad: A Psychoanalytic Biography*, 112.

3. Najder, *Joseph Conrad: A Chronicle*, 16.

4. Karl, *Joseph Conrad: The Three Lives*, 151, 152.

5. Conrad, *Lord Jim*, 134.

6. Conrad, *Youth: A Narrative and Two Other Stories: Heart of Darkness: The End of the Tether*, 267.

7. Conrad, *Almayer's Folly*, 22.

8. Conrad, *Chance: A Tale in Two Parts*, 38, 39.
9. The main difference between most critical discourse on *Chance* and my own lies in the reading of Captain Anthony's delay in his consummation of the marriage—my interpretation viewing him as a father-double who declines to exercise his autonomy until convinced of the mutual desire on the part of his wife. Significantly, this occurs simultaneously with the elimination of the "bad" father. Douglas Hewitt said of de Barral that "there is no possible contact between him and Anthony" (96), and of Anthony, that "we are not convinced of the reality of the man, nor, therefore, of the significance of the central situation" (95). Albert J. Guerard suggests that "the absurd final pages of *Chance* should simply be subtracted and ignored" (262), adding that "the essential fact about Captain Anthony is that he has refrained from sexual intercourse with his wife" (263), although he admits that "his determination not to stumble over the corpse of the father may suggest a determination not to fail sexually" (264). He fails to carry this to what, for me, is the logical conclusion—an archetypal reading in which the "good" father is only freed with the destruction of the "bad" father. Meyer perceptively concludes that "the idea that Captain Anthony should continue to enjoy his triumph was apparently unpalatable to Conrad, for he found it necessary to kill the captain off . . . after a few years of married life" (226). This supports my view of the elimination of the "good" father in favor of the young suitor—a transference clearly indicated in the text. Anthony, it should be remembered, is repeatedly identified as "the son of the poet" whose paternally incestuous inclinations have been clearly spelled out. Thomas Moser comes perhaps closest to my reading when he notes the repeated triangular pattern of "hero, heroine, and rival" (103), going on to say that "the later hero is always an eligible bachelor, not necessarily youthful" including Captain Anthony and Peyrol. This insight is somewhat undercut by the judgment that Conrad lacked a "genuine, dramatic interest in sexual problems" (128).
10. Bradbrook was possibly the first to designate *The Rover* as "Conrad's Tempest" (75), but she did not develop the analog as fully as Herbert Howarth did in "The Meaning of Conrad's *The Rover*" (692). He stands out among the critics for acknowledging the tie between Scevola's impotence and blood-lust (683). Although he too does not carry the parallels as far as I do, he does single Peyrol out as a special case: "The daughters of his books from 1895 to 1913 were baulked in their natural love by crazed and jealous fathers. . . . Now, arriving from *par dela les mers* to replace the massacred father, the surrogate father heals, protects, loves his daughter and eventually sacrifices himself to send her to her husband" (692).
11. Conrad, *The Rover*, 162.
12. Jessie Conrad, *Conrad As I Knew Him*, 105. Quoted in Meyer, *Joseph Conrad: A Psychoanalytic Biography*, 117.

Chapter 6

1. Brown, *James Joyce's Early Fiction: The Biography of a Form*, 6.
2. Perkins, *Joyce and Hauptmann: Before Sunrise*.
3. To Stanislaus from Pola, Austria, December 3, 1904, *Selected Joyce Letters*, 46.
4. To Stanislaus, May 2 or 3, 1905, *Selected Joyce Letters*, 61.
5. Maddox, *Nora: The Real Life of Molly Bloom*, 205; *U*, 12.1497.
6. Church, "*Dubliners* and Vico," 154.
7. Joyce, *Dubliners*, "The Dead," 180.
8. Joyce, *Stephen Hero*, 66.
9. Joyce, *A Portrait of the Artist as a Young Man*, 221.
10. Joyce, Zurich Notebook, 8.A.5 at SUNY Buffalo. Transcribed in Herring, *Studies in Bibliography* 22:309. The words "incest" and "suicide" are also mentioned. See Ford, "Why Is Milly in Mullingar?" *James Joyce Quarterly* 14, no. 4 (1977): 436–49.
11. Trilling, *The Opposing Self*, 149.
12. Shechner, *Joyce in Nighttown: A Psychoanalytic Inquiry into* Ulysses, 149.
13. Ford, "Why Is Milly in Mullingar?" Milly's exile is just one of many factors in Bloom's life to account for the recurrent suicide motif, especially in terms of drowning. Tiresias predicts of Odysseus that "in the end death would come to him from the sea" (Graves, 2:360). The deaths of Bloom's father, Mrs. Sinico, Ophelia, and the attempted death of Reuben J. Dodd's son are all related to unhappy love affairs. Bloom's dreamhouse is equipped with a "carbon monoxide gas supply throughout" (*U*, 17:1549–50), and he fears "the commital of homicide or suicide during sleep by an aberration of the light of reason" (*U*, 17:1765–68). In Conrad's "The End of the Tether" (122, 639, 665) the father, obsessively absorbed in love for his daughter, and distraught over his blindness, drowns himself. The man "found drowned" has disappeared off Maiden's rock (*U*, 3:322), and Bloom muses, "Drowning they say is the pleasantest" (*U*, 6:988).
14. Adams, *Surface and Symbol: The Consistency of James Joyce's* Ulysses, 88.
15. Shakespeare, *The Merchant of Venice*, 2.2.70–71.
16. *La Sonnambula: An Opera in 2 Acts*, music by Bellini, libretto by Feline Romani, 138.
17. I first noticed this in Joyce's proof sheet #262 which I viewed in 1989 at the Rosenbach Museum. This change is also documented in Joyce, *Ulysses: A Critical and Synoptic Edition*, ed. Gabler, 1.588.8.
18. "Circe" Buffalo TS V.B.13h, 15; *James Joyce Archive*, 168.
19. "Circe" Buffalo TS V.B.13h, 35; *James Joyce Archive*, 187.
20. Since I have adhered to the Gabler edition in this work, I should point out that in contrast to the Random House edition (372) which reads as "face," Gabler et al. have made the change to: "Me have a nice pace" (*U-G*, Historical Collation, 1797). While this is not the place to open up the endless question of

authoritative text, this should be noted, and, if valid, could have been Joyce's attempt to reproduce the baby talk of a three-year-old.

21. "Circe" Buffalo TS V.B.13h, 39; *James Joyce Archive*, 191. "She" in Joyce's insertion became "the young person" in the final version.

22. Landor, *Imaginary Conversations*, in *Complete Works*, 7:359.

23. See Benstock, *Joyce-Again's Wake: An Analysis of* Finnegans Wake (1965), Tindall, *A Reader's Guide to* Finnegans Wake (1972), and Senn, "Insects Appalling," in *Twelve and a Tilly*, ed. Jack P. Dalton and Clive Hart (1965), to name only a few. In Senn's essay we read: "Incest may be natural with gods, men and insects, but ultimately it is a crime and a sin. Thus it is not only one cause of perpetual crimean wars of opposing sect-arian fathers and sons and brothers, but it is also intimately involved in Earwicker-earwig's sinful crime in the park. From his name and from 'the bynames was put under him' we might indeed gauge that 'our old offender was humile, commune and ensectuous'" (*FW*, 29.30, Senn, 39). But the passage also states that he "will be ultimendly respunchable for the hubbub caused in Eden-borough" (*FW*, 29.34–36).

24. Glasheen, *A Second Census of* Finnegans Wake: *An Index of the Characters and Their Roles*, ix.

25. The significance of the Prankquean material was pointed out to me by William J. Ford, M.D., in an unpublished, 1971 essay.

26. McHugh, *Annotations to* Finnegans Wake, 527.25.

27. *The Barber of Seville*, in *The New Milton Cross' Complete Stories of the Great Operas*, ed. Kohrs, 79–89.

28. Ibsen, *The Master Builder*, in *When We Dead Awaken and Three Other Plays*, 215.

29. See Ford, "James Joyce and the Conrad Connection: The Anxiety of Influence."

Chapter 7

1. James, "The Tempest," in *Selected Literary Criticism*, ed. Shapira, 309–10.

2. Shakespeare, *King Henry VIII*, Prologue 1.1.1.

3. Kanfer, "The 110-Year-Old Murder" in *Time*, October 27, 1980, 100. Two versions appeared that year: *The Decoding of Edwin Drood* by Leon Garfield (Scribners); and *The Mystery of Edwin Drood* concluded by Leon Garfield (Andre Deutsch).

4. Dickens, *The Mystery of Edwin Drood*, 14.

5. Wall, *Charles Dickens: A Critical Anthology*, 173. From Forster's *Life of Charles Dickens*, vol. 2, chap. 2.

6. Henry James, *The Sense of the Past*, prefatory note by J. C. Squire, vi.

7. James, *The Ivory Tower*, 271.

8. James, Notes for *The Sense of the Past*, 285–351.

9. This could have one of two meanings: either it identifies Cantopher as the sort of Renaissance Man that Horace Walpole was, or it suggests the male character depicted in Walpole's Gothic novels. The Gothic novel often entailed incest as a plot component.

10. Jean-Aubry, *The Sea Dreamer*, from a letter to André Gide, January 30, 1921.

11. Conrad, *Suspense: A Novel of Napoleonic Times*, 22.

12. Guerard, *Conrad the Novelist*, 288.

13. Jean-Aubry, *The Sea Dreamer*, 280–81.

14. Curle, *The Last Twelve Years of Joseph Conrad*, 226.

15. Hart, *Structure and Motif in* Finnegans Wake, 53.

16. Nietzsche, *The Birth of Tragedy and the Genealogy of Morals*, 61.

17. Trilling, *The Liberal Imagination*, 80–81.

18. Norman Holland, introduction to *Shakespeare's Personality*, 7–8.

19. Jean-Aubry, *Joseph Conrad: Life and Letters*, February 26, 1899, 1:272. Also quoted in Meyer, *Joseph Conrad: A Psychoanalytic Biography*, 323n.k.

20. Beja, *James Joyce: A Literary Life*, 120.

21. Ralph Ellison's *Invisible Man* (1947), John Hawkes's *Second Skin* (1963), Alice Walker's *The Color Purple* (1982), Toni Morrison's *The Bluest Eye* (1970) and *Beloved*, Maya Angelou's *I Know Why the Caged Bird Sings* (1970), Anne Moody's *Coming of Age in Mississippi* (1968), and Gayl Jones's *Corregidora* (1975).

22. Shapiro, "They're Daddy's Little Girls," *Newsweek*, January 24, 1994, 66. Recently reviewed books on father/daughter incest have included Edna O'Brien's *Down by the River*, Kathryn Harrison's *The Kiss*, and Ann-Marie MacDonald's *Fall on Your Knees*.

Bibliography

Abenheimer, K. M. "Shakespeare's *Tempest*: A Psychological Analysis." *Psychoanalytic Review* 33 (1946): 399–415. Reprint, in Faber, *The Design Within: Psychoanalytic Approaches to Shakespeare*, 499-520.

Adams, Robert Martin. *Surface and Symbol: The Consistency of James Joyce's Ulysses*. New York: Oxford University Press, 1962.

Adrian, Arthur A. "Dickens and Inverted Parenthood." *Dickensian* 67 (1971): 3–11.

Arens, W. *The Original Sin: Incest and Its Meaning*. New York: Oxford University Press, 1986.

Atherton, James S. *The Books at the Wake: A Study of Literary Allusions in James Joyce's* Finnegans Wake. New York: Viking, 1960.

Beja, Morris. *James Joyce: A Literary Life*. Columbus: Ohio State University Press, 1992.

Ben-Merre, Diana Arbin. "Bloom and Milly: A Portrait of the Father and the 'Jew's Daughter'." *James Joyce Quarterly* 18, no. 4 (1981): 439–44.

Benstock, Bernard. *Joyce-Again's Wake: An Analysis of* Finnegans Wake. Seattle: University of Washington Press, 1965.

Bentham, Jeremy. *The Theory of Legislation*. London: Trabner, 1890.

Bernheimer, Charles, and Claire Kahane, eds. *In Dora's Case: Freud-Hysteria-Feminism*. New York: Columbia University Press, 1985.

Berrone, Louis, ed. and trans. Introduction to *James Joyce in Padua*. New York: Random House, 1977.

Beyle, Marie-Henri [De Stendhal]. "The Cenci." *The Abbess of Castro and Other Tales.* Trans. C. K. Scott Moncrieff, 165–203. 1837. New York: Boni and Liveright, 1926.

Bleich, David. "Artistic Form as Defensive Adaptation: Henry James and *The Golden Bowl.*" *Psychoanalytic Review* 58, no. 2 (1971): 223–44.

Blunden, Edmund. *Shelley: A Life Story.* London: Oxford University Press, 1965.

Boose, Lynda E. "The Father and the Bride in Shakespeare." *PMLA* 96 (1982): 325–47.

———. "The Father's House and the Daughter in It: The Structures of Western Culture's Daughter-Father Relationship." In Boose and Flowers, *Daughters and Fathers,* 19–74.

Boose, Lynda E., and Betty S. Flowers, eds. *Daughters and Fathers.* Baltimore: Johns Hopkins University Press, 1989.

Bowen, Zack. "The Bronzegold Sirensong: A Musical Analysis of the Sirens Episode in Joyce's *Ulysses.*" In *Literary Monographs.* Vol. 1. Ed. Eric Rothstein and Thomas Durseath, 245–300. Madison: University of Wisconsin Press, 1967.

Bradbrook, M. C. *Joseph Conrad: Poland's English Genius.* Cambridge: Cambridge University Press, 1942.

Brown, Homer Obed. *James Joyce's Early Fiction: The Biography of a Form.* Cleveland, Ohio: Case Western Reserve University Press, 1972.

Browning, Robert. "Cenciaja." In *The Poems and Plays of Robert Browning,* 1009. 1876. New York: Modern Library, 1934.

Brownstein, Marilyn L. "The Preservation of Tenderness: A Confusion of Tongues in *Ulysses* and *Finnegans Wake.*" In Friedman, *Joyce: The Return of the Repressed,* 225–56.

Bruni, Alessandro Francini. "Joyce Stripped Naked in the Piazza." Ed. and notes Willard Potts. *James Joyce Quarterly* 14, no. 2 (1977): 127–59. Reprint, *Portraits of the Artist in Exile: Recollections of James Joyce by Europeans,* ed. Willard Potts, trans. Camilla Rudolph et al., 7–38, Seattle: University of Washington Press, 1979.

Butt, John, and Kathleen Tillotson. *Dickens at Work.* Fairlawn, N.J.: Essential, 1958.

Cargill, Oscar. *The Novels of Henry James.* New York: Macmillan, 1961.

Caroselli, Susan L., ed. *Guido Reni 1575–1642.* Los Angeles: Los Angeles County Museum of Art; Bologna: Nuova Alfa Editoriale, 1994.

Carton, Evan. "'A Daughter of the Puritans' and Her Old Master: Hawthorne, Una, and the Sexuality of Romance." In Boose and Flowers, *Daughters and Fathers,* 208–32.

Caws, Mary Ann. "What Can a Woman Do for the Late Henry James?" *Raritan* 14, no. 1 (1994): 1–17.

Chambers, E. K. *Sources for a Biography of Shakespeare.* Oxford: Clarendon Press, 1946.

Chaucer, Geoffrey. *The Canterbury Tales.* c. 1390. Trans. Nevill Coghill. Baltimore: Penguin, 1952.

Cheng, Vincent J. *Shakespeare and Joyce: A Study of Finnegans Wake.* Philadelphia: University of Pennsylvania Press, 1984.

Church, Margaret. "*Dubliners* and Vico." *James Joyce Quarterly* 5 (1968): 150–56.
Clayton, Jay, and Eric Rothstein, eds. *Influence and Intertextuality in Literary History*. Madison: University of Wisconsin Press, 1991.
Clement, Catherine. *Opera of the Undoing of Women*. Trans. Betsy Wing. Minneapolis: University of Minnesota Press, 1988.
Cohen, Paula Marantz. *The Daughter's Dilemma: Family Process and the Nineteenth-Century Domestic Novel*. Ann Arbor: University of Michigan Press, 1993.
Connolly, Thomas E. *The Personal Library of James Joyce: A Descriptive Bibliography*. University of Buffalo Studies, Monographs in English 6. 1955. Vol. 22, no. 1.
Conrad, Joseph. *Almayer's Folly*. 1895. London: J. M. Dent and Sons, 1947.
———. *Chance: A Tale in Two Parts*. 1913. New York: W. W. Norton, 1968.
———. "The End of the Tether." 1903. In *Youth: A Narrative and Two Other Stories: Heart of Darkness—The End of the Tether*, ed. Morton Dauwen Zabel, 165–305. Garden City, N.Y.: Doubleday, 1959.
———. "Freya of the Seven Isles." In *'Twixt Land and Sea*, 145–238. London: J. M. Dent and Sons, 1947.
———. *Lord Jim*. Ed. Thomas Moser. 1899. New York: W. W. Norton, 1968.
———. *The Mirror of the Sea and A Personal Record*. 1906, 1912. London: J. M. Dent and Sons, 1946.
———. *Nostromo*. 1904. Introduction by Robert Penn Warren. New York: Random House, 1951.
———. *Notes on Life and Letters*. 1921. London: J. M. Dent and Sons, 1949.
———. *The Rover*. Garden City, N.Y.: Doubleday Page, 1923.
———. *Suspense: A Napoleonic Novel*. Garden City, N.Y.: Doubleday Page, 1925.
———. *Under Western Eyes*. 1911. Garden City, N.Y.: Doubleday, 1963.
Cory, Donald W., and R. E. L. Masters, eds. *Violation of Taboo: Incest in the Great Literature of the Past and Present*. New York: Julian Press, 1963.
Crawford, F. Marion. "Beatrice Cenci: The True Story of a Misunderstood Tragedy; With New Documents." *Century* 75, no. 3 (1908): 449–66.
Crews, Frederick C. *The Tragedy of Manners: Moral Drama in the Later Novels of Henry James*. 1957. Hamden, Conn.: Archon, 1971.
———, ed. *Psychoanalysis and Literary Process*. Cambridge, Mass.: Winthrop, 1970.
Curle, Richard. *The Last Twelve Years of Joseph Conrad*. London: Sampson, Low, Marston, 1928.
Curran, Stuart. *Shelley's "Cenci": Scorpions Ringed with Fire*. Princeton, N.J.: Princeton University Press, 1970.
Daly, Leo. *James Joyce and the Mullingar Connection*. Republic of Ireland: Dolmen Press, 1975.
Delimata, Bozena Berta. "Reminiscences of a Joyce Niece." *James Joyce Quarterly* 19, no. 1 (1981): 45–62.
Dickens, Charles. *American Notes and Pictures from Italy*. London: J. M. Dent and Co., 1908.
———. *Bleak House*. 1853. New York: New American Library, 1964.
———. *Dombey and Son*. 1848. New York: New American Library, 1964.

———. "George Silverman's Explanation." 1868. In *Charles Dickens' Best Stories*. Introduction by Morton Dauwen Zabel, ed., 611–34. Garden City, N.Y.: Hanover House, 1959.

———. "The Misplaced Attachment of Mr. John Dounce." In *Sketches by Boz*, 244–49.

———. "The Mistaken Milliner: A Tale of Ambition." In *Sketches by Boz*, 250–55.

———. *The Mystery of Edwin Drood*. 1870. New York: New American Library, 1961.

———. *The Old Curiosity Shop*. 1841. Middlesex, England: Penguin, 1972.

———. *Our Mutual Friend*. 1865. Middlesex, England: Penguin, 1971.

———. *The Posthumous Papers of the Pickwick Club*. 1837. New York: Modern Library, 1935.

———. *Sketches by Boz*. 1833–36. London: Oxford University Press, 1957.

Donnelly, John. "Incest . . . in Lear." *Psychoanalytic Review* 40 (1953): 149–55.

Dumas, Alexandre. *Crimes Célèbres* or *Celebrated Crimes*. Vol. 5. Trans. I. G. Burnham. London: W. and G. Foyle, 1895.

Dundes, Alan, ed. *Cinderella: A Folklore Casebook*. New York: Garland, 1982.

———. "'To Love My Father All'." In *Cinderella: A Folklore Casebook*, 229–44.

Durkheim, Emile. 1897. *Incest: The Nature and Origin of the Taboo*. Trans. Edward Sagarin. New York: L. Stuart, 1963.

Edel, Leon. *Henry James: The Untried Years—1843–1870*. New York: J. B. Lippincott, 1953.

———. *Henry James: The Conquest of London—1870–1881*. New York: Avon, 1962.

———. *Henry James: The Middle Years—1882–1895*. New York: Avon, 1978.

———. *Henry James: The Treacherous Years—1895–1901*. New York: Avon, 1978.

———. *Henry James: The Master—1901–1916*. Philadelphia: J. B. Lippincott, 1972.

———. Introduction to *Watch and Ward*, by Henry James. New York: Grove Press, 1960.

———. *The Psychological Novel: 1900–1950*. London: Rupert Hart-Davis, 1961.

Ehrsam, Theo. G. *A Bibliography of Joseph Conrad*. Metuchen, N.J.: Scarecrow Press, 1969.

Eliert-Schifferer, Syphille, et al. *Guido Reni e L'Europe: Fama e Fortuna* (Guido Reni and Europe: Fame and Fortune). Frankfurt: Schirn Kunsthalle; Bologna: Nuova Alfa Editoriale, 1988.

Ellmann, Richard. *The Consciousness of Joyce*. London: Oxford University Press, 1977.

———. *James Joyce*. New York: Oxford University Press, 1959.

———. *James Joyce: New and Revised Edition*. New York: Oxford University Press, 1982.

Erickson, Peter B. "Patriarchal Structures in *The Winter's Tale*." *PMLA* (1982): 819–29.

Erikson, Erik H. "Human Strength and the Cycle of Generations." In *Insight*, 109–58.

———. *Insight and Responsibility: Lectures on the Ethical Implications of Psychoanalytic Insight*. New York: W. W. Norton, 1964.

———. "Psychological Reality and Historical Actuality" [Dora Case]. In *Insight and Responsibility: Lectures on the Ethical Implications of Psychoanalytic Insight*, 161–77.

———. "Reality and Actuality: An Address." In Bernheimer and Kahane, *In Dora's Case: Freud-Hysteria-Feminism*, 44–55.

Erlich, Gloria. *Family Themes and Hawthorne's Fiction: The Tenacious Web.* New Brunswick, N.J.: Rutgers University Press, 1984.

Faber, M. D., ed. *The Design Within: Psychoanalytic Approaches to Shakespeare.* New York: Science House, 1970.

Feldman, A. Bronson. "Imaginary Incest." *American Imago* 12 (1955): 117–55.

Fenichel, Otto. "Specific Forms of the Oedipus Complex." 1931. *Collected Papers, First Series.* New York: W. W. Norton, 1953. 204–20.

Fiedler, Leslie. "Archetype and Signature." *Sewanee Review* 60 (1952): 253–73.

Firebaugh, Joseph J. "The Ververs." *Essays in Criticism* 4, no. 4 (1954): 400–10.

Fish, Charles. "Form and Revision: The Example of *Watch and Ward.*" *Nineteenth Century Fiction* 22 (1966): 173–190.

Fitch, Noel Riley. *Anaïs: The Erotic Life of Anaïs Nin.* New York: Little, Brown and Co., 1993.

Fitzgerald, F. Scott. *Tender Is the Night.* 1934. New York: Chas. Scribner's, 1962.

Fitzsimons, Raymund. *Garish Lights: The Public Reading Tours of Charles Dickens.* New York: J. B. Lippincott, 1970.

Flamm, Dudley. "The Prosecutor Within: Dickens's Final Explanation." *Dickensian* 66–67 (1970–71): 16–23.

Fleissner, Robert F. *Dickens and Shakespeare: A Study in Histrionic Contrasts.* New York: Haskell House, 1965.

Fogel, Daniel Mark. *Covert Relations: James Joyce, Virginia Woolf, and Henry James.* Charlottesville: University Press of Virginia, 1990.

Ford, Jane. "James Joyce and the Conrad Connection: The Anxiety of Influence." *Conradiana* 17, no. 1 (1985): 3–19.

———. "James Joyce's Trieste Library: Some Notes on Its Use." In *Joyce at Texas: Essays on the James Joyce Materials at the Humanities Research Center,* ed. Dave Oliphant and Thomas Zigal, 141–58. Austin: University of Texas at Austin, 1983.

———. "Why Is Milly in Mullingar?" *James Joyce Quarterly* 14, no. 4 (1977): 436–49.

Forster, John. *The Life of Charles Dickens.* 1903. 2 vols. London: J. M. Dent, 1966.

Fradin, Joseph I. "Will and Society in *Bleak House.*" *PMLA* 81 (1966): 95–109.

Frazer, Sir James G. *The Golden Bough: A Study in Magic and Religion.* 1922. Abridged edition. New York: Macmillan and Co., 1948.

Freud, Sigmund. "Beyond the Pleasure Principle." 1922. In *Standard Edition,* 18: 7–66. 1955.

———. "Civilization and Its Discontents." 1930. In *Standard Edition,* 21: 59–45. 1961.

———. "Fragment of an Analysis of a Case of Hysteria" [Dora]. 1905. In *Standard Edition,* 7: 1–122. 1953.

———. *A General Introduction to Psychoanalysis.* 1920. In *Standard Edition,* 17: 207. 1955.

———. *The Interpretation of Dreams*. 1900. In *Standard Edition*, 4. 1953.

———. "On the History of the Psycho-analytic Movement." 1914. In *Standard Edition*, 14: 7–66. 1957.

———. "On the Universal Tendency to Debasement in the Sphere of Love." 1915. In *Standard Edition*, 11: 179–90. 1957.

———. "The Paths to the Formation of Symptoms." Lecture 23. In *Standard Edition*, 16: 358–75. 1963.

———. "Some Character-Types Met with in Psycho-Analytic Work." 1916. In *Standard Edition*, 14: 311–33. 1957.

———. "A Special Type of Choice of Object Made by Men." (Contributions to the Psychology of Love I). 1910. In *Standard Edition*, 11: 165–175. 1957.

———. *The Standard Edition of the Complete Psychological Works of Sigmund Freud*. 24 vols. Trans. and ed. James Strachey et al. London: Hogarth and the Institute for Psycho-Analysis, 1953–74.

———. "The Taboo of Virginity." (Contributions to the Psychology of Love III). 1918 [1917]. In *Standard Edition*, 11: 193–208. 1957.

———. "Totem and Taboo." 1913. In *Standard Edition*, 13: ix–162. 1955.

Friedman, Neil, and Richard M. Jones. "On the Mutuality of the Oedipus Complex: Notes on the Hamlet Case." *American Imago* 20 (1963): 107–31. Reprinted in Faber, *The Design Within: Psychoanalytic Approaches to Shakespeare*, 121–46.

Friedman, Susan Stanford. "(Self)Censorship and the Making of Joyce's Modernism." In *Return of the Repressed*, 21–57.

———. "Weavings: Intertextuality and the (Re)Birth of the Author." In Clayton and Rothstein, *Influence and Intertextuality in Literary History*, 146–80.

———, ed. *Joyce: The Return of the Repressed*. Ithaca, N.Y.: Cornell University Press, 1993.

Froula, Christine. "The Daughter's Seduction: Sexual Violence and Literary History." In Boose and Flowers, *Daughters and Fathers*, 111–35.

Frye, Northrop. *Anatomy of Criticism: Four Essays*. 1957. New York: Atheneum, 1966.

———. "The Archetypes of Literature." *Kenyon Review* 13 (1951): 92–110.

Gay, Peter. *Freud: A Life for Our Time*. New York: W. W. Norton, 1988.

Gilbert, Sandra M. "Life's Empty Pack: Notes toward a Literary Daughteronomy." In Boose and Flowers, *Daughters and Fathers*, 256–77.

Gillon, Adam. *Conrad and Shakespeare and Other Essays*. New York: Astra, 1982.

Girard, René. *Deceit, Desire and the Novel: Self and Other in Literary Structure*. Trans. Yvonne Freccero. Baltimore: Johns Hopkins University Press, 1969.

Gissing, George. "Characterization." In Wall, *Charles Dickens: A Critical Anthology*, 222–39.

Glasheen, Adaline. *A Second Census of Finnegans Wake: An Index of the Characters and Their Roles*. Evanston, Ill.: Northwestern University Press, 1963.

Goethe, Johann Wolfgang von. *Elective Affinities*. 1809. Trans. R. J. Hollingdale. Harmondsworth, England: Penguin, 1978.

Gorky, Maxim. "The Hermit." In Cory and Masters, *Violation of Taboo: Incest in the Great Literature of the Past and Present*, 140–68.

Gower, John. *Confessio Amantis*. 1390. Ed. Russell A. Peck. New York: Holt, Rinehart and Winston, 1968.

Graves, Robert. *The Greek Myths*. 2 vols. 1955. Baltimore: Penguin, 1968.

Groden, Michael, et al., eds. *The James Joyce Archive*: Ulysses: 'Circe' and 'Eumaeus'. A Facsimile of Manuscripts & Typescripts for Episodes 15 (Part II) & 16. New York and London: Garland Publishing, 1977.

Guerard, Albert J. *Conrad the Novelist*. Cambridge: Harvard University Press, 1958.

Gunn, Ian, and Alistair McCleery, comps. *The Ulysses Pagefinder*. Edinburgh, Scotland: Split Pea Press, 1988.

Hanley, Miles L. *Word Index to James Joyce's* Ulysses. Madison: University of Wisconsin Press, 1965.

Harbage, Alfred. *A Kind of Power: The Shakespeare-Dickens Analogy*. Memoirs of the American Philosophical Society, vol. 105. Philadelphia: American Philosophical Society, 1975.

Hardwick, Mollie. "Born under Aquarius." *Dickensian* 62 (1966): 86–95.

Hart, Clive. *A Concordance to* Finnegans Wake. Minneapolis: University of Minnesota Press, 1963.

———. *Structure and Motif in* Finnegans Wake. London: Faber and Faber, 1962.

Harty, John, III, ed. *James Joyce's* Finnegans Wake: *A Casebook*. New York: Garland, 1991.

Hawthorne, Nathaniel. *The Marble Faun*. 1859. New York: Signet, 1961.

———. "Rappaccini's Daughter." 1844. In *The Complete Novels and Tales of Nathaniel Hawthorne*, ed. N. H. Pearson, 1043–65. New York: Modern Library, 1965.

Herman, Judith L., with Lisa Hirschman. *Father-Daughter Incest*. Cambridge: Harvard University Press, 1981.

Herring, Phillip F. "*Ulysses* Notebook VIII. A.5 at Buffalo." *Studies in Bibliography* 22 (1962): 287–310.

Hewitt, Douglas. *Conrad: A Reassessment*. Cambridge, England: Bowes and Bowes, 1952.

Holland, Laurence Bedwell. *The Expense of Vision: Essays on the Craft of Henry James*. Princeton, N.J.: Princeton University Press, 1964.

Holland, Norman N. "Caliban's Dream." *Psychoanalytic Quarterly* 37 (1968): 114–25. Reprint, in Faber, *The Design Within: Psychoanalytic Approaches to Shakespeare*, 521–34.

———. *The Dynamics of Literary Response*. New York: Oxford University Press, 1968.

———. *Psychoanalysis and Shakespeare*. New York: McGraw-Hill, 1966.

———. Introduction to *Shakespeare's Personality*, ed. with Sidney Homan and Bernard J. Paris, 1–15. Berkeley: University of California Press, 1989.

Homer. *The Odyssey*. Trans. E. V. Rieu. Baltimore: Penguin, 1956.

House, Humphrey. "The Changing Scene." 1898. In Wall, *Charles Dickens: A Critical Anthology*, 323–48.

Howarth, Herbert. "The Meaning of Conrad's *The Rover*." *Southern Review* 6 (1970): 682–97.

Howells, Mildred. *Life in Letters of W. D. Howells*. New York: n.p., 1928.

Hutter, Albert. "Psychoanalysis and Biography: Dickens' Experience at Warren's Blacking." *Hartford Studies in Literature* 8, no. 1 (1976): 23–37.

Ibsen, Henrik. *The Master Builder*. 1892. In *When We Dead Awaken and Three Other Plays*, trans. Michael Meyer. Garden City, N.Y.: Doubleday and Co., 1960.

———. *Rosmersholm*. 1892. In *Six Plays by Henrik Ibsen*, trans. Eva Le Gallienne. New York: Modern Library, 1957.

James, Henry. *The American*. 1877. Boston: Houghton Mifflin, 1962.

———. *The Bostonians*. 1886. New York: Random House, 1956.

———. *The Golden Bowl*. 1904. Ed. John Halperin. New York: Meridian, 1972.

———. *Italian Hours*. 1909. Ed. John Auchard. University Park: Pennsylvania State University Press, 1992.

———. *The Ivory Tower*. 1910. New York: Chas. Scribner's Sons, 1917.

———. *The Notebooks of Henry James*. Ed. F. O. Matthiessen and Kenneth B. Murdock. New York: Oxford University Press, 1947.

———. *The Portrait of a Lady*. 1880. Boston: Houghton Mifflin, 1963.

———. "The Real Thing." 1892. In *The Portable Henry James*, ed. Morton Dauwen Zabel. Revised Lyall H. P. Powers. New York: Viking Press, 1972.

———. *Roderick Hudson*. 1875. Introduction by Leon Edel. Boston: Houghton Mifflin, 1977.

———. *The Sense of the Past*. Notes for *The Sense of the Past*. Prefatory note by J. C. Squire. London: W. Collins Sons, n.d.

———. *A Small Boy and Others*. 1913. New York: Chas. Scribner's Sons, 1941.

———. "The Tempest." 1907. In *Selected Literary Criticism*, ed. Morris Shapira, 297–310. New York: McGraw-Hill, 1965.

———. Preface to *The Turn of the Screw*. *The Aspern Papers, The Turn of the Screw, The Liar, and The Two Faces*, xxiv. London: Macmillan, 1922.

———. *Washington Square and The Europeans*. 1878. New York: Dell Publishers, 1969.

———. *Watch and Ward*. 1871. London: Macmillan, 1923.

———. *What Maisie Knew*. 1897. Harmondsworth, England: Penguin, 1973.

———. *Wings of the Dove*. 1902. New York: New American Library, 1964.

Jean-Aubry, Gerard. *Joseph Conrad: Life and Letters*. 2 vols. Garden City, N.Y.: Doubleday, Page, 1927.

———. *The Sea Dreamer: Joseph Conrad*. Garden City, N.Y.: Doubleday and Co., 1957.

Johnson, Edgar. *Charles Dickens: His Tragedy and Triumph*. 2 vols. New York: Simon and Schuster, 1952.

Jones, Ernest. *Papers on Psycho-Analysis*. 2nd ed. New York: Wm. Wood and Co., 1919.

Josephson, Matthew. *Stendhal: Or the Pursuit of Happiness*. Garden City, N.Y.: Doubleday, 1946.

Joyce, James. "The Centenary of Charles Dickens." In *James Joyce in Padua*, Introduction by Louis Berrone, ed. and trans., 25–37. New York: Random House, 1977.

———. *Dubliners.* 1916. New York: Viking Press, 1968.

———. *Finnegans Wake.* 1939. New York: Viking Press, 1966.

———. *Giacomo Joyce.* 1914. Introduction and Notes by Richard Ellmann. London: Faber and Faber, 1984.

———. *Letters of James Joyce.* Vol. 1. Ed. Stuart Gilbert. New York: Viking Press, 1966.

———. *Letters of James Joyce.* Vols. 2 and 3. Ed. Richard Ellmann. New York: Viking Press, 1966.

———. *A Portrait of the Artist as a Young Man.* 1916. New York: Viking Press, 1968.

———. *Selected Letters of James Joyce.* Ed. Richard Ellmann. New York: Viking Press, 1975.

———. *Stephen Hero.* 1903. New edition. Ed. John J. Slocum and Herbert Cahoon. New York: New Directions, 1963.

———. *Ulysses.* 1922. New York: Random House, 1961.

———. *Ulysses: A Critical and Synoptic Edition.* 1922. Ed. Hans Walter Gabler et al. 3 vols. New York: Garland, 1984.

———. Zurich Notebook, VIII. A.5. 1918. Lockwood Library, State University of New York at Buffalo.

Kanfer, Stefan. "The 110-Year-Old Murder." *Time* (October 27, 1980): 100–101.

Karl, Frederick R., and Laurence Davies, eds. *The Collected Letters of Joseph Conrad.* 5 vols. 1861–1916. New York: Cambridge University Press, 1983–1996.

———. *Joseph Conrad: The Three Lives.* New York: Farrar, Straus and Giroux, 1979.

———. *A Reader's Guide to Joseph Conrad.* New York: Noonday Press, 1960.

Kay, Dennis. *Shakespeare: His Life, Work and Era.* New York: Morrow and Co., 1992.

Kiell, Norman, ed. *Psychoanalysis, Psychology and Literature: A Bibliography.* Madison: University of Wisconsin Press, 1963.

Kimball, Jean. "Autobiography as Epic: Freud's Three-Time Scheme in Joyce's *Ulysses." Texas Studies in Literature and Language* 31 (1989): 475–90.

———. "Henry James's Last Portrait of a Lady: Charlotte Stant in *The Golden Bowl." American Literature* 28, no. 4 (1957): 449–68.

———. "James Joyce and Otto Rank: The Incest Motif in *Ulysses." James Joyce Quarterly* 13, no. 3 (1976): 366–82.

Kincaid, James. *Dickens and the Rhetoric of Laughter.* Oxford, England: Clarendon, 1971.

Kleinberg, Seymour. "Ambiguity and Ambivalence: The Psychology of Sexuality in Henry James's *The Portrait of a Lady." Markham Review* 5 (1968): 2–7.

Kohrs, Karl, ed. *The New Milton Cross' Complete Stories of the Great Operas.* Garden City, N.Y.: Doubleday, 1955.

Kris, Ernest. *Psychoanalytic Explorations in Art.* 1952. New York: Schocken, 1971.

Krook, Dorothea. *The Ordeal of Consciousness in Henry James.* Cambridge: Cambridge University Press, 1962.

Landor, Walter Savage. *Complete Works.* 8 vols. London: Chapman and Hall, 1876.

La Sonnambula: An Opera in 2 Acts (The sleepwalker). By Vincenzo Bellini (music); Feline Romani (libretto). The English version by Natalia Macferren; essay by H. E. Krebiel. New York: G. Schirmer, 1901.

Leavis, F. R. *The Great Tradition*. New York: Geo. W. Stewart, 1949.

Lebowitz, Naomi. "Magic and Metamorphosis in *The Golden Bowl*." *Sewanee Review* 73 (1965): 58–73.

Lenormand, H.-R. "Note sur un séjour de Conrad en Corse" (Note on a sojourn of Conrad in Corsica). "Hommage à Joseph Conrad, 1857–1924." *La Nouvelle Revue Française* ns 135 (1924): 666–71. Reprint, *Joseph Conrad: A Critical Symposium*, ed. R. W. Stallman, trans. Charles Owen, 5–8.

Lesser, Simon O. *Fiction and the Unconscious*. New York: Vintage, 1957.

Levi-Strauss, Claude. "The Structural Study of Myth." In *The Structuralists from Marx to Levi-Strauss*, ed. Richard and Fernande De George. Garden City, N.Y.: Anchor, 1972.

Lewin, Karl Kay. "Freud's Own *Negative* Counter-transference." *Psychoanalytic Review* 60, no. 4 (1973–74): 519–32.

Lewis, R. B. *The Jameses: A Family Narrative*. New York: Farrar, Straus, and Giroux, 1991.

Lieberman, E. James. *Acts of Will: The Life and Work of Otto Rank*. New York: Macmillan, 1985.

MacKenzie, Norman, and Jeanne MacKenzie. *Dickens: A Life*. New York: Oxford University Press, 1979.

Maddox, Brenda. *Nora: The Real Life of Molly Bloom*. Boston: Houghton Mifflin, 1988.

Maisch, Herbert. *Incest*. Trans. Colin Bearne. New York: Stein and Day, 1972.

Mallett, Michael. *The Borgias*. London: Bodley Head, 1969. Reprint, Chicago: Academy Chicago Pub., 1987.

Manheim, Leonard, and Eleanor Manheim, eds. *Hidden Patterns: Studies in Psychoanalytic Literary Criticism*. New York: Macmillan, 1966.

Manning, Sylvia Bank. *Dickens as Satirist*. New Haven, Conn.: Yale University Press, 1971.

———. "Dickens, January, and May." *Dickensian* 71 (1975): 67–75.

Marcham, Frank. *William Shakespeare and His Daughter Susannah*. London: Grafton, 1931.

Marcus, Steven. "Dickens: From Pickwick to Dombey." *A Pickwick Portrait Gallery: From the Pens of Divers Admirers*. Port Washington, N.Y.: Kennikat Press, 1970.

———. "Freud and Dora: Story, History, Case History." In Bernheimer and Kahane, *In Dora's Case: Freud-Hysteria-Feminism*, 56–91.

Masson, Jeffrey M., ed. and trans. *The Complete Letters of Sigmund Freud to Wilhelm Fliess, 1887–1904*. Cambridge: Harvard University Press, 1985.

Masters, R. E. L. *Patterns of Incest: A Psycho-Social Study of Incest Based on Clinical and Historic Data*. New York: Julian Press, 1964.

Maves, Carl. *Sensuous Pessimism: Italy in the Work of Henry James*. Bloomington: Indiana University Press, 1973.

McBride, Margaret. "*Finnegans Wake*: The Issue of Issy's Schizophrenia." In *Joyce Studies Annual 1996*, ed. Thomas F. Staley, 145–75. Austin: University of Texas

Press in cooperation with the Harry Ransom Humanities Research Center, University of Texas, 1996.

McCurdy, Harold Grier. *The Personality of Shakespeare: A Venture in Psychological Method*. New Haven, Conn.: Yale University Press, 1953.

McHugh, Roland. *Annotations to Finnegans Wake*. Baltimore: Johns Hopkins University Press, 1980.

Mead, Margaret. *Sex and Temperament*. New York: Mentor, 1950.

Meiselman, Karin C. *Incest: A Psychological Study of Causes and Effects with Treatment Recommendations*. San Francisco: Jossey-Bass, 1978.

Melville, Herman. *Pierre or the Ambiguities*. 1852. New York: Grove Press, 1957.

Menaker, Esther. *Otto Rank: A Rediscovered Legacy*. New York: Columbia University Press, 1982.

Meyer, Bernard C. *Joseph Conrad: A Psychoanalytic Biography*. Princeton, N.J.: Princeton University Press, 1967.

Miller, Ian. "The Dickens Dramas: Mr. Dombey." In *Dickens Centennial Essays*, ed. Ada Nisbet and Blake Nevius, 155–65. Berkeley: University of California Press, 1971.

Miller, J. Hillis. *The Form of Victorian Fiction*. Notre Dame, Ind.: Notre Dame University Press, 1968.

———. "Georges Poulet's Criticism of Identification." *Modern Language Notes* 78, no. 5 (1969): 471–88.

Mueller, Martin. "Hermione's Wrinkles, or, Ovid Transformed: An Essay on *The Winter's Tale*." *Comparative Drama* 5, no.3 (1971): 226–39.

Moser, Thomas. *Joseph Conrad: Achievement and Decline*. Cambridge: Harvard University Press, 1957.

Najder, Zdzislaw. *Joseph Conrad: A Chronicle*. Trans. Halina Caroll-Najder. New Brunswick, N.J.: Rutgers University Press, 1983.

de Navarre, Marguerite. "A Tale of Incest," from *The Heptameron*. In Cory and Masters, *Violation of Taboo: Incest in the Great Literature of the Past and Present*, 100–104.

Nietzsche, Friedrich. *The Birth of Tragedy and the Genealogy of Morals* (in German). 1872, 1887. Trans. Francis Golffing. Garden City, N.Y.: Doubleday Anchor, 1956.

Nin, Anaïs. *Incest: From a Journal of Love. The Unexpurgated Diary of Anaïs Nin, 1932–1934*. Introduction by Rupert Pole. New York: Harcourt Brace Jovanovich, 1992.

Norris, Margot. *The Decentered Universe of Finnegans Wake: A Structuralist Analysis*. Baltimore: Johns Hopkins University Press, 1976.

Nuhn, Ferner. *The Wind Blew from the East: A Study in the Orientation of American Culture*. New York: Harper, 1940.

O'Toole, Patricia. *The Five of Hearts: An Intimate Portrait of Henry Adams and His Friends, 1880–1918*. New York: Clarkson Potter, 1990.

Ovid. *The Metamorphoses*. Trans. Mary M. Innes. Baltimore: Penguin, 1962.

The Oxford Companion to English Literature. Ed. Sir Paul Harvey, 4th ed. New York: Oxford University Press, 1967.

Paris, Bernard J. "*The Tempest*: Shakespeare's Ideal Solution." In *Shakespeare's Personality*, ed. Norman Holland et al., 206–25.

Parsons, Anne. "Is the Oedipus Complex Universal?" In *The Psychoanalytical Study of Society*, ed. Werner Muensterberger et al., 3–278. New York: International University Press, 1964.

Pauncz, Arpad. "The Lear Complex in World Literature." *American Imago* 40 (1954): 51–83.

Pearson, Gabriel. "The Novel to End All Novels." In *The Air of Reality: New Essays on Henry James*, ed. John Goode, 301–62. London: Methuen, 1972.

Pepper, Stephen. *Guido Reni*. Oxford: Phaidon, 1984.

Perkins, Jill. *Joyce and Hauptmann: Before Sunrise—James Joyce's Translation with an Introduction and Notes*. San Marino, Calif.: Huntington Library, 1978.

Portigliotti, Giuseppi. *The Borgias: Alexander VI, Caesar, Lucrezia*. Trans. Bernard Miall. New York: Alfred A. Knopf, 1927.

Potts, Willard, ed. *Portraits of the Artist in Exile: Recollections of James Joyce by Europeans*. Seattle: University of Washington Press, 1979.

Price, Martin, ed. *Dickens: A Collection of Critical Essays*. Englewood Cliffs, N.J.: Prentice-Hall, 1967.

Rank, Otto. *Das Inzest-Motiv in Dichtung und Sage* (The incest theme in literature and legend). Leipzig and Vienna: Franz Deuticke, 1912.

———. *The Incest Theme in Literature and Legend: Fundamentals of a Psychology of Literary Creation*. 1912. Introduction by Peter L. Rudnytsky. Trans Gregory C. Richter. Baltimore: Johns Hopkins University Press, 1992.

Renvoize, Jean. *Incest: A Family Pattern*. London: Routledge and Kegan Paul, 1982.

Ricci, Corrado. *Beatrice Cenci*. 1923. Trans. Morris Bishop and Henry Longan Stuart. 2 vols. New York: Boni and Liveright, 1925.

Rieff, Philip, ed. Introduction to *Dora: An Analysis of a Case of Hysteria*, by Sigmund Freud. New York: Collier, 1971.

Robert, Paul Le. *Le Grand Robert de la langue française: dictionnaire alphabétique et analogique de la langue française*. 2nd ed. Paris: Le Robert, 1985.

Roussel, Royal. *The Metaphysics of Darkness: A Study in the Unity and Development of Conrad's Fiction*. Baltimore: Johns Hopkins University Press, 1971.

Rudnytsky, Peter L. Introductory essay. *The Incest Theme in Literature and Legend: Fundamentals of a Psychology of Literary Creation*, by Otto Rank, trans. Gregory C. Richter, xi–xxxv. Baltimore: Johns Hopkins University Press, 1992.

de Sade, the Marquis. *Eugénie de Franval*. 1788. In *The Marquis de Sade: The Complete Justine, Philosophy in the Bedroom and Other Writings*, trans. Richard Seaver and Austryn Wainhouse, 375–445. New York: Grove Press, 1966.

Sadoff, Dianne F. "The Clergyman's Daughters: Anne Bronte, Elizabeth Gaskell, and George Eliot." In Boose and Flowers, *Daughters and Fathers*, 303–25.

Samuels, Charles Thomas. *The Ambiguity of Henry James*. Urbana: University of Illinois Press, 1971.

Schoenbaum, Samuel. *William Shakespeare: A Compact Documentary Life*. New York: Oxford University Press, 1977.

Schutte, William. *Joyce and Shakespeare: A Study in the Meaning of Ulysses*. New Haven, Conn.: Yale University Press, 1957.

Schwartz, Murray M. "Leontes' Jealousy in *The Winter's Tale*." *American Imago* 30, no. 3 (1973): 250–75.

————. *The Winter's Tale:* "Loss and Transformation." *American Imago* 32 (1975): 145–99.

Schwartz, Murray M., and Coppélia Kahn, eds. *Representing Shakespeare: New Psychoanalytic Essays.* Baltimore: Johns Hopkins University Press, 1980.

Scofield, C. I., ed. *The Holy Bible.* 1909. New York: Oxford University Press, 1945.

Scott, Bonnie Kime. *Joyce and Feminism.* Bloomington: Indiana University Press, 1984.

Scott, W. I. D. "Pericles the Schizophrenic." In *Shakespeare's Melancholics,* chap. 9, p. 140. London: Mills and Bron, 1962.

Sears, Sallie. *The Negative Imagination: Form and Perspective in the Novels of Henry James.* Ithaca, N.Y.: Cornell University Press, 1968.

Senn, Fritz. "Insects Appalling." In *Twelve and a Tilly,* ed. Jack P. Dalton and Clive Hart, 36–39. Evanston, Ill.: Northwestern University Press, 1965.

Seymour, Miranda. *A Ring of Conspirators: Henry James and His Literary Circle, 1895–1915.* London: Hodder and Stoughton, 1988.

Shakespeare, William. *King Henry VIII.* c. 1613. Ed. R. A. Foakes. Arden Shakespeare. London: Methuen, 1968.

————. *King Lear.* c. 1605. Ed. Kenneth Muir. Arden Shakespeare. London: Methuen, 1972.

————. *Love's Labour's Lost. The Complete Works of William Shakespeare.* Cambridge Edition Text. Ed. William Addis Wright. New York: Garden City Pub., 1936.

————. *The Merchant of Venice.* 1596. Baltimore: Penguin, 1959.

————. *A Midsummer Night's Dream.* c. 1595. Ed. Madeleine Doran. Baltimore: Penguin, 1967.

————. *Othello.* c. 1604. Ed. Oscar James Campbell et al. New York: Bantam, 1962.

————. *Pericles.* c. 1608. Arden Shakespeare. Ed. F. D. Hoenigar. London: Methuen, 1969.

————. *Romeo and Juliet.* c. 1596. Ed. J. A. Bryant, Jr. New York: New American Library, 1964.

————. *The Tempest.* c. 1611. Ed. Frank Kermode. Arden Shakespeare. London: Methuen, 1972.

————. *The Winter's Tale.* 1611. Ed. J. H. P. Pafford. Arden Shakespeare. London: Methuen, 1978.

Shapiro, Laura. "They're Daddy's Little Girls." *Newsweek* (January 24, 1994): 66.

Sharpe, Ella Freeman. "From *King Lear* to *The Tempest.*" In *Collected Papers on Psycho-Analysis,* ed. Marjorie Brierley, 214–41. London: Hogarth Press, 1950.

Shaw, George Bernard. Foreword to *Great Expectations,* by Charles Dickens. 1947. Reprinted in Wall, *Charles Dickens: A Critical Anthology,* 284–97.

Shechner, Mark. *Joyce in Nighttown: A Psychoanalytic Inquiry into Ulysses.* Berkeley: University of California Press, 1974.

Shelley, Mary. *Mary Shelley's Journal.* Ed. Frederick L. Jones. Norman: University Press of Oklahoma, 1947.

————. *Mathilda.* Written 1819. Ed. Elizabeth Nitchie. Chapel Hill: University of North Carolina Press, 1959.

Shelley, Percy Bysshe. *The Cenci.* 1819. Ed. George E. Woodberry. Boston: D. C. Heath, 1909.

——. *The Cenci.* 1819. Ed. Roland A. Duerksen. New York: Bobbs-Merrill, 1970.

——. *The Cenci.* 1819. In *The Selected Prose and Poetry*, ed. Carlos Baker, 132–99. New York: Modern Library, 1951.

Shore, W. Teignmouth. *Shakespeare's Self.* New York: Haskell House, 1971.

Smith, David. "Incest Patterns in Two Victorian Novels: 1. Her Master's Voice: *Jane Eyre* and the Incest Taboo." *Literature and Psychology* 15, no. 3 (1965): 135–44.

Solomon, Margaret C. *Eternal Geomater: The Sexual Universe of* Finnegans Wake. Carbondale: Southern Illinois University Press, 1969.

Sophocles. *Oedipus at Colonus.* c. 470 B.C. Trans. F. Storr. Vol. 1. London: Wm. Heinemann, 1946.

Sprengnether, Madelon. "Enforcing Oedipus: Freud and Dora." In Bernheimer and Kahane, *In Dora's Case: Freud-Hysteria-Feminism*, 254–76.

Stallman, R. W., ed. *Joseph Conrad: A Critical Symposium.* "Note on a sojourn of Conrad in Corsica" (Trans. of H.-R. Lenormand, "Note sur un séjour de Conrad en Corse"), by Charles Owen, 5–8. 1960. Encore Ed. Athens: Ohio University Press, 1982.

Steffan, Truman Guy. "Seven Accounts of the Cenci and Shelley's Drama." *Studies in English Literature, 1500–1900* 9, no. 4 (1969): 601–18.

Taylor, G. Rattray. *Sex in History.* New York: Vanguard Press, 1970.

Terry, Patricia, trans. Introduction to *The Honeysuckle and the Hazel Tree: Medieval Stories of Men and Women.* Berkeley, Calif.: University of California Press, 1995.

Thomas, Dylan. "The Burning Baby." In Cory and Masters, *Violation of Taboo: Incest in the Great Literature of the Past and Present*, 133–39.

Thorne, W. B. "*Pericles* and the Incest-Fertility Opposition." *Shakespeare Quarterly* 22, no. 1 (1971): 43–56.

Thornton, Weldon. *Allusions in* Ulysses. Chapel Hill: University of North Carolina Press, 1968.

Tick, Stanley. "On Not Being Charles Dickens." *Bucknell Review* 16, no. 1 (1968): 85–95.

——. "The Unfinished Business of *Dombey and Son*." *Modern Language Quarterly* 36, no. 4 (1975): 391–402.

Tindall, William York. *A Reader's Guide to* Finnegans Wake. New York: Farrar, Straus and Giroux, 1972.

——. *A Reader's Guide to James Joyce.* New York: Noonday Press, 1959.

Tolstoy, Leo Nikolayevich. *The Power of Darkness.* 1888. Trans. George Rapall Noyes and George Z. Patrick. In *A Treasury of the Theatre Vol. 2: From Henrik Ibsen to Robert Lowell*, ed. John Gassner and Bernard F. Dukore, 115–44. 4th ed. New York: Simon and Schuster, 1970.

Tomalin, Claire. *The Invisible Woman: The Story of Nelly Ternan and Charles Dickens.* New York: Knopf, 1991.

Torsney, Cheryl B. "Prince Amerigo's Borgia Heritage." *Henry James Review* 2 (1981): 126–31.

Tresize, Simon. Review of *Beatrice Cenci*, by Goldschmidt (opera [CD]). *Opera Now* (August–September 1995). Based on Shelley's *Beatrice Cenci*. Estes, Jones, Alexander, Kimm, Rose. Rundfunkchor Berlin, Deutches Symphonie-Orchester Berlin. Written 1951, performed 1980s.

Trilling, Lionel. *The Liberal Imagination*. Garden City, N.Y.: Doubleday Anchor, 1953.

———. *The Opposing Self*. New York: Viking, 1955.

Twitchell, James B. *Forbidden Partners: The Incest Taboo in Modern Culture*. New York: Columbia University Press, 1987.

Tysdahl, B. J. *Joyce and Ibsen: A Study in Literary Influence*. New York: Humanities Press, 1968.

Vanderbilt, Heidi. "Incest: A Chilling Report." *Lear's* (February 1992): 49–77.

Van Ghent, Dorothy. "The Dickens World: A View from Todgers's." *Sewanee Review* 58 (1950): 419–38. Reprint, Price, *Dickens: A Collection of Critical Essays*, 4–38.

———. *The English Novel: Form and Function*. 1953. New York: Harper and Row, 1967.

Wall, Stephen, ed. *Charles Dickens: A Critical Anthology*. Harmondsworth, England: Penguin, 1970.

Ward, Elizabeth. *Father-Daughter Rape*. London: Women's Press, 1984.

Ward, J. A. *The Search for Form: Studies in the Structure of James's Fiction*. Chapel Hill: University of North Carolina Press, 1967.

Weinberg, Samuel Kirson. *Incest Behavior*. New York: Citadel Press, 1955.

Westermarck, Edward A. *The History of Human Marriage*. 5th ed. New York: Allerton, 1922.

Whaley, Helen. "The Role of the Blind Piano Tuner in *Ulysses*." *Modern Fiction Studies* 16 (1971): 531–35.

Wharton, Edith. *Summer*. 1918. Introduction by Cynthia Griffin Wolff. New York: Harper and Row, 1979.

Willbern, David. "*Filia Oedipi*: Father and Daughter in Freudian Theory." In Boose and Flowers, *Daughters and Fathers*, 75–96.

Yaeger, Patricia, and Beth Kowalski-Wallace, eds. *Refiguring the Father: New Feminist Readings of Patriarchy*. Carbondale: Southern Illinois University Press, 1989.

Yost, George. *Pieracci and Shelley: An Italian Ur-Cenci*. Potomac, Md.: Scripta Humanistica, 1986.

Young, Philip. *Hawthorne's Secret: An Un-Told Tale*. New York: David R. Godine, 1989.

Zabel, Morton Dauwen, ed. Introduction to *Charles Dickens' Best Stories*. Garden City, N.Y.: Hanover House, 1959.

Zwinger, Lynda. *Fathers, Daughters, and the Novel: The Sentimental Romance of Heterosexuality*. Madison: University of Wisconsin Press, 1991.

Index